Praise for *Island*

"Angel Island is now an idyllic state park out in San Francisco Bay. But for many of the 175,000 Chinese immigrants arriving from 1910 to 1940, it served as one final obstacle in their long journey to Gam San, the Golden Mountain and the Land of the Flowery Flag. . . . This attractive volume of oral histories, photographs, and poems gleaned from the walls . . . unveils a fascinating story of raw courage and delicate sensibility which should make Chinese-Americans proud they descend from such 'pioneers.'" —*Christian Science Monitor*

"The poems, which appear both in Chinese characters and in English translation, speak effectively of loneliness, frustration and bitterness, as the immigrants awaited the medical examinations and interrogations that were designed more to keep them out of the United States than help them enter." —*San Francisco Chronicle*

"A sad and touching book that is yet oddly exhilarating as well, because it is primary history of the highest order." —*New York Times*

"*Island* is a unique work of history using the annotated poetry of Chinese immigrants to reveal a long-forgotten aspect of the American dream." —*London Times*

"That suffering can beget art is perhaps one of the most hopeful facts about the human psyche. . . . The creative act['s] . . . flourishing in the midst of despair is a tribute not only to humanity's endurance, but to its possibilities for triumph. These thoughts are occasioned by [this] book." —*San Francisco Examiner*

"An exquisite volume, handsomely designed and illustrated, rich with the resonant verse of the anonymous poets of Angel Island." —*Los Angeles Times*

"Many of the writers [on Angel Island] were laborers who had received little education. They expressed their anguish and anger by writing verses on the wall, without concern for the styles or rigid forms of poetry. As a result their writing is an artless art, and in that sense, may be the most genuine art or literary form." —*Pacific Affairs*

"With *Island* a new chapter has been written in the history of the Chinese in America, one which . . . will remind future generations of the tenacity Chinese immigrants displayed against the adversity which greeted them upon their arrival in America."

—*Berkeley Gazette*

"The editors of *Island*, themselves children of former Angel Island detainees, have done groundbreaking primary research and yeoman's literary work. . . . *Island* should be on the bookshelves of scholars and students interested in immigrant literature and required reading for those specializing in Asian American literature and history." —*Melus*

"The book is both educational and uplifting. . . . The reader is given an intimate view of the Chinese immigrants' experience, and while the injustice is obvious, even more so is a noble sense of honor and of destiny which tempered the detainees' frustration." —*East West*

"A passionate and immensely talented work of translation. Most of the poems would stand on their own in any context, and the accounts by survivors, all old now, will reacquaint anyone whose forebears came over on a boat with the tribulations of the newcomer." —*Focus*

ISLAND

埃崙詩集

POETRY AND HISTORY OF

CHINESE IMMIGRANTS ON

ANGEL ISLAND, 1910–1940

SECOND EDITION

EDITED BY

HIM MARK LAI

GENNY LIM

JUDY YUNG

University of Washington Press

Seattle and London

Island: Poetry and History of Chinese Immigrants on Angel Island, 1910–1940 is published with the assistance of a grant from the Naomi B. Pascal Editor's Endowment, supported through the generosity of Janet and John Creighton, Patti Knowles, Mary McLellan Williams, and other donors.

© 2014 by HOC DOI (History of Chinese Detained on Island) Project
Printed and bound in the United States
Design: Dustin Kilgore
Composed in Warnock, a typeface designed by Robert Slimbach
18 17 16 15 14   5 4 3 2 1

University of Washington Press
www.washington.edu/uwpress

Library of Congress Cataloging-in-Publication Data
Island : poetry and history of Chinese immigrants on Angel Island, 1910–1940 / edited by Him Mark Lai, Genny Lim, and Judy Yung. — Second edition.
    pages   cm. — (Naomi B. Pascal Editor's Endowment)
    Island was self-published in 1980 with partial funding from the Zellerbach Family Fund and the Wallace Alexander Gerbode Foundation, as well as the assistance of the San Francisco Study Center and Chinese Culture Foundation of San Francisco under the publisher's name—HOC DOI, which stands for "History of Chinese Detained on Island." It went into a second printing in 1983 and was republished by the University of Washington Press in 1991.
    In this revised edition sixty-nine poems in the main text have been combined with the sixty-six poems in the appendix into one section. Chinese poems that had been found on the walls of the immigration stations at Ellis Island in New York and at Victoria, B.C. in Canada are also included. Charles Egan, David Chuenyan Lai, Marlon K. Hom, and Ellen Yeung helped with the new translations and corrected any errors in the poems based on a report commissioned by the Angel Island Immigration Foundation. The historical introduction is rewritten to include the new research that has been done since *Island* was first published; excerpts of oral histories are replaced with twenty full profiles and stories drawn from our oral history collection and the immigration files at the National Archives, San Francisco).
    Unlike the first edition of *Island*, this revised edition uses the real names of our interviewees and includes photographs of them. Volunteers pored over twenty-seven rolls of microfilm that had been scanned by Ancestry.com in an effort to determine the actual detention time, exclusions, and appeals for Chinese applicants at Angel Island (see tables 1 and 2 in the appendix). The bibliography is updated; a map showing the emigrant districts in Guangdong has been added, as well as a glossary of Chinese names and terms mentioned in the book.
    Includes bibliographical references and index.
    Bilingual text in English and Chinese.
    ISBN 978-0-295-99407-9 (pbk. : alk. paper) 1. Chinese poetry—United States—Translations into English. 2. Chinese poetry—20th century—Translations into English. 3. Immigrants' writings, Chinese. 4. Chinese—United States—History. 5. Immigrants—United States—History. 6. United States—Emigration and immigration—History. I. Lai, H. Mark, editor, translator. II. Lim, Genny, editor. III. Yung, Judy editor. IV. Title: Poetry and history of Chinese immigrants on Angel Island, 1910-1940.
  PL3164.5.E5I85 2014
  895.11'51—dc23
                2014020568

Dedicated to the pioneers who passed through Angel Island

and

in memory of Him Mark Lai

CONTENTS

ORAL HISTORIES

PREFACE

IN 1940, AFTER A FIRE SHUT DOWN THE IMMIGRATION STATION on Angel Island in San Francisco Bay, one of the bitterest chapters in the history of Chinese immigration to America came to a close. The detention building, where Chinese men had been held, was spared by the fire and put to use by the U.S. Army for housing prisoners of war during World War II. It then stood abandoned for three decades, until it was finally marked for demolition by the California Department of Parks and Recreation. As luck would have it, the order was never carried out, thanks to the foresight of Alexander Weiss, a park ranger.

In 1970, while making his rounds on the island, Weiss noticed Chinese calligraphy inscribed all over the walls of the detention building. Although he could not read any of the writing, he knew it must have been left by Chinese immigrants who were once detained there. Weiss informed his superiors of his discovery, but they shared neither his enthusiasm nor his belief that the graffiti on the walls had any significance. He then contacted his biology professor at San Francisco State College, George Araki. Araki went to the island with San Francisco photographer Mak Takahashi, who brought floodlights and photographed practically every inch of wall that bore writing, most of which was poetry.

Their discovery, which occurred at a time of intense Asian American activism around issues of racial equality and social justice, soon sparked enough interest that the local community lobbied for preservation of the writings. *East West*, a bilingual Chinese American newspaper, published some of the Angel Island poems that Takahashi had photographed. Once we became aware of them, we embarked on a quest to collect and translate the poems and make them known to the world. Many of the poems on the walls had been partially obliterated by layers of paint and natural deterioration, and we were working against time to preserve as many as we could before the building was destroyed. We invited Chris Huie, a local photographer, and other members of Kearny Street Workshop (KSW) to help make wall rubbings of the poems. In 1976, KSW mounted a traveling exhibit about Chinese immigrants on Angel Island at a gallery in San Francisco Chinatown. The exhibition, which featured artwork, historical photographs, and reproductions of the poems, helped spread the word about the poetry and the existence of the abandoned immigration station.

Since there was hardly anything written about Angel Island, we decided to conduct oral history interviews with former detainees and employees of the immigration station. Finding subjects willing to talk proved difficult, however, as no one wanted to recall such a painful and shameful experience. In the process, we were fortunate to find two immigrants, Smiley Jann and Tet Yee, who had meticulously copied down close to one hundred poems in their notebooks while detained on Angel Island in the early 1930s.

In 1976, California appropriated $250,000 for the preservation of the poetry and the building. Over the next forty years, community activists and descendants of Angel Island detainees, ourselves included, worked to recover the immigration history of Angel Island. Key to this was acquiring National Historic Landmark status for the immigration station and securing funds to preserve the poetry and restore the detention center as a symbol of America's history of racial exclusion and a site of conscience and reconciliation for all.

The research project, which started out as a personal quest to reclaim our history as Chinese Americans, soon evolved into a book project. Despite the fact that we all had full-time jobs at the time—Him Mark was working as a mechanical engineer at Bechtel, Genny was a television producer and poet, and Judy was heading the Asian Community Library in Oakland—we were able to finish the book in three years' time. Him Mark, who among the three of us was the most proficient in the Chinese language and the most knowledgeable about Chinese and Chinese American history, did the lion's share of the work. Aside from conducting archival research and oral history interviews, he translated all the poems we had from the Takahashi photographs, Jann and Yee collections, Chinese-language newspapers, and KSW rubbings. Him Mark also wrote the historical introduction and all the footnotes, which were necessary for understanding the colloquial expressions and allusions to historical figures and events in the poems. Genny, an accomplished poet in the English language, spent hours refining Him Mark's translations, adding feeling and depth to them. She also helped with the oral history interviews. Judy concentrated on finding people to interview, transcribing the interviews, and selecting excerpts to complement the poems in the book. We all shared in the work of selecting photographs and preparing the manuscript for publication.

As enthused as we were about the importance of our book, no publisher was interested in it. None of us were published scholars, and, we were told, there was no market for a bilingual collection of Chinese American poetry. Undeterred, we decided to self-publish with partial funding from the Zellerbach Family Fund and the Wallace Alexander Gerbode Foundation, as well as the assistance of the San Francisco Study Center and Chinese Culture Foundation of San Francisco. Genny came up with our publisher's name—HOC DOI, which stands for "History of Chinese Detained on Island" and is the colloquial Cantonese term for a sojourner.

Island: Poetry and History of Chinese Immigrants on Angel Island, 1910–1940—consisting of a historical introduction, 135 poems in Chinese and English, excerpts from thirty-nine oral history interviews, and twenty-two photographs of the period—was published in 1980. It was designed by Harry Driggs in two-colored paper with an understated cover showing a ship approaching the island in the fog. The book won an Award of Merit for book design from the Western Art Directors Club in 1981. *Island* went into a second printing in 1983 and was republished by the University of Washington Press in 1991. It has remained in print until its replacement by this updated, expanded edition.

The book was not a best seller, but it had a profound impact in the fields of American literature and U.S. history. Fred Ferretti of the *New York Times* described it as "an exquisite volume, handsomely designed and illustrated, rich with the resonant verse of the anonymous poets of Angel Island." The Before Columbus Foundation, in awarding the volume the American Book Award in 1982 for excellence in literature, had this to say: "*Island* is a model of editing, presentation, and books that give meaning and visibility to a larger and more complete history of the United States." In 1993, the Angel Island poems joined the American literary canon when thirteen poems were included in the second edition of the *Heath Anthology of American Literature*, intended for use in high schools and colleges throughout the country. Since its publication, *Island* has become a literary staple in Asian American studies, ethnic studies, U.S. immigration history, and American literature classes, and the Angel Island story is starting to be included in social studies textbooks for public schools.

More important has been the book's impact on both the Chinese American community and the United States at large. By openly airing the dark secrets of racial exclusion and illegal immigration, the book served as a catharsis as well as an exoneration of those who had been imprisoned on Angel Island. It legitimized the Angel Island experience to the degree that our immigrant parents no longer felt ashamed or afraid of sharing their stories. As for their children, brought up under the shadow of exclusion,

Island allowed them to reclaim their history, reconcile with their immigration past, and take pride in their ethnic heritage. To the rest of America, *Island* succeeded in calling attention to a shameful chapter in our country's immigration history and the need to safeguard against its reoccurrence. This became evident when President Obama included the Angel Island story in his major speech on immigration reform in 2009 and when Congress formally apologized in 2012 for the Chinese Exclusion Acts.

Through the years, *Island* has inspired and spawned other research, publications, and multimedia productions (films, plays, songs, dance, and operas) about the Angel Island experience. Of particular importance has been the new research done by Erika Lee based on the Chinese exclusion files at the National Archives at San Francisco (NARA-SF), Nayan Shah on public health issues and medical practices at Angel Island, Estelle Lau on the paper son immigration strategy and Confession Program, and Robert Barde on passenger ships and Angel Island, as well as Erika Lee and Judy Yung's comprehensive history of Angel Island immigration.

Moreover, the Angel Island Immigration Station Foundation and California State Parks, in their efforts to preserve the poetry and restore the immigration station as a historical monument and museum, commissioned the Architectural Resources Group to conduct feasibility studies on the immigration station's buildings, cultural artifacts, history, and grounds. They also hired a team of Chinese scholars to do a comprehensive study of all the poems and inscriptions on the walls. So much more is now known about the history and wall inscriptions of Angel Island that we felt a second edition of *Island* was warranted.

Although Him Mark did not live long enough to work on the new edition with us, we have felt his spirit guiding us throughout the project. Before he died in 2009, he told us to combine the sixty-nine poems in the main text with the sixty-six poems in the appendix into one section. He also instructed us to include the Chinese poems that had been found on the walls of the immigration stations at Ellis Island in New York and at Victoria, B.C. in Canada, in order to show the similar responses of Chinese immigrants to racial exclusion and detention in different parts of the country and the world. Left without the benefit of his Chinese-language skills, we called on the expertise of Charles Egan, David Chuenyan Lai, Marlon K. Hom, and Ellen Yeung for help with the new translations and to correct any errors in the poems based on "Poetry and Inscriptions," the research team's report.

We also rewrote the historical introduction to include the new research that has been done since *Island* was first published and replaced the excerpts of oral histories with twenty full profiles and poignant stories drawn from our oral history collection and the immigration files at NARA-SF.

Unlike the first edition of *Island*, this revised edition uses the real names of our interviewees and includes photographs of them.

Volunteers spent many hours poring over twenty-seven rolls of microfilm that had been scanned by Ancestry.com in an effort to determine the actual detention time, exclusions, and appeals for Chinese applicants at Angel Island (see tables 1 and 2 in the appendix). We also updated the bibliography of sources and added a map showing the emigrant districts in Guangdong, as well as a glossary of Chinese names and terms mentioned in the book. We believe that these changes will contribute to a fuller picture and deeper understanding of the poetry and experiences of Chinese immigrants on Angel Island than ever before.

Judy Yung and Genny Lim
June 1, 2014

ACKNOWLEDGMENTS

THIS REVISED EDITION OF *ISLAND* WOULD NOT HAVE BEEN POS-sible without the support and assistance of many organizations, colleagues, volunteers, archivists, families, and individuals who generously shared their time, energy, knowledge, expertise, and stories with us.

We wish to thank the following people for their research assistance and prompt responses to our many queries: Marisa Louie and Bill Greene at the National Archives at San Francisco (NARA-SF); Wei Chi Poon at the Ethnic Studies Library, University of California, Berkeley; Eddie Wong, Grant Din, and Julie Phuong at the Angel Island Immigration Station Foundation; Al Cheng and Steve Owyang with the Friends of the Roots project at the Chinese Historical Society of America; and Robert Barde, Ben Fenkell, Sandra Gin, Felicia Lowe, Marlon K. Hom, Derek Lang, Erika Lee, Larry Lew, Bill Lowe, Shirley Mow, Anna Pegler-Gordon, Dan Quan, Maria Sakovitch, Jack Tchen, Doris Tseng, Germaine Wong, and Ellen Yeung.

In our efforts to revise *Island*, we sorely missed the involvement and contributions of Him Mark Lai, who died in 2009. Our gratitude goes to Charles Egan, Marlon K. Hom, and David Chuenyan Lai for their translations of the new poems in *Island*; to Ellen Yeung for her meticulous work in editing the poems, footnotes, bibliography, and glossary; to the wonderful staff at the University of Washington Press—Lorri Hagman, Tim Zimmerman, Mary C. Ribesky, Laura Iwasaki, and Dustin Kilgore—for the special care they gave to this book; and to Laura Lai and Ruthanne Lum McCunn for their support and sound advice throughout this project.

Almost all of the detainees whom we interviewed for *Island* and whose stories are included in this revised edition have passed away. In their absence, we were fortunate to locate their families and obtain their help in filling the gaps in their parents' stories. They also provided us with documents and photographs and granted us permission to use their real names in *Island*. Our heartfelt thanks go to Kathy and David Ang, Dennis and

Robert Fong, Daisy and Debbie Gin, Joyce Horowitz, Cynthia Ip and David Lau, Andrea and Alvin Ja, Peter Ja and Mary Fong, Arliss Jann, Laura Lai, James Poy Wong, Victor Low and Pearl Chinn, Linelle Marshall, John Mock, Penelope Wong, and Irene Yee.

Many volunteers assisted with the graphics and appendix material in this book. Our special thanks to Vincent Chin for scanning the certificates of identity and many documents at NARA-SF; Daniel Quan for sharing digital copies of the Angel Island poems and photographs from his collection; Andrea Ja for enhancing old photographs for publication; Xing Chu Wang for typing the Chinese poems from Victoria, B.C.; Jamie Hawk for drawing the map of Guangdong; Jianye He and Ellen Yeung for compiling the bibliography of Chinese sources; Eddie Fung, Kelsey Owyang, Vincent Chin, Kathy Ang, and Ben Lee for tallying the detention time for 95,687 applicants; and Robert Barde for calculating the median days of detention.

Our family histories are linked to the Angel Island Immigration Station, and it is to our parents, who made the journey to America and endured confinement on Angel Island for our sake, that we owe our deepest gratitude: Lai Bing and Dong Hing Mui, Lim Tai Go and Lin Sun Lim, and Tom Yip Jing and Jew Law Ying.

ISLAND

埃崙诗集

INTRODUCTION

Under the Shadow of Exclusion:

Chinese Immigrants on Angel Island

A NGEL ISLAND, NOW AN IDYLLIC STATE PARK IN SAN FRAN-cisco Bay, not far from Alcatraz, was the point of entry for more than half a million immigrants, including one hundred thousand Chinese, who came to the United States between 1910 and 1940.[1] Modeled after New York's Ellis Island, the site was used as the detention center for newcomers awaiting decisions on medical and immigration inspections. But whereas Ellis Island was built to welcome European immigrants to the United States, the Angel Island Immigration Station was built to enforce the Chinese exclusion laws and to keep Chinese and other Asians out of the country. As a rule, Chinese applicants, who made up 70 percent of the de-

FIG. 1.1
Panoramic view of the Angel Island
Immigration Station,
c. 1910. Courtesy of California
State Parks, 2014.

tainee population on Angel Island, were subjected to longer examinations, interrogations, and detentions than any other immigrant group.

The ordeal of immigration and incarceration left an indelible mark in the minds of many Chinese, a number of whom wrote poetry on the barracks walls, recording their voyages to America, their longing for families back home, and the outrage and humiliation they felt at the treatment they received upon arriving in America. Others kept their sad stories hidden from their children until, with the gentle coaxing of oral historians, they were able to talk about their experiences many years later. This collection of poetry and oral histories is a testament to the hardships they endured on Angel Island, their perseverance, and their determination to make a new life in America.

"FOR THE SAKE OF THE STOMACH"

The first Chinese to immigrate to the United States in the mid-nineteenth century came principally from the Pearl River Delta of Guangdong in southeastern China. Attracted by stories of the gold rush in Gold Mountain (Gam Saan, the common Chinese name for California), they came not only as prospectors but also as artisans, merchants, and students. Many more arrived as laborers to work in Hawaii's sugar plantations and the mines, railroad lines, farmlands, fisheries, and factories of the American West.

1 New research has revealed that 550,469 people arrived and 665,430 departed through the port of San Francisco between 1910 and 1940. An estimated 300,000 people were detained at Angel Island, including 100,000 Chinese, 85,000 Japanese, 8,000 South Asians, 8,000 Russians and Jews, 1,000 Koreans, and 1,000 Filipinos. See Lee and Yung, *Angel Island*, 17–20, 69. Additional research for this book shows that half of the Chinese applicants were landed from the ship, and only 50,000 Chinese spent any time on Angel Island (see table 1 in the appendix).

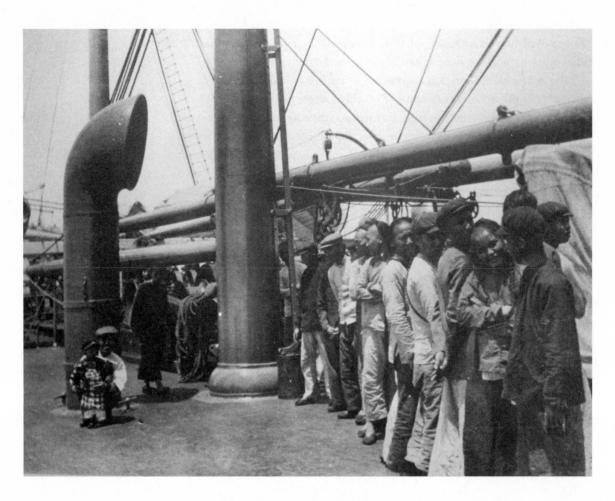

FIG 1.2
En route to Gold Mountain.
Courtesy of San Francisco
Maritime Museum, K9.17265.

From 1852 until 1882, when the Chinese Exclusion Act was passed, more than three hundred thousand Chinese entered the United States. They helped fuel the global expansion of Western capitalism by providing a continuous stream of labor from Asia to drive its burgeoning industries and profits.

After China's defeat by the British in the Opium Wars (1839–42, 1856–60), a weakened China was forced to open its ports to foreign trade, pay indemnities of 20 million silver dollars, and, most damaging of all, grant Great Britain and its allies extraterritorial rights, which made them immune to Chinese law. Life for the Chinese people, especially in the rural south, deteriorated as a result. Aside from suffering increased taxes, forfeiture of land, competition from imported manufactured goods, and unemployment, they also had to contend with problems of overpopulation, floods and famines, bandits, and the devastation caused by peasant rebellions and the ongoing Punti-Hakka interethnic conflict. Because of their coastal location and early contact with foreign traders, many were drawn to America by

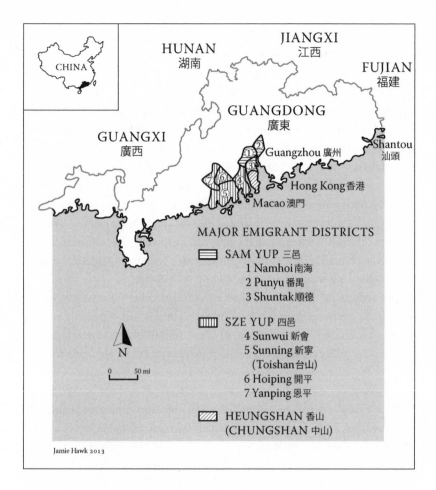

FIG. 1.3
From the mid-nineteenth century until World War II, most Chinese in the United States came from these emigrant districts in Guangdong.

Map labels:

CHINA

HUNAN 湖南
JIANGXI 江西
FUJIAN 福建
GUANGDONG 廣東
GUANGXI 廣西

Guangzhou 廣州
Shantou 汕頭
Hong Kong 香港
Macao 澳門

MAJOR EMIGRANT DISTRICTS

SAM YUP 三邑
1 Namhoi 南海
2 Punyu 番禺
3 Shuntak 順德

SZE YUP 四邑
4 Sunwui 新會
5 Sunning 新寧
  (Toishan 台山)
6 Hoiping 開平
7 Yanping 恩平

HEUNGSHAN 香山
(CHUNGSHAN 中山)

N
0   50 mi

Jamie Hawk 2013

news of the gold rush and labor contractors in search of young, able-bodied men to work in the New World.

The Chinese received a hostile reception in the United States almost from the start. Arriving at a time of western expansion, when European Americans, imbued with a strong sense of Manifest Destiny and white superiority, were laying claim to its lands and riches, Chinese immigrants fell victim to racial discrimination and class exploitation. Although some white Americans welcomed the Chinese as new members of the American family, many saw them as the Yellow Peril—a moral, racial, and economic threat to the American way of life. Even before the Chinese began to arrive, many white Americans held fast to their assumption that China was a backward, heathen, and degenerate country populated by the dregs of humanity. Moreover, the racial and cultural differences of the Chinese set them worlds apart. They were stereotyped in the mass media and in the halls of Congress as immoral and vice ridden, "full of filth and diseases," slave labor, and "wholly unfit to become citizens." White Americans considered them to be racial subordinates, akin to Africans, Mexicans, and American Indians, and mistreated them accordingly.

Although Chinese were not welcomed or treated as equals, their contributions to the United States were critical to its emergence as an economic and political world power. They were instrumental in building the transcontinental railroad and provided the bulk of labor that helped lay down the industrial infrastructure of the American West. Chinese laborers laid the tracks and telegraph lines; reclaimed swamplands in the Sacramento–San Joaquin Delta; developed the shrimp and abalone fisheries, the opulent Napa-Sonoma vineyards, and new strains of fruits and vegetables; and proved to be a reliable workforce for mining companies, salmon canneries in the Pacific Northwest, and California's growing agriculture and light industries. Nonetheless, Chinese newcomers remained targets of ethnic stereotyping, discriminatory laws, and racial violence.

As early as 1852, California enacted a foreign miners' license tax, which was aimed particularly at Chinese miners. Until it was repealed in 1870, the tax accounted for $5 million, or close to half of the state's revenue. As the gold rush petered out, hostile miners resorted to physical violence to drive the Chinese from the mines. San Francisco, where many Chinese chose to settle, passed ordinances intended to deprive them of their livelihoods and make their lives miserable: the Cubic Air Ordinance prohibited Chinese from renting rooms that allowed less than 500 cubic feet of air per person; the Sidewalk Ordinance stopped Chinese from using poles to carry laundry loads on the sidewalk; and the Queue Ordinance required Chinese prisoners to cut their hair short, a disgrace for Chinese in those early days, when the queue symbolized their national identity. California also passed anti–civil rights legislation that prohibited Chinese from immigrating to the state, testifying against a white person in court, applying for jobs in public works, marrying whites, and owning land.

But the worst was yet to come. When an economic depression hit the West in the 1870s, anti-Chinese violence broke out among white workers who blamed the Chinese for driving down wages and stealing their jobs. Throughout the American West, bloodthirsty mobs stormed Chinese settlements, looting, lynching, burning, and driving the Chinese out. So cruelly did America treat them that it caused humorist Mark Twain to wince and write wryly of the Chinese, "They are a harmless race when white men either let them alone or treat them no worse than dogs."[2]

The slogan coined by Denis Kearney and the Workingman's Party at their sandlot rallies—"The Chinese must go!"—became a reality when labor leaders and opportunistic politicians pressured Congress to pass the Chinese Exclusion Act of 1882, which suspended the immigration of Chinese

2   See Pfaelzer, *Driven Out*;
    Twain, *Roughing It*, 350.

laborers for ten years and barred Chinese from becoming naturalized U.S. citizens. At the same time, the federal government established the Court of Indian Offenses to prosecute Native Americans for practicing "heathenish rites" and ordered that Indian children be removed from their families and placed in boarding schools designed to strip them of their Indian identity and assimilate them into white society. It was in this oppressive racial climate that Chinese exclusion was legislated into federal law.

The Chinese Exclusion Act heralded a change in the nation's immigration policy, from one that had been free and unrestricted to one of restriction and exclusion. In subsequent years, Congress passed additional laws to bar South Asians, Japanese, Koreans, and Filipinos and to limit immigration from southern and eastern European countries.[3] For the first time in U.S. history, members of a specific immigrant group were refused entry on the basis of their race and class. Only government officials, merchants, students, teachers, travelers, and those claiming U.S. citizenship were exempted. The Exclusion Act was extended and revised several times over subsequent years, closing loopholes and becoming stricter in its provisions and enforcement. As one Chinese immigrant remarked in 1904, when Congress extended the law indefinitely, "They call it exclusion, but it is not exclusion, it is extermination."[4] In 1887, only ten Chinese were admitted into the country.

The exclusion laws, which were not repealed until 1943, had a devastating impact on the Chinese community in America. Its population plummeted from 105,000 in 1880 to 77,000 in 1940, and many men were forced to endure long separations from their wives and children in China. Chinatowns became "bachelor societies" with all the attendant social vices—prostitution, gambling, illegal drugs, and tong wars—and Chinese Americans everywhere were made to feel like social pariahs and second-class citizens.

"TAKING THE CROOKED PATH"

During these same years, however, life in China was becoming increasingly difficult. As political and economic conditions in China continued to decline under the pressures of Western imperialism, and as fighting flared between warlords, followed by internal rivalry between Nationalists and Communists in the 1920s and a full-scale war with Japan in the 1930s, many people were willing to sacrifice their life savings and risk exclusion in the hope of making better lives in America. Some Chinese traveled to Canada, Mexico, or the Caribbean islands and were then smuggled into the United States. Many more took the "crooked path" by falsely claiming to be members of the exempt classes—most often merchants or U.S. citizens. As one

3   The Immigration Act of 1917 denied entry to immigrants from the "Asiatic Barred Zone," which encompassed India, Burma, Siam, the Malay States, Arabia, Afghanistan, Russia, and the Polynesian Islands. The Immigration Act of 1924, which set annual quotas for each immigrant group, was designed to limit arrivals from southern and eastern Europe. It also closed the door on Japanese and Korean immigration by denying admission to all aliens who were "ineligible to citizenship." The Tydings-McDuffie Act of 1934 changed the status of Filipinos from American nationals to aliens and assigned the Philippines a measly quota of fifty immigrants per year.

4   Chan Kiu Sing, cited in Coolidge, *Chinese Immigration*, 302.

former detainee put it, "We didn't want to come illegally, but we were forced to by the exclusion laws. If we told the truth, it won't work, so we had to take the crooked path."[5]

A lucrative business in false papers sprang up on both sides of the Pacific. Chinese companies in the United States sold fictitious partnerships to immigrants seeking to claim merchant status. Chinese entering the country for the first time or returning from visits to China often claimed more sons than they had in order to create immigration slots that could be sold to prospective migrants known as "paper sons"—individuals who were offspring not in reality but on paper only.[6] The 1906 earthquake and fire, which destroyed the city hall and all of San Francisco's birth records, enabled many more Chinese to claim birthright and derivative citizenships. So successful were they at circumventing the Chinese exclusion laws that more Chinese immigrants were admitted into the United States during the exclusion period (303,000) than in the period before exclusion (258,000).[7] Chinese immigrants and immigration officials both estimated that 80 to 90 percent of these applicants were most likely paper sons or paper daughters.

U.S. immigration officials were aware of the methods used by Chinese immigrants to evade the exclusion laws. According to Luther Steward, acting commissioner of immigration, "If their claims [as natives of Chinese descent] are true, every Chinese woman who had ever resided in the U.S. would have had in excess of fifty children."[8] They also pointed to the preponderance of claimed sons over claimed daughters as evidence of deception. The Immigration Service reacted with harsh measures. Frequent sweeps through Chinese business establishments, schools, and churches ensnared illegal immigrants. During the 1920s, the Chinese community complained of a "veritable Reign of Terror" against them.[9] The common sight of immigration officials dressed in green uniforms arresting Chinese gave rise to the Cantonese term *luk yi*, or "green clothes man," which eventually became the colloquial name for a police officer. At the port of entry, immigrant inspectors held all Chinese claims for right of admission suspect until applicants' identities could be verified through cross-examinations. Designed to exclude rather than to admit, routine interrogations of new arrivals became more intensive and detailed.

The Chinese viewed the exclusion laws and regulations as unfair and discriminatory and termed the statutes *kelü*, meaning "tyrannical laws." They addressed numerous complaints to the U.S. government through diplomatic channels, objecting to the harsh treatment of the Chinese in general and protesting in particular the suspicious and discourteous behavior of immigration officials toward women and members of the exempt classes.[10] In 1892, after Congress passed the Geary Act to extend the exclu-

5 Ted Chan interview.
6 In the 1920s, the average cost of a partnership was $1,000, while the going rate for paper son slots was $1,500 to $2,000.
7 Lee and Yung, *Angel Island*, 76.
8 Committee Representing the Down Town Association of San Francisco, "Transcript of Stenographic Notes Taken on the Occasion of a Visit Paid the Angel Island Immigration Station, June 6, 1911," file 52961/24-D, Central Office Subject Correspondence and Case Files, RG 85, NARA-DC.
9 Erika Lee, *At America's Gates*, 228.

sion law for another ten years and, additionally, to require that all Chinese aliens register for certificates of residence or risk deportation, the entire Chinese community refused to comply, hoping that the U.S. Supreme Court would rule in its favor. Instead, the high court declared the law constitutional. The Chinese lost that legal battle but were able to claim victory in the 1905 boycott of U.S. goods, which started in Shanghai and quickly spread to other Chinese cities and overseas Chinese communities. The boycott succeeded in forcing the U.S. government to relax some of its more objectionable regulations.[11]

FIG. 1.4
Pacific Mail Steamship Company detention shed at Pier 40. Source: *Chinese World,* January 21, 1913, 3.

From the late 1880s until 1910, Chinese ship passengers arriving at San Francisco were detained in a two-story shed at the Pacific Mail Steamship Company dock (known to Cantonese immigrants as *muk uk,* or "wooden house"), until immigrant inspectors could examine them and determine the validity of their claims. As many as four hundred to five hundred people at a time were crammed into the ramshackle facility with no access to sunshine, fresh air, or exercise. Chinese community leaders, alarmed at the unsafe and unsanitary conditions of the structure, complained frequently to U.S. officials. According to an editorial published in the *Chinese World* newspaper, "The mistreatment of us Chinese confined there was worse than for jailed prisoners. The walls were covered with poems of anguish; traces of tears soaked the floor. There were even some who could not endure the cruel abuse and took their own lives. . . . Those seeing this cannot help but feel aggrieved and gnash their teeth in anger." Some grew so frustrated that they risked their lives to escape. In the fall of 1908 alone, thirty-two Chinese succeeded in escaping from the shed by cutting a hole in the wall.[12]

Upon investigation, the Bureau of Immigration declared the shed "a veritable fire trap" and the deplorable conditions beyond repair. It recommended that a new immigration station be erected on Angel Island to better accommodate the growing numbers of aliens, chiefly Chinese and other Asians. The subsequent decision to relocate the station to Angel Island was not altogether humanitarian. Officials also felt that the island location would prevent Chinese immigrants from being coached by friends and relatives on the outside as well as protect Americans from contagious diseases that Asians allegedly carried. Moreover, the immigration station, like Alcatraz prison, would be escape-proof.[13]

10   U.S. Department of Commerce and Labor, *Annual Report,* 1904–5, 81; *Chinese World,* May 2, 1910, 3.
11   Tsai, *China and the Overseas Chinese,* 121–22.
12   *Chinese World,* January 22, 1910, 3; *San Francisco Call,* September 9, 1908, 4, and November 29, 1908, 17.
13   Richard Taylor to Commissioner-General of Immigration, March 25, 1909, file 52270/21, Central Office Subject Correspondence and Case Files, RG 85, NARA-DC; H. H. North to George C. Perkins, December 7, 1903, box 1, Hart Hyatt North Papers, Bancroft Library, University of California, Berkeley.

14 Such lavish praise for the
    immigration station was pub-
    lished in the local newspapers
    before it was even opened:
    "Indeed, the newcomers from
    foreign shores, will prob-
    ably think they have struck
    paradise when they emerge
    from the steerage quarters
    of an ocean liner and land at
    the summer resort which the
    Immigration Bureau has pro-
    vided for them." *San Francisco
    Chronicle*, August 18, 1907, 4.

15 M. W. Glover to Acting
    Commissioner of Immigra-
    tion, November 21, 1910, file
    52961/26F, and Acting Com-
    missioner Luther C. Steward
    to Commissioner-General of
    Immigration, December 19,
    1910, Central Office Subject
    Correspondence and Case
    Files, RG 85, NARA-DC; *San
    Francisco Chronicle*, August
    8, 1920, 52, and November 1,
    1922, 8.

16 After the fire, the deten-
    tion center was moved to
    temporary quarters at 801
    Silver Avenue, relocated to
    Sharp Park in the spring of
    1942, and finally settled in the
    Appraiser's Building at 630
    Sansome Street in 1944.

On January 21, 1910, the "finest immigration station in the world" opened at Angel Island, despite complaints by Chinatown leaders that its location was inconvenient for witnesses.[14] The government quickly discovered that the station's insular location was far from satisfactory. Fresh water was scarce, and the station was expensive to operate since all essentials had to be shipped from the mainland. A few months after the facility opened, the authorities already had second thoughts. Surgeon Melvin Glover and Acting Commissioner of Immigration Luther Steward submitted reports highly critical of the many physical and sanitary drawbacks in the design and construction of the hospital and immigration station. In 1920, Commissioner of Immigration Edward White declared that the facility's structures were "virtual tinderboxes" and proposed that the station be moved back to the mainland in order to cut expenses. Two years later, Commissioner-General of Immigration W. W. Husband called the Angel Island buildings "the worst immigration station I have ever seen, . . . filthy and unfit for habitation."[15] But it was not until November of 1940, three months after a fire destroyed the administration building, that the government finally abandoned the site and moved the immigration station back to San Francisco.[16]

"HUNDREDS OF DESPOTIC ACTS"

The Angel Island Immigration Station proved to be a global crossroads for immigrants from eighty countries around the world. Two-thirds of the newcomers came from China and Japan, but there were also immigrants from India, Korea, Russia, the Philippines, Great Britain, Germany, Spain, Mexico, Central and South America, the Pacific Islands, Australia, and New Zealand.[17] From the moment that their ships landed in San Francisco, it became apparent that their treatment and their chances of being admitted into the country all hinged on immigration policies that discriminated against individuals on the basis of race, class, gender, and nationality.

The differential treatment began during primary inspection, when immigration and medical officials climbed aboard the ships to inspect the papers and health of all the passengers and crew. First-class passengers, who were mostly white and wealthy, were given a cursory examination in the privacy of their cabins. They, along with returning residents and those traveling in second class, were usually allowed to land directly from the ship. Third-class and steerage passengers, who were mainly Asians and poor, along with sick passengers and anyone whose papers were in question, were

FIG. 1.6
Fire in 1940 that destroyed the administration building. Courtesy of San Francisco History Center, San Francisco Public Library.

17 See map and table 2 in Lee and Yung, *Angel Island*, 2–3, 328–29.

all required to take the ferry to Angel Island for a more thorough inspection. Most non-Asians were thus able to avoid Angel Island altogether or had a very short stay there. In contrast, at least half of the Chinese passengers were usually transported to Angel Island and detained there for weeks and months while awaiting decisions on their applications.[18]

Upon arriving at Angel Island, passengers deposited their luggage in the baggage shed and were shepherded to the immigration station. From then on, segregation policies were strictly enforced to create spatial distance between the races and to protect whites from the "contamination" of Asians. Men and women, including husbands and wives, were separated and not allowed to see or communicate with each other until their cases had been settled. Children under age twelve were assigned to the care of their mothers. There were also separate living quarters, dining halls and eating times, recreation areas, and hospital entrances and wards—all designed to keep the different classes, races, and genders apart. Superior detention quarters and dining facilities and better food and treatment for whites reflected the racial favoritism embedded in U.S. immigration policies.

18   See table 1 in the appendix.

FIG. 1.8
Chinese detainees on the hospital
steps. Courtesy of National
Archives, Washington, D.C.

The first stop for the new arrivals was the administration building,
which housed the registration rooms, offices, medical exam room, four
dining rooms, dormitories for employees, and detention quarters for one
hundred people. There they were segregated into waiting areas, given a
quick look-over, registered, and assigned to their living quarters. Chinese
and Japanese men were kept in separate sections of the detention barracks;
all others, including women and children, were housed on the second floor
of the administration building in segregated quarters.

The next day, they were taken to the hospital, located northeast of the
administration building, for the medical exam. While non-Asians were

FIG. 1.9
Chinese women's infirmary.
Courtesy of National Archives,
Washington, D.C.

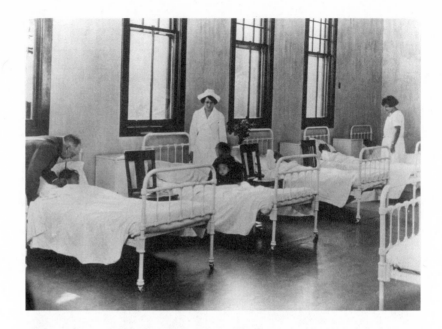

19   Shah, *Contagious Divides*,
     179–203; Mr. Leung inter-
     view; Chen Wen-hsien,
     "Chinese under Both Exclu-
     sion and Immigration Laws,"
     392–95.

given a cursory line inspection and eye exam for any medical defects or signs of trachoma, Asian immigrants were subjected to more intensive and invasive examinations of their blood and waste products intended to detect traces of intestinal parasites that they were known to carry. Before 1910, immigrants could be excluded for having such "loathsome and dangerously contagious diseases" as trachoma, tuberculosis, syphilis, gonorrhea, and leprosy. In 1910, uncinariasis (hookworm infection) and filariasis (thread-worm infection) were added to the list of excludable diseases, and in 1917, clonorchiasis (liver fluke infection) was also classified as reason for exclusion. Because of poor sanitation in rural parts of Asia, immigrants from China, Japan, Korea, and India were most commonly diagnosed with these parasitic diseases and denied entry. The men were required to strip naked in order to reveal any abnormalities. Women were not required to disrobe, unless the doctors detected specific signs of disease. However, if there were any doubts about the claimed age of an applicant, both male and female applicants were subjected to a nude inspection of their body parts, which caused great anguish among the Chinese. Unaccustomed to exposing themselves in public, many, like Mr. Leung, felt "red faced and hot eared" during the exam. A group of female students complained bitterly about the rude nurses who demanded they produce stool specimens on the spot.[19]

The Chinese reacted strongly to these humiliating and discriminatory procedures. An editorial in the *Chinese Defender* sarcastically accused the Public Health Service of inventing the hookworm diagnosis as a way of barring Chinese entry to the country. "So arriving immigrants now have hookworms. Somebody must have stayed awake nights to think that out; it surely was a stroke of genius!"[20] After considerable protest from Chinese organizations and among diplomatic circles, the U.S. government reclassified the parasitic diseases and allowed immigrants to seek medical treatment at the immigration hospital, but at their own expense. It is no wonder that Asian immigrants had higher rates of medical exclusion, longer stays on the island, and more added expenses than their European counterparts. Those fortunate enough to pass the medical hurdle returned to their dormitories to await hearings on their applications.

"LAWS HARSH AS TIGERS"

During the early years of the immigration station's operations, this waiting period could stretch into months and became a source of many complaints. By the mid-1920s, however, the delay averaged two to three weeks. Overall, the median days of detention for Chinese immigrants was sixteen days.[21] The Chinese also complained that the examination procedure for Chinese applicants and witnesses was unfair. In response, the Immigration Service modified regulations to require that Chinese cases be heard by Boards of Special Inquiry instead of by just one inspector. This change put Chinese on the same footing with other aliens. The board was made up of two immigrant inspectors and a stenographer. It was not bound by technical rules of procedure or evidence as applied by the federal courts, but it was allowed to use any means it deemed fit to ascertain the legitimacy of the immigrant's application to enter the United States under the Chinese exclusion acts and general immigration laws.[22] For Chinese applicants, this meant longer and more exhaustive interrogations than for any other immigrant group on Angel Island.

Chinese immigrants who claimed merchant status were asked to provide detailed documentation of their business activities and volume of merchandise, a list of all partners, and two white witnesses to testify on their behalf. Their appearance, handwriting, clothing, and hands (whether callous or smooth) were all used as evidence to determine whether they were really merchants or were instead laborers in disguise. Wong Chung Hong, the first recorded person to be admitted into the country through Angel Island, met all of these criteria. He showed immigration officials his "section 6" exempt-class certificate signed by the Chinese viceroy and U.S. consul general in Canton, verifying his status as a merchant. Moreover, he was dressed in richly embroidered robes and had $500 in U.S. currency that he planned to invest in a grocery business. Inspector Lorenzen noted that the applicant's appearance was "conclusively" not that of a laborer, and

20 *Chinese Defender*, November 1910, 1, as quoted in Shah, *Contagious Divides*, 192.

21 Commissioner of Immigration Luther Seward to the Commissioner-General of Immigration, January 9, 1911, file 52999/44-B, Central Office Subject Correspondence and Case Files, RG 85, NARA-DC; *Chinese World*, November 8, 1913, 3, and March 1, 1916, 3; table 1 in the appendix.

22 *U.S. Immigration Service Bulletin* 1, no. 12 (March 1, 1919); Edward Haff, *Boards of Special Inquiry*, 2nd ser., Lecture No. 24, November 26, 1934; Emery Sims interview.

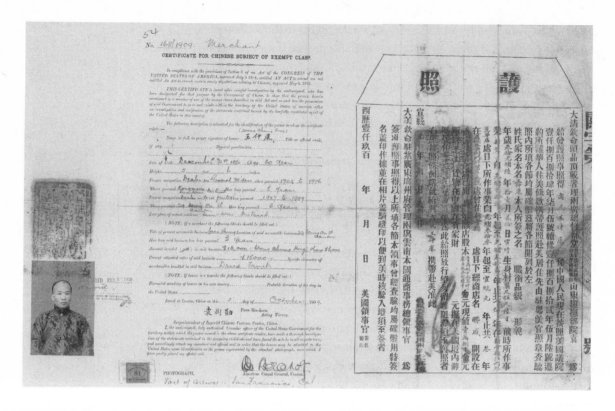

FIG. 1.10
Wong Chung Hong's "section 6"
certificate attesting to his exempt
status as a merchant, September
11, 1909. Courtesy of National
Archives, San Francisco.

Wong was landed three days later.[23] Once admitted, however, a merchant's dealings with the Immigration Service did not end. All Chinese businesses were required to send an up-to-date list of their partners to immigration authorities on a regular basis, and investigators were often sent into the Chinese community to ascertain whether merchants were maintaining the exempt status under which they had been admitted. If they were not, they could face deportation.

By the 1920s, more Chinese were claiming to be sons of native-born citizens than any other immigration status. Because there were usually no documents to corroborate or disprove these claims, the scope and method of examination for Chinese cases were different from those for other nationalities. Evidence was often confined to the detailed testimony given by the applicant and his witness concerning family history, relationships, living arrangements, and everyday life in the village. Applicants were sometimes asked to identify family pictures and draw maps of their ancestral villages and the surrounding countryside. Any discrepancies in the answers of the applicant and the witness could mean exclusion and deportation. In the absence of any witnesses, as in the case of a returning native U.S. citizen who claimed to have left for China at a young age, authorities asked questions that tested his English-language proficiency and recollections of life

23 File 10382/54 (Wong Chung
Hong), Immigration Arrival
Investigation Case Files, RG
85, NARA-SF.

in America: "Have you ever ridden in a streetcar?" "Does it snow here in winter?" "Do you know of any Chinese restaurants or joss houses in this city?" "Which store was opposite the one in which you lived?" "Do Jackson Street and Dupont Street run in the same direction?"[24]

Chinese women, who were entering the country primarily as the dependent wives or daughters of a merchant or U.S. citizen, were given a harder time than the men. They had to first prove to immigration officials that their husbands or fathers still qualified as members of the exempt classes. They had to also prove that their identities and relationships were real. Lacking official records of their births or marriages, the women were required to answer detailed and intimate questions about their living environments and marital relations. A wife who had moved to her husband's village only briefly before immigrating to the United States could have difficulty answering these questions. Women suspected of being prostitutes or having committed an act of "moral turpitude" were subjected to longer interviews and asked more intrusive questions about their sexual history than were men.

Aware of the interrogation procedures employed at Angel Island, Chinese immigrants prepared by memorizing information provided to them and their witnesses by immigration brokers months before the voyage. Facts pertaining to family history, home life, and even personal habits were studied from coaching books, which could run several dozen pages. This was particularly true when applicants and their witnesses claimed fictitious relationships. One interviewee told us that her mother, who was illiterate, committed the coaching book to memory by putting it into a song. "She had another woman read it to her, and she would sing it to herself like she would Chinese opera," said Ruth Chan Jang. Coaching papers were frequently taken aboard ship for review and thrown overboard or destroyed as the ship approached the U.S. harbor. Mr. Wong, who was twelve years old when detained on Angel Island in 1933, told us that his father had repeatedly nagged him about studying the coaching book well. He even hid coaching notes in his son's cap for him to review. Wong's worst moment at Angel Island came when other children got hold of his cap and started playing catch with it. "They didn't understand why I was so upset, but I was scared to tears!"[25]

Some inspectors were strict but fair, others delighted in matching wits with the applicant, and still others used intimidation to test applicants. From the perspective of immigration officials, such actions were necessary to ferret out discrepancies and frauds. Chinese, however, viewed the dreaded interrogation process as unreasonable and harsh. Over the years, they persistently complained that the detailed questions asked of them had no apparent relevance to the board's objectives. Some queries would have

24 Jorae, *The Children of China-town*, 25.
25 Ruth Chan Jang interview; Mr. Wong interview.

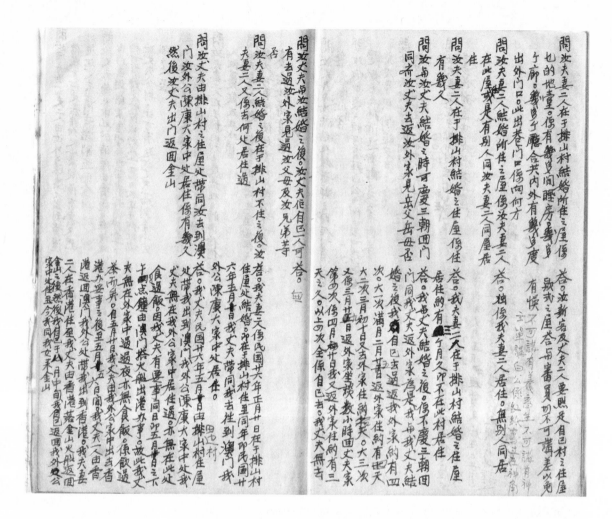

been difficult for anyone to answer: "What are the birth and marriage dates of your family members?" "How many times a year did you receive letters from your father?" "How many steps are there leading to your attic?" "Who lived in the third house in the second row of houses in your village?" "Of what material is the ancestral hall built?" "How many guests were at your wedding?" Real sons and daughters, even those who had studied coaching books beforehand, were known to have failed the test.

Because Chinese immigrants usually did not understand English and the inspectors did not speak Chinese, the board provided an interpreter at the hearing. During the early years of the exclusion era, the hiring of Chinese as interpreters was expressly prohibited because government officials believed that they could not be trusted in immigration work. By the time the Angel Island Immigration Station opened in 1910, government policies had changed, partly because it was almost impossible to find qualified whites to fill the positions. Most of the Chinese interpreters who were hired

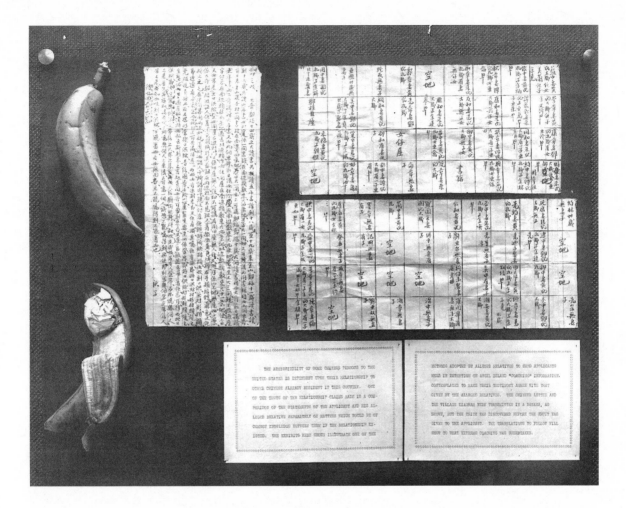

had college degrees, spoke a number of Chinese dialects, and came highly recommended by white missionaries or trustworthy citizens like Donaldina Cameron, superintendent of the Presbyterian Mission Home in San Francisco. Even so, to forestall collusion between the applicant, witness, and interpreter, the board used a different interpreter for each session of the hearing. At the end of each session, the board chairman usually asked the interpreter to identify the dialect being spoken in order to ascertain whether the applicant and witnesses alleged to be members of the same family were speaking the same dialect. Chinese interpreters had no say in the board's final decision, but their attitudes and demeanor at the hearings could help or hinder applicants during the interrogations.

Corruption in the Immigration Service was pervasive throughout the country, and it was no different at Angel Island. Immigrant inspectors and interpreters were known to accept bribes to render favorable decisions and interpretations. One of the biggest scandals broke in 1917 when a federal

FIG. 1.12
Coaching note and detailed village map found inside a banana. Courtesy of National Archives, Washington, D.C.

FIG. 1.13
Chinese kitchen staff. Courtesy of
National Archives, Washington,
D.C.

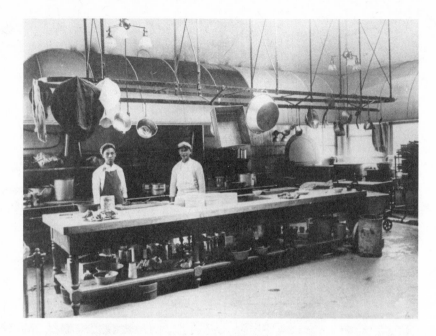

grand jury exposed a smuggling ring that was netting hundreds of thousands of dollars each year. Employees at Angel Island were caught stealing and manipulating Chinese records in connection with illegal entries. Duplicate copies of records were being sold to Chinese for $100, and immigrant inspectors were charging $200 for substituting a photograph in a Chinese file. The grand jury indicted thirty people, including immigrant inspectors, lawyers, and Chinese immigration brokers. Twenty-five employees were dismissed, transferred, or forced to resign as a result of the investigation.[26]

A typical proceeding usually lasted two or three days, longer if witnesses had to be interviewed in distant cities or if applicants and witnesses had to be recalled and reinterrogated about inconsistencies in their answers. Applicants were asked two hundred to one thousand questions, and transcripts ran between twenty to eighty typewritten pages.[27] During these hearings, memories might fail, wrong answers might be given, and unforeseen questions might be asked. Hence, it was often necessary to smuggle coaching information into the detention quarters so that there would be no discrepancies. One method was to hide coaching notes in gift packages sent by relatives in the city. Immigration officials who routinely inspected letters and packages found contraband messages inside hollow oranges, bananas, pork buns, and even peanuts whose shells had been pried apart and glued back together again. A second method involved the Chinese kitchen staff stopping by specified stores in Chinatown on their days off to pick up coaching messages left by relatives of detainees. For a small fee, they would smuggle the messages into the station and pass them at mealtimes to officers of the

26 Erika Lee, *At America's Gate*, 198–200.
27 Wen-hsien Chen, "Chinese under Both Exclusion and Immigration Laws," 107.

Self-governing Association (Zizhihui), a mutual aid organization formed by Chinese male detainees. The note was then taken upstairs to the detention barracks and delivered to the designated person.

In the event that someone was caught passing a note, everyone was instructed to help destroy the evidence. One such incident made the newspaper headlines in 1928. While escorting a Chinese girl to the dining room as the men were leaving, Chief Matron Mary L. Green saw the girl pick up a folded piece of paper dropped by one of the men. As soon as she seized the message from the girl and hid it in her dress, the men quickly turned and pounced on her. According to a newspaper account of the incident, "Fifty Chinese men attacked Mary L. Green. Her arms were pinioned and hands pulled her head back by her ears. They tore at her dress, ripping it away from her chest and body, fingers scratching the flesh, hands pummeling the woman's arms and shoulder—seeking at any cost a mysterious note. . . . The men found the note, tore it to bits. Then the bits disappeared, chewed and swallowed by the Orientals."[28] Another riot was reported in the *San Francisco Chronicle* on July 2, 1925, when Chinese detainees beat up a white attendant for being an informer. Soldiers from Fort McDowell were called in to quell the rioters with fixed bayonets.

If the applicant's testimony largely corroborated that of the witnesses, the authorities would render a favorable decision and land him or her. An unfavorable decision, however, would result in deportation, unless the applicant chose to appeal the decision to higher authorities in Washington, D.C., or the federal courts. Of all the immigrant groups on Angel Island, the Chinese were the most adept at taking advantage of the legal channels open to them, sparing no expense in the process. Many hired such well-known immigration attorneys as Joseph P. Fallon, George A. McGowan, Alfred L. Worley, and Oliver P. Stidger to prepare their applications and represent them at Angel Island. Attorney fees ran from $100 to $1,000, with an additional $500 to $700 if the case was appealed to Washington, D.C.[29]

From 1910 to 1940, immigrant inspectors on Angel Island rejected 9 percent or 8,672 out of 95,687 Chinese applicants. Of these, 88 percent retained attorneys to appeal the decisions, and 55 percent of the appeals were successful. In many cases, higher authorities found that the interrogation process at Angel Island was unfair. Only 5 percent of all Chinese applicants ended up being deported, but because of the lengthy appeals process, 6 percent of the immigrants languished on Angel Island for more than a year before their cases were finally decided.[30]

Kong Din Quong, a grandson of a native, holds the record for the longest known detention at the immigration station. He arrived on the *President Coolidge* on November 9, 1938, claiming to have been born on December

28 "Immigrants Fight Matron in Bay Riot," *San Francisco Examiner*, March 20, 1928, 4.

29 Wen-hsien Chen, "Chinese under Both Exclusion and Immigration Laws," 431.

30 See tables 1 and 2 in the appendix.

31 Based on an examination of 95,687 applicants who appeared in U.S. Department of Immigration and Naturalization Service, *Lists of Chinese*; also "*In the Matter of Kong Din Quong on Habeas Corpus*," file 22974, U.S. District Court, Northern District of California, Admiralty Case Files, 1851–1966, RG 21, NARA-SF; and "*Kong Din Quong v. Hall, District Director of Immigration*," No. 9250, U.S. Court of Appeals for the Ninth Circuit, 112 F.2d 96, 1940 U.S. App. LEXUS 4233 (Lexis Nexis Academic Web). According to Chen Wen-hsien, there were two cases of Chinese boys who had stayed in detention for more than three years—one for 1,136 days and the other for 1,635 days—but we were not able to verify her findings (see "Chinese under Both Exclusion and Immigration Laws, 405).

32 See Lee and Yung, *Angel Island*, chapter 4.

33 See ibid., chapter 3.

34 *San Francisco Chronicle*, October 7, 1919, 7; *South China Morning Post*, May 1, 2004, C5; Edwar Lee interview, May 8, 1976; *Chinese World*, May 18, 1926, 4; Lee and Yung, *Angel Island*, 101–2; poems 64, 111, 112, and the suicide poem that Xie Chuang recalled on p. 282. For details of a suicide committed with chopsticks by a Chinese woman at the temporary immigration station in San Francisco, see file 41369/11–29 (Wong Shee), Immigration Arrival Investigation Case Files, RG 85, NARA-SF.

29, 1921—eight months after his father, a son of a native who was born in China, was first admitted into the United States. Based on its observations and physical exams of the applicant by three doctors, the Board of Special Inquiry concluded that Kong was several years older than he claimed to be and that he had been born before his father came to reside in the United States. Kong was denied admission on grounds that a father cannot transfer citizenship rights to his children until he becomes a resident of the United States. Kong's attempts to appeal his case to the U.S. district court and circuit court of appeals failed, and he was deported on December 4, 1940, after spending 756 days, or twenty-five months, in detention on Angel Island.[31]

Only one other immigrant group, South Asians (mostly Sikhs), had a higher rate of rejection and deportation than the Chinese. From 1910 to 1932, 25 percent of all Asian Indian applicants were rejected, usually on grounds that they had hookworms or were "likely to become public charges," a clause that applied to applicants with little funds or chances of finding employment. Lacking financial resources and the support of ethnic organizations and a home government, most did not appeal the decisions and were sent back to India.[32]

At the opposite extreme, Japanese applicants had the shortest stay and the lowest rate of deportations (less than 1 percent), because Japan was a powerful nation at the time, having defeated China and Russia in two separate wars. To forestall Congress from passing legislation against Japanese immigration, in 1907–8 the Japanese government negotiated an understanding with the United States known as the Gentlemen's Agreement, whereby Japan would stop issuing passports to laborers. The agreement permitted all Japanese aliens in the United States to send for their wives and children, a privilege denied Chinese laborers under the Chinese Exclusion Act. Armed with passports issued by the Japanese government and marriage and birth records proving their right to enter, the overwhelming majority, including ten thousand picture brides, were admitted into the country within a day or two of their arrival.[33]

Most of the Chinese applicants who were denied entry swallowed their disappointment and stolidly awaited their fate. According to the testimony of former detainees, quite a few committed suicide aboard returning ships or in the detention barracks, but our research turned up evidence of only a handful of suicide cases. On October 7, 1919, the *San Francisco Chronicle* reported that Fong Fook, who was en route from China to Mexico, hanged himself with a towel tied to a gas fixture after just a few days in detention. Lester Tom and Gerald Won, two boys who were detained on Angel Island in 1931 and 1936, respectively, recalled actually witnessing the suicides of two men who hanged themselves in the lavatory because they could not face the prospect of deportation. Interpreter Edwar Lee told us the story of a Chinese woman who was so distraught about being deported that "she sharpened a chopstick and stuck it in her brain through the ear and died." Her two alleged sons were landed immediately upon her death. At least two other Chinese women were known to have attempted suicide, one by jumping from the administration building and the other by trying to hang herself in the women's lavatory. Additional evidence was found in the poems carved into the barracks walls attesting to the deaths and suicides of fellow detainees.[34]

"IMPRISONED IN THE WOODEN BUILDING DAY AFTER DAY"

At any one time, between two hundred and three hundred males and thirty to fifty females were detained at Angel Island. Most were new arrivals, but some were returning residents with questionable documents. Also

FIG. 1.14
Chinese men's dormitory, 1910.
Courtesy of California State Parks, 2014.

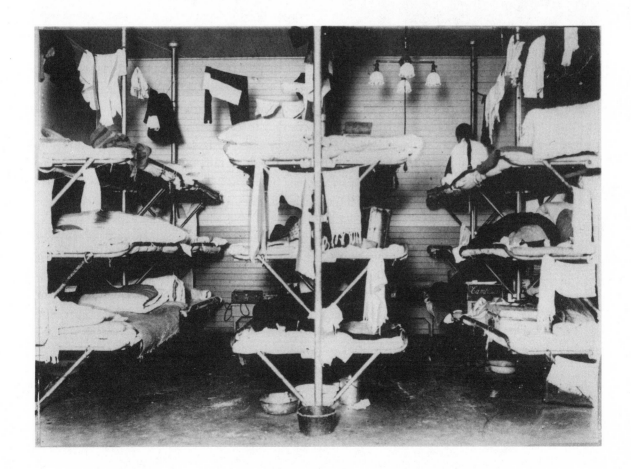

FIG. 1.15
Charles Schulze, immigrant
inspector, and Tye Leung,
interpreter and assistant matron,
1912. Courtesy of Theodore F.
Schulze.

confined were earlier arrivals whose applications
had been denied and who were waiting decisions
on their appeals, Chinese residents who had been
arrested and sentenced to be deported, and tran-
sients en route to and from countries neighboring
the United States, especially Mexico and Cuba. In
1932, for example, the detention center held more
than four hundred Chinese refugees from Mexico
waiting to be deported to China because of Mexi-
co's Expulsion Order of 1931.[35]

Men and women lived in separate, sparsely
furnished communal rooms filled with rows of
double-deck or triple-deck metal bunks. Each bunk
had a blanket, mattress, and pillow. The rooms were
dark, overcrowded, poorly ventilated, and fire haz-
ards. Privacy was minimal. Chinese men generally
were kept in two large rooms in the detention bar-
racks under lock and key, with wire-meshed win-
dows and barbed-wire fences to prevent escapes.
Each room contained 192 beds, each measuring six
feet long and two feet wide, and set two feet apart.
The crowded conditions were deemed unsanitary
and conducive to the spread of communicable dis-
eases like meningitis, according to one study by the Public Health Service.[36]
Chinese women, originally detained in the same building, were moved to
the second story of the administration building sometime before 1911. The
daily routine for both men and women was marked by "wake-up" calls in
the morning, three meals a day in the dining hall, and "lights out" in the
evening.

Guards sat outside the dormitories and generally left the Chinese alone.
During the first year of operation, Tye Leung, an American-born Chinese
from the Presbyterian Mission Home in San Francisco, was hired as inter-
preter and assistant to the matrons. The home was well known for rescuing
Chinese prostitutes and abused slave girls, and Leung came highly recom-
mended by its superintendent, Donaldina Cameron. She was specifically
instructed by Commissioner H. H. North to look out for prostitutes at-
tempting to enter the country. While working on Angel Island, Tye Leung
met and fell in love with immigrant inspector Charles Frederick Schulze.
Because of California's anti-miscegenation law, they had to go to the state of
Washington to get married. In the prevailing racist atmosphere of the times,
the two were soon forced to resign their positions. No Chinese-speaking

35 Camacho, *Chinese Mexicans*,
    86.
36 Bolten, "Cerebrospinal Men-
    ingitis at Angel Island."

FIG. 1.16
Chinese men's recreation yard.
Courtesy of California State Parks,
2014.

matron was ever hired to replace Tye Leung at Angel Island, but under pressure from the Japanese community, Fuku Terasawa was employed as a Japanese interpreter and matron from 1912 to 1925, during a period of the greatest influx of Japanese women to the United States.[37]

Confined inside the dormitory, the men languished on their bunks, spending their waking hours daydreaming or worrying about the future. Some passed the time gambling, but stakes were usually small because inmates had little pocket money. The literate read Chinese newspapers sent from San Francisco and books brought from home. They must have also spent a great deal of time writing and carving hundreds of poems and pictures on the walls, usually under cover because of the stern regulations posted in the barracks: "This building belongs to the United States government. It is unlawful to write on or disfigure the walls or to destroy any property on these premises."[38] The signs evidently failed to deter them. By the late 1920s, a phonograph, Chinese opera records, and musical instruments purchased by the Self-governing Association were also available for their amusement. A separate, fenced, outdoor recreation yard that was open for most of the day except during the rainy season afforded the men some fresh air and exercise. Once a week, they were

37 Lee and Yung, *Angel Island*, 81–82, 120–22; Yung, Chang, and Lai, *Unbound Voices*, 282–88.

38 Frank Hays, Inspector in Charge, to Edward White, Commissioner of Immigration, March 4, 1916, file 12030/24, Central Office Subject Correspondence and Case Files, RG 85, NARA-SF.

FIG. 1.17
Women out on a walk with
missionary worker Eleanor
Schoeraff (far right), c. 1930.
Courtesy of California State Parks,
2014.

escorted to the baggage shed at the dock, where they could select needed items from their luggage.

Women marked their time in detention differently. Many lacked formal education and were unable to read Chinese newspapers and books sent from San Francisco. Some knitted or did needlework. A few attended English-language and Americanization classes organized by social workers. Women and children were periodically allowed to walk the grounds in a supervised group—a privilege denied Chinese men. Although they did not form an organization as did the men, women told us that they supported one another in their own ways—by sharing food that had been sent by relatives in the city, reading and writing letters for those who were illiterate, consoling the aggrieved, and accompanying one another to the lavatory because they were afraid of seeing the ghosts of women who had committed suicide there. Chinese women were kept in the administration building that was destroyed in the 1940 fire, so we have no record of poems written by women, but more than one detainee recalled seeing many sad and bitter poems on the walls of the women's lavatory and dormitory.[39]

Unlike the other nationalities, Chinese were not allowed visitors for fear they would collude on interrogations. Other than immigration officials,

39 Lee Puey You interview; Lee
Suk Wan interview; and Con-
nie Young Yu, "Rediscovered
Voices," 134.

FIG. 1.18
Deaconess Katharine Maurer with
women and children on rooftop
of the administration building, c.
1930. Courtesy of California State
Parks, 2014.

the outsider they saw most often was Deaconess Katharine Maurer, who
had been appointed in 1912 by the Women's Home Missionary Society
of the Methodist Episcopal Church to tend to the welfare and needs of
all immigrants on Angel Island. Her work was also supported by funds
and gifts from the Daughters of the American Revolution. Maurer, who
became known as the "Angel of Angel Island" and who was called "Ma" by
the Chinese women, helped detainees write letters, taught them English,
organized Christmas parties, and provided women and children with toi-
letries, clothing, sewing and knitting materials, books, and toys. Until she
retired in 1951, she also distributed Bibles and promoted Christianity at
the immigration station.[40]

The San Francisco Chinese Young Men's Christian Association (YMCA),
at Maurer's request, also made regular visits to the men's detention barracks.
From the 1920s until the station closed in 1940, visitors from the YMCA
showed movies, taught English, brought newspapers and recreational equip-
ment, and prepared the immigrants for life in America. Chinese clergymen
often came on these visits to preach to the inmates.[41] Sometimes staff from
the Chinese Young Women's Christian Association would visit the women.
However, neither Maurer nor these visitors could change the basic prison-

40 Lee and Yung, *Angel Island*,
    64–66; Sakovitch, "Deacon-
    ess Katharine Maurer."
41 Among the most frequent
    visitors were the Reverend
    Daniel Wu of the Episcopal
    Mission, K. Y. Tse of the
    Presbyterian Mission, and B.
    Y. Leong of the Congrega-
    tional Mission.

FIG. 1.19
A Chinese minister talking to
detainees in the recreation yard.
Courtesy of Chris K.D. Huie.

like conditions created by discriminatory exclusion laws, and, despite their persistence, they converted few inmates to Christianity.

"TO REDRESS GRIEVANCES AND AVENGE WRONGS"

The Chinese held at Angel Island understandably resented their long confinement, particularly because they knew that immigrants from other countries, like Japan and Russia, were processed and released within a day or two. Their disgruntlement was fueled by the enforced idleness and dismal conditions at the station. Unable to change or improve their situation, they frequently petitioned the Chinese Consolidated Benevolent Association, Chinese Chamber of Commerce, and Chinese consul general for help. The first petition charging mistreatment was sent only a few days after the station opened in 1910.[42]

The detainees' major complaint was the poor quality of food that they were served. The government awarded concessions for providing meals to private firms based on competitive bids, with the stipulation that less money be spent on meals for Asian detainees than for Europeans or employees.[43] In

42 *Chung Sai Yat Po* (Chinese American Daily), January 27, 1910, 2.

43 In 1909, concessionaires were allotted 14 cents per meal for Asian detainees, 15 cents for European detainees, and 25 cents for employees. See Architectural Resources Group and Daniel Quan Design, "Final Interpretive Plan," C5–C7.

FIG. 1.20
Chinese dining hall with
concession in back, 1929. Courtesy
of San Francisco History Center,
San Francisco Public Library.

FIG. 1.21
Meals were noisy, crowded affairs
in the Chinese dining hall in the
administration building. Courtesy
of California Historical Society,
CHS2010.307.

1916, the average cost per Chinese meal dropped from 14 cents to 8 cents, and the quality of food got worse as a result. In response, male detainees protested by staging a disturbance in the dining hall, turning over their bowls and throwing utensils and food at the guards. There were enough of these disturbances to precipitate the posting of a sign in Chinese warning diners not to make trouble or spill food on the floor. In 1919, a full-fledged riot broke out, and federal troops had to be called in from Fort McDowell on the east side of the island to restore order. A year later, authorities in Washington, D.C., finally decided to improve the situation, and the station began to serve better food. As reported in the *Chinese World* newspaper, the new menu after the riot was as follows:

BREAKFAST—Tea and rice with the following dishes: Pork with preserved stem cabbage, greens (Mon.); pork and mustard greens soup, fermented bean curd (Tue.); pork with greens, salted fish (Wed.); pork with dried bean sticks, plum sauce (Thur.); pork and winter melon soup, bean curd with soy sauce (Fri.); beef steamed with sweet pickles, greens (Sat.); bean vermicelli with pork, fermented bean paste (Sun.).

LUNCH—Biscuits, bread, and tea with the following: Pork congee (Mon.); sweet tapioca soup (Tue., Thur., Sat.); pork and fish congee (Wed.); pork congee (Fri.); pork noodles (Sun.).

DINNER—Tea and rice with the following: Bean vermicelli with pork, salted fish (Mon.); fish with dried lily flowers, preserved olives (Tue.); beef with potatoes (Wed.); beef with bean sprouts, salted fish (Thur.); codfish with dried lily flowers, preserved olives (Fri.); pork with white beans, preserved olives (Sat.); beef with turnips or cloud fungus, beef with onions, salted fish (Sun.).[44]

The men were better organized than the women. In 1918, they formed the Self-governing Association with the purpose of providing mutual aid and maintaining order in the barracks. Its Anglicized name, ironically, was Angel Island Liberty Association. Officers generally were elected from the people who had been detained the longest, particularly those whose cases were on appeal, and, on occasion, respected intellectuals. The scope of the association's activities varied from one administration to another. As new immigrants arrived, the officers welcomed them and oriented them to life on the island and the rules in the dormitory. With the meager funds collected from membership dues, the association bought records, books, school supplies, and recreational equipment for the detainees. When talent was available, it scheduled weekly skits, operas, or musical concerts for evening diversions. At times, officers organized classes for children, curtailed gambling, and arbitrated fights that broke out in the dormitory. If immigrants had complaints or requests, the organization's spokesman, who usually knew some English, negotiated with the authorities. For example, when Tet Yee was chairman of the Self-governing Association in 1932, he

44 *Chinese World*, March 19, 1920, 3–4. The newspaper published the following menu before the riot: "BREAKFAST—Tea, rice, pork with bok choy, winter melon, dried lily flowers, Chinese cabbage, mustard greens, or dried bean sticks, plus one small dish. LUNCH—Congee with pork and dried shrimps, congee with beef and dried bok choy, sweet congee with green beans, sweet congee with red beans, coffee and bread, or sweet tapioca soup. DINNER—Tea, rice, beef cooked with cabbage, dried bamboo shoots, potatoes or turnips, plus one side dish (salted fish, preserved olives, fermented bean curd, sweet pickles or plum sauce). On Friday, fresh fish or bean vermicelli with dried shrimp." See *Chinese World*, February 28, 1910, 3.

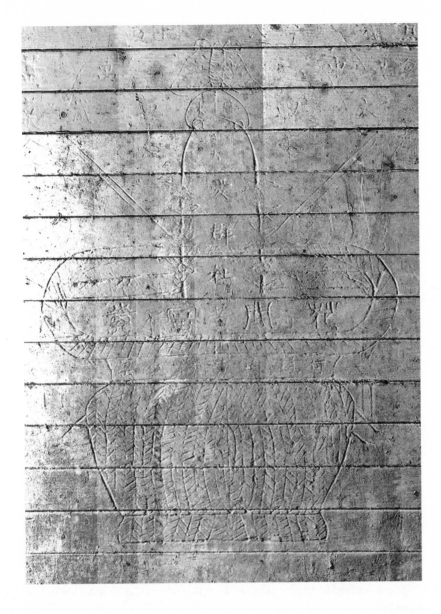

FIG. 1.22

Drawing of a Chinese ancestral altar with stele in basket that was found on the second floor of the men's barracks. Chinese flags, a butterfly, and the following Chinese inscriptions appear in the drawing: Long live the Republic of China; China; Guangdong; Remember the 6th day of the 4th month (Qingming Festival); Society for Love of the Multitude (on stele); and Prosperity in bloom. Courtesy of Architectural Resources Group and Charles Egan.

negotiated successfully with immigration officials to provide Chinese detainees with toilet paper and soap as they did for other immigrant groups. The organization also maintained communication with the Chinese community in San Francisco and helped smuggle coaching notes into the barracks. It reflected the united and collective spirit of the male detainees and helped make life on the island more bearable for them.[45]

Many other discouraged applicants vented their frustrations and lodged their complaints by writing poems on the walls as they waited for the results of their appeals. "There are tens of thousands of poems com-

45 Information about the Self-governing Association comes from interviews with Ted Chan, Tet Yee, Ja Kew Yuen, and Lee Show Nam.

posed on these walls. They are all cries of complaint and sadness." Some poems dwell on wives and families left behind and debts incurred in making the voyage. "My parents wait at the door but there is no news. / My wife and child wrap themselves in quilts, sighing with loneliness." Others reflect a strong sense of national consciousness, decrying the unjust exclusion laws and bemoaning a weak motherland incapable of intervening on their behalf. "I thoroughly hate the barbarians because they do not respect justice. / They continually promulgate harsh laws to show off their prowess. / They oppress the overseas Chinese and also violate treaties." There are also angry poems that speak of revenge. "The day our nation becomes strong, / I swear we will cut off the barbarians' heads." And farewell messages offer advice and encouragement to fellow travelers. "Let this be an expression of the torment that fills my belly. / Leave this as a memento to encourage fellow souls."[46] As the earliest literary expressions of Chinese immigrants, these poems not only bear witness to the indignities they suffered in coming to Gold Mountain but also serve as a reminder of the futility and folly of the exclusion laws themselves.

"ALWAYS REMEMBER THE TIME THEY SPENT HERE"

The irony of exclusion was that it did not improve the white working-man's lot. In reality, the Chinese were never a threat. At the peak of their immigration, they numbered about 1 percent of California's population. Unemployment remained high, and the wage level did not rise after the "cheap" competition had been virtually eliminated. In 1943, Congress repealed the Chinese Exclusion Act as a goodwill gesture to China, a U.S. ally in World War II. Chinese immigration resumed, albeit at the slow rate of 105 Chinese per year, and Chinese aliens were finally granted the right to naturalization. But the ordeal of interrogation and detention did not come to an end until 1952, when the burden of screening prospective immigrants shifted from U.S. immigration stations to U.S. consular officials overseas.

The irreparable damage of Chinese exclusion and incarceration was deep and long-lasting. Paper sons and paper daughters had to live out their lives under pseudo-identities, in constant fear of detection by immigration authorities. Unpleasant memories as well as their shaky legal status led many Chinese to fear the law, to avoid political activities, and to hide the truth about their immigration past from their children. Moreover, the feeling that they were allowed into this country only at the sufferance of the dominant white majority worked to foster alienation and delay their assimilation into the larger society. Most damaging were the psychological

46 Lines of poetry from poems 42, 65, 92, 118, and 114.

32

wounds inflicted by exclusion upon generations of Chinese Americans—the implication that they were racial inferiors, unwanted immigrants, and unassimilable aliens.

In 1956, in an effort to clear up the backlog of paper son cases and end the practice once and for all, the Immigration and Naturalization Service (INS) established the Confession Program, whereby Chinese who admitted their fraudulent entry could have their status adjusted and their real names restored. The program wreaked havoc in the Chinese community, as those who confessed were asked to provide the names and addresses of their real and fictitious families as well as those of other illegal immigrants. The government also attempted to force confessions and deport those known to be "pro-Communists" by conducting immigration raids in Chinatown and subpoenaing family and district association records. In the end, only 11,336 people confessed to being paper sons or paper daughters, but the illegal status of an additional 19,124 people was exposed in the process.[47]

It was not until Congress passed the Immigration Act of 1965 that the last vestige of racism was removed from U.S. immigration laws and Chinese immigration was put on a par with that of other nations. The floodgates opened, and thousands upon thousands of Chinese immigrants were admitted based on a system favoring family reunification, skilled and professional workers, and refugee resettlement. As a result, the Chinese population in the United States doubled every decade, growing from 237,000 in 1960 to 3.3 million in 2010, families were reunited, and a second generation of Chinese Americans emerged to realize the American Dream.

On the 130th anniversary of the Chinese Exclusion Act of 1882, the House of Representatives joined the Senate in passing a resolution introduced by Judy Chu, the first Chinese American woman elected to Congress, "expressing regret" for the Chinese Exclusion Acts. Senate Resolution 201 not only acknowledges that the discriminatory laws had "resulted in the persecution and political alienation of persons of Chinese descent, unfairly limited their civil rights, legitimized racial discrimination, and induced trauma that persists with the Chinese community today"; it also reaffirmed Congress's commitment "to preserve and protect the civil rights of all people."[48] The apology came too late for those who had been most directly affected by the exclusion laws, and it did not erase past wrongs or their effects. But by acknowledging a legislative mistake in retrospect, Congress has made it possible for Chinese Americans to reconcile with the dark secrets of their immigration past.

Discriminatory immigration laws are now a part of the past, but the lonely hulk of the Angel Island detention building, with its carved walls

47 Lau, *Paper Families*, 118.
48 Senate Resolution 201, 112th Congress, in 157 *Congressional Record*, S6352–54, October 6, 2011.

expressing the hopes and sorrows of nameless Chinese immigrants, stands as a stark reminder of America's history of racial exclusion. It further serves as a cautionary tale of the tragic consequences that befall a civilized society when it shuts its doors to outsiders by erecting an immigration system that fosters racism and intolerance and, ultimately, compromises its own moral ethics and humanity.

Today, as our country suffers the worst economic crisis since the Great Depression, and as Americans are once again stoking the flames of xenophobia by blaming immigrants for taking away jobs and being a drain on the American economy, we should not forget that, with the exception of Native Americans, we are a nation of immigrants, exiles, refugees, and transplants who together built this great nation. As we search for a way to fix our broken immigration system, we would do well to heed the lessons of Angel Island and remember to uphold the founding principles of our nation—a democracy based on the ideal of liberty and justice for all.

POETRY

Carved on the Walls:
Poetry of Chinese Immigrants on Angel Island

HIM MARK LAI AND GENNY LIM

FIG. 2.1
Abandoned detention building
with walls covered with Chinese
poetry, 1970. Photo by Leland
Wong.

WHEN THE DOORS OF THE ANGEL ISLAND IMMIGRATION STA-
tion shut in 1940, hundreds of poems that had been carved on the
barracks walls by Chinese immigrants were locked inside and for-
gotten. The poems, expressing their thoughts and feelings during
confinement, have been resurrected and preserved in this book. It was by
accident that they survived. After park ranger Alexander Weiss discovered
the poems in 1970, we began conducting oral history interviews. As luck
would have it, we also happened upon the poems transcribed by Smiley
Jann and Tet Yee during their detention in the 1930s.

Jann copied ninety-two poems in a manuscript he titled "A Collection
of Autumn Grass: Voices from the Hearts of the Weak." He later wrote an
article that was published in a Shanghai periodical recounting his experi-
ences in detention and quoted five poems from his collection. Yee tran-
scribed ninety-six poems in all, seventy-eight of which are also in Jann's
collection. We found numerous textual differences between Jann's and
Yee's poems, which may have been due in part to different interpretations
of barely legible characters on the walls and to further editing and refining
by the compilers.[1]

Today, more than 200 poems from the Angel Island barracks have been
recorded. These include the Jann and Yee collections, Mak Takahashi's
photographs, KSW rubbings, poems printed in various Chinese newspa-
pers, and the findings of four poetry consultants (Charles Egan, Wan Liu,
Newton Liu, and Xing Chu Wang) who were commissioned in 2003 by the
Angel Island Immigration Station Foundation to do a comprehensive study
of the poems and inscriptions on the walls of the detention barracks. Using
the latest computer graphics technology, the research team discovered a
treasure trove of 172 Chinese poems, 33 graphic images, and 300 inscrip-
tions in Chinese, Japanese, Korean, Russian, Punjabi, Spanish, Italian, Ger-
man, and English, which they transcribed, translated, and analyzed in their
monumental report "Poetry and Inscriptions: Translation and Analysis."[2]
Included in the report are the exact locations of 75 percent of the *Island*
poems, comparisons of these poems to the wall inscriptions, and seventy
new poems not published in *Island*.

The Chinese poems appear to have been written for the most part ei-
ther by those detained for a long time or by those awaiting deportation.
The poets were largely Cantonese villagers from the Pearl River Delta re-
gion in Guangdong who sought to impart their experiences to country-
men following in their footsteps. Their feelings of anger and frustration,
hope and despair, homesickness and loneliness covered the walls of the
detention barracks. Many of the poems were originally written in pencil or

[1] For Smiley Jann's article and
     story, see pp. 274–78, and
     for Tet Yee's story, see pp.
     287–91.
[2] See Architectural Resources
     Group and Daniel Quan
     Design, "Poetry and
     Inscriptions."

ink. Within a few months of the immigration station's opening, Commissioner North ordered the walls repainted to cover up what he considered graffiti. Undeterred, the poets began carving the outlines of the Chinese calligraphy with a knife to create impressions of each of the words. The maintenance crew, ordered to cover the writing, filled in the words with putty before applying a new coat of paint over them. Although the putty and paint succeeded in obliterating many of the carved poems, they also served as sealers that helped preserve the wood from further deterioration. Over the years, the putty shrank and the different layers of paint cracked, revealing the carved poems underneath.

All of the poems were written in the classical style of Chinese poetry—the traditional medium of artistic self-expression and protest used for centuries by Chinese scholars and commoners alike. Most adhered to the strict form of classical poetry and were written with four or eight lines per poem, with five or seven characters per line. In this form, the Chinese character at the end of every even-numbered line usually rhymes. Parallel couplets were often employed within the poems. There were also a few poems with lines consisting of four characters each, several couplets, and poems cast in the sophisticated form of *lüshi*, regulated verse characterized by a pattern of tonal variations and rhetorical parallelisms (poems 32, 37, and 91).[3]

The poets borrowed liberally from one another, repeating phrases and allusions. At least two poems (26 and 44) are imitative of works well known in classical Chinese literature. There are frequent references and allusions to famous heroic figures in Chinese legend and history, especially those who had overcome adversity: King Wen, who was thrown in prison before his son founded the Zhou dynasty; Su Wu, who was detained by nomads in the north for nineteen years but never gave up hope; and Zu Ti, a general who succeeded in recovering the Yellow River Valley seized by invaders in the fourth century. Such literary references may make it difficult for the non-Chinese reader to follow the drift of some poems. For this reason, we have provided annotations where necessary.

Some poems might have been written by one person and revised by another at some later date. An obvious example is poem 117. Today, the poem found on the wall has ten lines of four characters each, yet both Jann and Yee apparently saw and copied a similar poem with twelve lines of five characters per line (poem 118). The meaning of each corresponding line, however, whether written with four or five characters, is the same in the three different versions.

The research team of consultants also found evidence of dialogic poems, reflecting the tradition of Chinese scholars, who often met to compose

3 For a discussion of *lüshi*, see ibid., IV-19–21.

poetry using the same rhyming patterns and themes. Poems 111 and 112 provide a good example. They appear close together on the wall and match each other in rhyming words, poetic style, and message. They are among the most elegant and moving poems in the collection, both lamenting the death of a fellow detainee. The pair of poems was either written by the same person or written by two poets who were responding to each other's poems.[4]

The early twentieth century saw an increasing national consciousness among the Chinese, and that spirit is reflected in the subject matter of the poems. At least half of them voice resentment at being confined and bitterness that their weak motherland cannot intervene on their behalf. There is the recurring defiant wish for China to become powerful enough to one day wreak vengeance on America. Aside from these basic sentiments, the poems as a whole are not strikingly political. There were political differences among the inmates—some were more Marxist and leftist leaning, like Xie Chuang, while others were staunch supporters of the Nationalist Party.[5] Regardless, the men were wise to keep their own counsel, as the Immigration Act of 1917 added radical politics to the list of deportable offenses. The classical metaphors and historical allegories embedded in these poems, which were written anonymously in a language the jailers couldn't understand, would have been familiar to the writers' kinsmen. Most bemoan the writer's own situation. A few are farewell verses written by deportees, while others are accounts of tribulations by transients bound to or from Mexico and Cuba.

The literary quality of the poems varies greatly. The style, form, language, and use of literary allusions in some works indicate that the poets were well versed in the linguistic intricacies of poetic expression and well read in Chinese history and literature, while others could only be characterized as rudimentary attempts or graffiti, at best. Most of the poems were written in the *kaishu* calligraphy style, which was used in woodblock books and government documents of the Qing dynasty (1644–1911). The excellent calligraphy in which many of the poems were written is a strong indication that not all of the men were poorly educated village bumpkins (see poem 135 on p. 163, for example). By examining clusters of poems with identical calligraphy styles, the research team was able to conclude that some of the poems must have been inscribed by the same calligrapher, regardless of their authorship or dates of composition. One poem found on the second floor of the detention barracks was skillfully carved in reverse, perhaps because the author wanted other detainees to be able to make copies to take with them when they left the island (see poem 74 on p. 107).

However, most immigrants at that time did not have a formal educa-

4   Other examples include poems 21 and 22; 78 and 79; 86 and 87. For a discussion of dialogic poems, see ibid., IV-5–48.

5   For Xie Chuang's story, see pp. 279–86.

tion beyond the elementary school level. They were also not equipped with rhyme books or dictionaries. Created under such circumstances, many poems violate rules of rhyme and tone required in Chinese poetry. Incorrect characters and usages are common. (These have been corrected and noted in the printed versions.) Some works have obscure meanings because of the frequent inclusion of Cantonese vernacular expressions as well as Chinese American colloquialisms. Such flaws, if such they are, are not evident in the English-language versions, because the translations preserve the meanings of the original Chinese poems while masking some of their defects.

The majority of the poems are undated and unsigned, most likely for fear of retribution from the authorities. Only one poet was courageous enough to sign his full name to two poems—Lee Gengbo of Toishan District (see poems 41 and 109). The Self-governing Association signed off on poem 69, encouraging people to contribute to war relief in China. A few of the poets used pen names or included their family names and places of origin. Judging from the few that are dated and the fact that 75 percent of the poems in the Jann and Yee collections can still be identified on the walls, a great number of them were written before the 1930s. By that time, the writing of classical poetry was already on the wane, and young immigrants coming after 1930 seldom wrote in that style.

Regrettably, none of the collected poems were written by women. Former women detainees have referred to poems on the walls of the dormitory. Lee Puey You recalled that "the bathroom was filled with poems expressing sadness and bitterness" and told us that she wrote poems during her twenty-month stay on Angel Island.[6] Unfortunately, a window into their innermost thoughts and feelings has disappeared, as their writings on Angel Island have not been preserved. Given that the great majority of detainees were males and Chinese women at that time did not have many educational opportunities, it is doubtful there were very many poems written by women. Whatever poems did exist, however, have been lost forever, since the women's quarters were located in the administration building, which was destroyed by fire in 1940.

This second edition of *Island* includes the same 135 poems that were published in the first edition. Based on discrepancies in the wording of the poems and the additional signature lines and poem titles that the research team found in comparing the poems on the wall with the published poems, we have made minor corrections in some and have combined, rearranged, and renumbered the poems into one continuous sequence under the five original subject headings. An effort was made to keep dialogic and similar poems together.

6   For Lee Puey You's story and her poetry, see pp. 330–38.

Our translation of "Imprisonment in the Wooden Building," the long poem that was originally published in the newspaper *Chinese World* in 1910, has been replaced in this edition with Marlon K. Hom's translation of a more complete version that was published in *Xinning Magazine* (Xinning zazhi) in 1911. Fifteen lines that advocated the overthrow of the Manchu Qing dynasty and restoration of Han rule had been deleted from the poem, most likely because *Chinese World* supported reform, rather than obliteration, of Qing rule. *Xinning Magazine*, which was intended for the emigrant community in Toishan District (previously Xinning District), printed the poem in its entirety with minor textual differences from *Chinese World*'s version. According to the magazine's editorial note, the poem was published to arouse the sympathy and appreciation of the sons of overseas Chinese so that they would not squander their fathers' hard-earned money. Written in the classical style and rich with allusions to heroic figures who had overcome adversity, it is the earliest and longest extant poem expressing the Chinese response to their detention on Angel Island.

In 1985, during the renovation of the immigration station on Ellis Island in New York Harbor, workers found Chinese writing etched on the washroom's marble walls. Some of the poems were partially illegible, and a few were political slogans written in the 1930s with references to the war against fascism: "Long live China! Down with imperialism! Victory to China!" Four of the poems from the Ellis Island collection are included here for comparison's sake.

Like many of the Angel Island poems, these works are rough and unpolished, and the sentiments expressed have a familiar ring. This should come as no surprise, since the writers were from the same socioeconomic strata and geographic region in China. One major difference, however, was the predominance of Chinese seamen, who were awaiting deportation at Ellis Island. Most were Cantonese, followed by seamen from Hainan, Fuzhou, and Shanghai. Away from home for six months at a stretch and lonely for female companionship, they were probably the ones who drew the lewd sketches of nude women and wrote the poem about lovemaking in a brothel. No such drawings or poems of a sexual nature have been found on the barracks walls at Angel Island.

There were only a few thousand Chinese among the twelve million European immigrants who were processed through Ellis Island from 1892 to 1954. But because of the Chinese exclusion laws, they were all subjected to the same harsh treatment as their counterparts on Angel Island—invasive physical exams, intense interrogations, and longer detentions than for other immigrants. According to Mr. Chow, who was detained on Ellis

Island for two weeks in 1950, the Chinese were kept in a large dormitory with several hundred bunk beds. Some had been imprisoned there for more than a year. Although the facilities were clean, the food was adequate, and the detainees were not mistreated, many people were depressed about not being allowed visitors, restrictions in their movement, and their uncertain futures. Because there was no privacy in their living quarters, detainees resorted to using the washroom to vent their frustrations and to scrawl messages all over the walls, complaining about the "oppressive laws" and their "bitter imprisonment" and expressing their yearning for the comforts of home and women.[7]

Aside from the immigration stations at Angel Island and Ellis Island, Chinese poems by immigrants were also found in the two-story immigration building in Victoria Island, British Columbia. In 1977, Professor David Chuenyan Lai of the University of Victoria, B.C. was able to rescue a dozen poems from the walls of the immigration station before the facility was demolished. He knew from his research and interviews with former detainees that upon arrival, they had all been taken to the *chu jai uk* (pigpen) in the city, where they were given a physical exam, interrogated, and asked to pay a $500 head tax.[8] Confined in jail cells for anywhere between a few days to a month or more, they could only express their shock and anger by writing poems on the walls of their cells. Sure enough, Lai was able to expose the Chinese texts by removing layers of paint from the walls. He copied as many poems as he could, and when the construction foreman told him to leave before the building collapsed on him, he managed to cut off three pieces of the wall to take with him (see p. 185).

The writing style and themes of the poems, seven of which are included here, are very similar to poems found at Angel Island and Ellis Island. Signature lines indicate that most were written during the first decade of the twentieth century, before Canada passed its Chinese exclusion law in 1923. Adhering to the strict form of regulated verse, the poems speak of the poverty that drove immigrants overseas and the torture of being "locked up in a cage" upon arrival. One poem, "My Wife's Admonishment," written by Lee from Toishan, is reminiscent of the "wooden fish songs" sung by wives left behind, reminding their husbands to be diligent, frugal, and faithful. Another poem that was carved into a column of the building and titled "Notice to fellow countrymen" turned out to be a popular folk song from Toishan. We have also included an inscription that is prose, not poetry, in order to show the similarity between the experiences and sentiments of Chinese detainees in Canada and those of their counterparts in the United States.

7   Jian Ni, "Ailisidao yimin shichao"; Him Mark Lai, "Chinese Detainees at NY's Ellis Island."

8   In an effort to discourage Chinese immigration, the Canadian parliament passed the Chinese Immigration Act of 1885, which required every Chinese person entering Canada to pay a $50 head tax. It was increased to $500 in 1903. Following the example of the United States, the Canadian parliament passed its Chinese exclusion law in 1923, repealed it in 1947, and established the Chinese Adjustment Statement Program in 1960, granting amnesty to eleven thousand paper sons and daughters.

These poems from Angel Island, Ellis Island, and Victoria, B.C. are remarkable for several reasons. Together, they represent the first literary body of work by Chinese in North America. Often haunting and poignant in their directness and simplicity of language, the poems express a vitality and spirit of indomitability never before identified with Chinese America. The stereotyped image of a passive, complacent race of lotus eaters will hardly find substantiation in the defiant tone and narratives of these writings. The poems chronicle the indignity and trauma suffered at the hands of racist immigration systems that operated throughout North America. They define what it meant to be Chinese in America. As such, the wall inscriptions are seminal artifacts that locate and establish the genesis of Asian American literature.

These immigrant poets unconsciously created a new sensibility and a new and emerging Chinese American individuality, which drew on China as the source and America as the bridge to spawn a new cultural identity. Their narratives of self-determination and resistance rank alongside African slave narratives as a legacy for Chinese Americans. Indeed, their wall calligraphy represents some of the earliest American graffiti and occupies a unique place in the literary annals of America. Their poetry is a vivid fragment of Chinese American history and a mirror that holds an undistorted image of that past.

TRANSLATORS' NOTE

These translations of the Angel Island poems follow the original meanings as closely as possible. As Chinese and English are culturally distinct and idiosyncratic languages, a word-for-word literal translation would have been unfeasible. Often, when dealing with Chinese characters for which there seemingly were no satisfactory English substitutes, we selected a culturally equivalent word or words that we believed best serves the author's intent.

The act of interpretation itself implies creation. One should bear in mind that translation involves subtle choices and compromises. Poetic translation is a complex and subjective process of mediation between culturally dissimilar and distinct linguistic and aesthetic frameworks. While the poems in this book express the thoughts of the individuals who wrote them, they do not reflect the original poetic meter or rhyme scheme. The literary form is generally subservient to the content, which, for historic reasons, is our first priority.

Chinese names and terms are transliterated in the pinyin system; however, as in our oral history transcriptions, we have retained the Cantonese spelling of people's names and place-names in Guangdong in order to reflect the region's spoken dialect and for consistency with our primary sources.

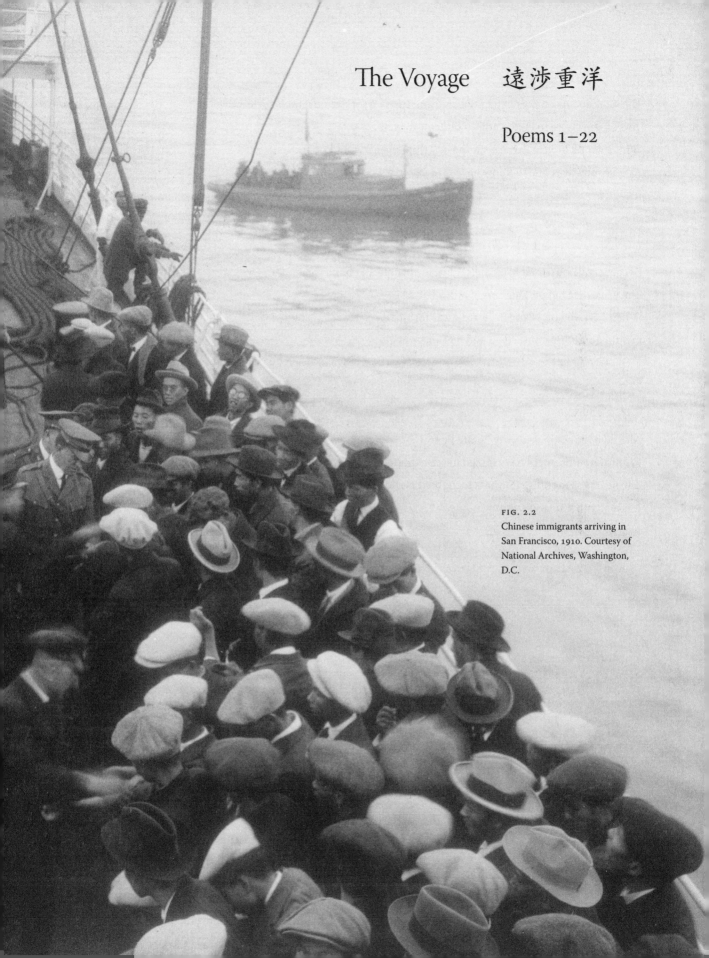

The Voyage 遠涉重洋

Poems 1–22

FIG. 2.2
Chinese immigrants arriving in
San Francisco, 1910. Courtesy of
National Archives, Washington,
D.C.

1.

The seascape resembles lichen twisting and turning for a thousand *li*.[1]
There is no shore to land, and it is difficult to walk.
With a gentle breeze I arrived at the city thinking all would be so.
At ease, how was one to know he was to live in a wooden building?

2.

Because my house had bare walls, I began rushing all about.
The waves are happy, laughing "Ha-ha!"
When I arrived on Island,[2] I heard I was forbidden to land.
I could do nothing but frown and feel angry at Heaven.

3.

As a rule, a person is twenty before he starts making a living.
Family circumstances have forced me to experience wind and dust.[3]
The heartless months and years seem bent on defeating me.
It is a pity that time quickly ages one.

---

1   One *li* is approximately one-third of a mile.
2   The colloquial name given to Angel Island by Cantonese
     immigrants.
3   The rigors of travel.

1.

水景如苔千里曲，
陸路無涯[1]路步難。
平風到埠心如是，
安樂誰知住木樓。

2.

家徒壁立[2]始奔波，
浪聲歡同笑呵呵。
埃崙念到聞禁往，
無非皺額奈天何。

3.

生平廿載始謀生，
家計逼我歷風塵。
無情歲月偏負我，
可[3]惜光陰易邁人。

1　余本作「崖」
2　舊金山週報作「天」
3　原作「省」

4.

The gold and silver of America is very appealing.

Jabbing an awl into the thigh[4] in search of glory,

   I embarked on the journey.

Not only are my one thousand pieces of gold already depleted, but

My countenance is blackened. It is surely for the sake of the family.

5.

Four days before the Qiqiao Festival,[5]

I boarded the steamship for America.

Time flew like a shooting arrow.

Already, a cool autumn has passed.

Counting on my fingers, several months have elapsed.

Still I am at the beginning of the road.

I have yet to be interrogated.

My heart is nervous with anticipation.

---

4 Su Qin (d. 317 BCE), a scholar during the period of the Warring States (475–221 BCE), was unsuccessful in gaining a post in the courts upon finishing his studies. After he returned home, the contempt of his family drove him to study harder. To keep awake at night, he would hold an awl over a thigh so that his hand would drop as he became drowsy, jabbing the awl into his flesh. Later, Su Qin became the prime minister of six states concurrently. The expression thus means to make a determined effort.

5 Better known as the Festival of the Seventh Day of the Seventh Moon, the Qiqiao Festival is widely celebrated among the Cantonese. In the legend of the Cowherd and the Weaver Maiden (Niulang Zhinü), the Weaver Maiden in heaven one day fell in love with a mortal Cowherd. After their marriage, her loom, which once wove garments for the gods, fell silent. Angered by her dereliction of duty, the gods ordered her back to work. She was separated from the Cowherd by the Silver Stream, or Milky Way, with the Cowherd in the constellation Aquila, while she was across the Heavenly River in the constellation Lyra. The couple was allowed to meet only once a year on the seventh day of the seventh moon, when the Silver Stream is spanned by a bridge of magpies. On this day, maidens display toys, figurines, artificial fruits and flowers, embroidery, and other examples of their handiwork, so that men can judge their skills. It is also customary for girls to worship the gods and make offerings of fruit to them.

4.
美洲金銀實可愛，
錐[4]股求榮動程來。
不第千金曾用盡，
犁黑面目為家哉。

5.
乞巧少四日，
搭輪來美洲。
光陰似箭射，
又已過涼秋。
屈指經數月，
尚在此路頭。
至今未曾審，
懸望心悠悠。

---

4 原作「椎」

6.

Everyone says traveling to North America is a pleasure.

I suffered misery on the ship and sadness in the wooden building.

After several interrogations, still I am not done.

I sigh because my compatriots are being forcibly detained.

By one from Heungshan[6]

7.

Originally, I had intended to come to America last year.

Lack of money delayed me until early autumn.

It was on the day that the Weaver Maiden met the Cowherd[7]

That I took passage on the *President Lincoln*.

I ate wind and tasted waves for more than twenty days.

Fortunately, I arrived safely on the American continent.

I thought I could land in a few days.

How was I to know I would become a prisoner suffering in the
   wooden building?

The barbarians' abuse is really difficult to take.

When my family's circumstances stir my emotions, a double stream
   of tears flows.

I only wish I can land in San Francisco soon,

Thus sparing me this additional sorrow here.

---

6   A district in the Pearl River Delta, Heungshan is the
    birthplace of Sun Yat-sen (Sun Zhongshan [1866–1925]), the
    first president of the Republic of China. After his death in
    1925, the district name was changed to Chungshan in Sun's
    memory (see map on p. 5.)
7   See n. 5.

6.

北遊咸道樂悠悠，
船中苦楚木樓愁。
數次審查猶未了，
太息[5]同胞被逼留。

　　香山人題

7.

本擬舊歲來美洲，
洋蚨迫阻到初秋。
織女會牛郎哥日，
乃搭林肯總統舟。
餐風嘗浪廿餘日，
幸得平安抵美洲。
以為數日可上埠，
點知苦困木樓囚。
番奴苛待真難受，
感觸家境淚雙流。
但願早登三藩市，
免在此間倍添愁。

5　余本作「惜」

8.

Instead of remaining a citizen of China, I willingly became an ox.

I intended to come to America to earn a living.

The Western-style buildings are lofty, but I have not the luck to live in them.

How was anyone to know that my dwelling place would be a prison?

9.

I used to admire the land of the Flowery Flag[8] as a country of abundance.

I immediately raised money and started my journey.

For over a month, I have experienced enough winds and waves.

Now on an extended sojourn in jail, I am subject to the ordeals of prison life.

I look up and see Oakland so close by.

I wish to go back to my motherland to carry the farmer's hoe.

Discontent fills my belly, and it is difficult for me to sleep.

I just write these few lines to express what is on my mind.

---

8   Cantonese colloquial term for the United States.

8.
國民不為甘為牛，
意至美洲作營謀。
洋樓高聳無緣住，
誰知樓所是監牢？

9.
夙慕花旗幾優哉，
即時籌款動程來。
風波閱月已歷盡，
監牢居所受災磨。
仰望屋崙相咫尺，
願回祖國負耕鋤。
滿腹牢騷難寢寐，
聊書數句表心裁。

10.

Poem by One Named Huie from Heungshan Encouraging the Traveler

Just talk about going to the land of the Flowery Flag

    and my countenance fills with happiness.

Not without hard work were one thousand pieces of gold

    dug up and gathered together.

There were words of farewell to the parents,

    but the throat choked up first.

There were many feelings, many tears flowing face to face,

    when parting with the wife.

Waves big as mountains often astonished this traveler.

With laws harsh as tigers,[9] I had a taste of all the barbarities.

Do not forget this day when you land ashore.

Push yourself ahead and do not be lazy or idle.

11.

I think back on the past when I had not experienced hardship.

I resolved to go and seek Taogong.[10]

The months and years are wasted, and still it has not ended.

Up to now, I am still trapped on a lonely island.

---

9 From "Tangong," a chapter in the *Book of Rites*: Confucius was passing Mount Tai and saw a woman weeping and wailing at a grave. Confucius asked why she was wailing so sadly. She said, "My father-in-law and my husband were killed by tigers. Now my son has also been killed by a tiger." Confucius asked why she didn't leave this dangerous place. She replied that it was because there was no oppressive rule here. Confucius remarked, "Oppressive rule is surely fiercer than any tiger."

10 Also known as Taozhugong, a wealthy merchant who lived during the fifth century BCE. His name is symbolic of wealth. Taozhugong was also known as Fan Li, a minister who once served King Goujian of the state of Yue. After aiding the king in defeating the enemy state of Wu, Fan resigned from his post to become a merchant.

10.

香山許生勉客題

說去花旗喜溢顏，
千金羅掘不辭艱。
親離有話喉先哽，[6]
妻別多情淚對潸。

浪大如山頻駭客，
政苛似虎倍嘗蠻。
毋忘此日君登岸，
發奮前程莫懶閒。

11.

憶昔當年苦未從，
堅心出外覓陶公。
歲月蹉跎仍未了，
至今猶困島孤中。

6　太平洋週報作「梗」

12.

People who enter this country

Come only because the family is poor.

Selling their fields and lands,

They wanted to come to the land of the Flowery Flag.

The family all looks to you.

Who is to understand it is the most difficult of difficulties!

13.

Living at home, there were no prospects for advancement.

The situation forced one to go to another country.

Separated from the clan, a thousand miles away,

Apart from the ancestors, we are no longer close to one another.

14.

It was four days before the Chongyang Festival[11]

When I transferred to a ship in Hong Kong.

Everybody is still here.

Our feet have been bound here for almost half an autumn.

    Written by one going to Mexico

---

11   A festival that occurs on the ninth day of the ninth moon,
when families visit ancestral graves.

12.

凡我國之人；
因謂家分起。
賣田又賣地；
欲往來花旗。
家人向住[7]汝；
誰知難上難。

13.

居家無步進；
他邦勢逼趁。
離宗千里遠；
別祖不相近。

14.

重陽少四日；
香港付輪舟。
大家仍在此；
繫足將半秋。

　　往墨客題

7　舊金山週報作「治」

15.

Abandoning wife and child, I crossed an entire ocean. I do not know
    how much wind and frost I've weathered; it was because my
    family was poor that I searched for white jade.[12]

Bidding farewell to relatives and friends, I drifted ten thousand *li*. It is
    difficult to keep track of all the rain and snow I've endured; it is all
    due to an empty purse and my reverence for copper coins.

16.

Flocks of fellow villagers do not refrain from spending thousands of
    gold pieces to get to America.

Several hundred compatriots invested huge sums but are now
    imprisoned on Island.

17.

As a traveler in wind and dust, half the time it was difficult.

In one month, I crossed to the end of the ocean.

I told myself that going by this way would be easy.

Who was to know that I would be imprisoned at Devil's Pass?

---

12   A precious variety of jade.

15.

拋妻子，重洋歷盡，不知受幾多風霜，
　　　　祇為家貧求白璧；
別親朋，萬里飄流，難計捱一切雨雪，
　　　　都緣囊澀重青蚨。

16.

梓里成群，千金不惜，圖走美；
同胞數百，巨資投擲，困埃崙。

17.

風塵作客半時難；
涉盡重洋一月間。
自問假途容易事；
誰知就困鬼門關。

18.

When I left, my parents regretted it was so hurried.

The reason I tearfully swallow my resentment is because of poverty.

Wishing to escape permanent poverty, I fled overseas.

Who caused my destiny to be so perverse that I would become imprisoned?

Victims of aggression, the people of our nation mourn the desperate times.

I feel sorely guilty for having not yet repaid my parents' kindness.

The chirping insects moan in the cold night.

Not only do I sob silently, but my throat tastes bitter.

 By Smiley Jann[13]

19.

Since our parting, another autumn has yet arrived.

I have become a distant traveler of faraway places.

Remembering your great kindness, I know in my heart I have not repaid you.

Hoping to send good tidings, I'll depend on writing letters.

20.

I left my native village and drifted to the American continent.

The moon has waned and waxed in turn several times.

My family anxiously waits for me to mail them news.

It is difficult to meet the wild geese,[14] and my sorrow is unending.

---

13 Smiley Jann included this poem in his collection, but it was not originally on the wall.

14 The mail service.

18.

離時父母恨忽忽；
飲怨漣漣也為窮。
欲免長貧奔海外；
誰教命舛困囚中？
侵凌國族悲時切；
未報親恩抱罪隆。
今也鳴蟲哀冷夜；
不單幽咽苦喉嚨。

　鄭文舫題[8]

19.

握別依然又一秋；
天涯作客遠方遊。
回憶高情心未償；
望傳佳語藉書郵[9]。

20.

離鄉飄流到美洲；
月缺重圓數輪流。
家人切望音信寄；
鴻雁難逢恨悠悠。

8　此詩收錄於鄭文舫之《秋蓬集》裡，
　　沒出現牆上。

9　余本作「賴」

21.

I remember since boarding a ship to America

Till now, the moon has waned twice.

There is no mail service to send a letter telling of my safe arrival.

The family is expectant, but their hopes are in vain.

22.

The ship set sail last year in the sixth moon.

I did not expect to be in this prison now.

I squandered a thousand and several hundred coins.

All my life I have been wretched, helpless, and now my troubles have
    implicated my elder brother.

21.

憶自動輪來美洲；
迄今月缺兩輪流。
欲寄安書恨郵乏；
家人懸望空悠悠。

22.

上年六月始揚帆；
不料今時到此監。
耗費金錢千數百；
生平孤苦累家兄。

In Detention 羈禁木屋

Poems 23–64

23.

Today is the last day of winter;

Tomorrow morning is the vernal equinox.

One year's prospects have changed to another.

Sadness kills the person in the wooden building.

24.

Random Thoughts Deep at Night

In the quiet of night, I heard, faintly, the whistling of wind.

The forms and shadows saddened me; upon seeing the landscape,

    I composed a poem.

The floating clouds, the fog, darken the sky.

The moon shines faintly as the insects chirp.

Grief and bitterness entwined are heaven sent.

The sad person sits alone, leaning by a window.

    Written by Yee of Toishan[15]

---

15 The largest percentage of Chinese in the continental United States and Canada came from Toishan District, located southwest of the Pearl River Delta (see map on p. 5).

23.

今日為冬末，
明朝是春分。
交替兩年景，
愁煞木樓人。

24.
深夜偶感

夜靜微聞風嘯聲，
形影傷情見景詠。
雲霧潺潺也暗天，
蟲聲唧唧月微明。
悲苦相連天相遣，
愁人獨坐倚[10]窗邊。

台山余題

---

10 原作「椅」

25.

Random Thoughts at Mid-autumn Festival[16]

The night is cool as I lie stiff on the steel bunk.

Before the window, the moon lady shines on me.

Bored, I get up and stand beneath the cold window.

Sadly, I count the time that's elapsed; it is already mid-autumn.

We should all honor and enjoy her.

But I have not prepared even the most trifling gift,

    and I feel embarrassed.

26.

The insects chirp outside the four walls.[17]

The inmates often sigh.

Thinking of affairs back home,

Unconscious tears wet my lapel.

27.

Depressed from living on Island, I sought the Sleeping Village.

The uncertain future altogether wounds my spirit.

When I see my old country fraught with chaos,

I, a drifting leaf, become doubly saddened.

---

16   The Mid-autumn Festival is celebrated on the fifteenth day of the eighth lunar month, when Chinese families observe the end of the harvest by sending wishes to the Moon Goddess, sharing moon cakes with family and friends, and worshipping the year's brightest moon.

17   This poem imitates the "Mulan Ci" (Poem of Mulan), which some judge to be a work dating back to the sixth century.

25.
中秋偶感

夜涼僵臥鐵床中，
窗前月姊透照儂。
悶來起立寒窗下，
愁把時計已秋中。
吾儕也應同敬賞，
菲儀無備亦羞容。

26.
四壁蟲唧唧，
居人多歎息。
思及家中事，
不覺淚沾滴。[11]

27.
悶處埃崙尋睡鄉，
前途渺渺總神傷。
眼看故國危變亂，
一葉飄零倍感長。

_____

11 余本作「襟」

28.

My belly is so full of discontent it is really difficult to relax.

I can only worry silently to myself.

At times I gaze at the cloud- and fog-enshrouded mountain-front.

It only deepens my sadness.

    By a wanderer from Heungshan

29.

Sadly, I listen to the sounds of insects and angry surf.

The harsh laws pile layer upon layer; how can I dissipate my hatred?

Drifting in as a traveler, I met with this calamity.

It is more miserable than owning only a flute in the marketplace of Wu.[18]

30.

Living on Island away from home elicits a hundred feelings.

My chest is filled with a sadness and anger I cannot bear to explain.

Night and day, I sit passively and listlessly.

Fortunately, I have a novel as my companion.

---

18 Wu Yun (d. 485 BCE), or Wu Zixu, was the son of a high
official serving the King of Chu (a state in the central Yangzi
River basin). His father fell into disfavor with the king and
was killed together with his family. Wu Zixu, however, fled
to the state of Wu (in present-day Jiangsu). He arrived with
only a flute, which he played in the marketplace to beg for
food. Later, he became an important official who served
the Wu king and led an army to defeat the state of Chu.
His victorious legions entered the Chu capital in 506 BCE,
whereupon he dug up the corpse of the former king and
whipped it three hundred times.

28.

牢騷滿腹甚難休，
默默沉沉祇自憂。
時望山前雲霧鎖，
恰似更加一點愁。

　　香山流蕩子題

29.

愁聽蟲聲與怒潮，
苛例重重恨怎消？
飄流為客遭此劫，
慘逾吳市一枝簫。

30.

旅居埃崙百感生，
滿懷悲憤不堪陳。
日夜靜坐[12]無聊[13]賴，
幸有小說可為朋。

12　余本作「在」
13　余本作「了」

31.

Imprisonment at Youli,[19] when will it end?

Fur and linen garments have been exchanged; it is already another autumn.

My belly brims with discontents, too numerous to inscribe on bamboo slips.[20]

Snow falls, flowers wilt, expressing sorrow through the ages.

32.

The west wind ruffles my thin gauze clothing.

On the hill sits a tall building with a room of wooden planks.

I wish I could travel on a cloud far away, reunite with my wife and son.

When the moonlight shines on me alone, the night seems even longer.

At the head of the bed there is wine, and my heart is constantly drunk.

There is no flower beneath my pillow, and my dreams are not sweet.

To whom can I confide my innermost feelings?

I rely solely on close friends to relieve my loneliness.

33.

America has power, but not justice.

In prison, we were victimized as if we were guilty.

Given no opportunity to explain, it was really brutal.

I bow my head in reflection, but there is nothing I can do.

    By Chan

---

19 King Wen (ca. 12th century BCE), founder of the Zhou
state, was held captive at Youli because the last Shang king
regarded him as a potential threat to Shang rule. His son,
King Wu (1134–1115 BCE), later defeated the Shang and
established the Zhou dynasty (1122–249 BCE).

20 This idea is taken from a proverb, which alludes to crimes so
numerous they will not fit on slips made from all the bamboo
in the Zhongnan Mountains. The ancient Chinese often
wrote on bamboo slips.

31.

羑里受囚何日休?
裘葛已更又一秋。
滿腹牢騷難罄竹,
雪落花殘千古愁。

32.

西風吹動薄羅裳,[14]
山坐高樓板木房。
意好子娘雲欲遠,
月明偏受夜更長。
床頭有酒心常醉,
枕底無花夢不香。
一幅幽情何心寄,
全憑知己解淒涼。

33.

美有強權無公理,
囹圄吾人也罹辜。
不由分說真殘酷,
俯首回思莫奈何。

　　　陳題

---

14 原作「常」

34.

This place is called an island of immortals,

When, in fact, this mountain wilderness is a prison.

Once you see the open net, why throw yourself in?

It is only because of empty pockets I can do nothing else.

35.

I, a seven-foot man, am ashamed I cannot stand tall.

Curled up in an enclosure,[21] my movements are dictated by others.

Enduring a hundred humiliations, I can only cry in vain.

This person's tears fall, but what can the blue heavens do?

36.

I have infinite feelings that the ocean has changed into a mulberry grove.[22]

My body is detained in this building.

I cannot fly from this grassy hill,

And green waters block the hero.

Impetuously, I threw away my writing brush.

My efforts have all been in vain.

It is up to me to answer carefully.

I have no words to murmur against the east wind.

    By Yuen

---

21 Like a worm.
22 Great changes.

34.

埃崙此地為¹⁵仙島，
山野原來是監牢。
既望張網焉投入？
祇為囊空莫奈何。

35.

鬚眉七尺愧無伸，
蜷伏圈中俯仰人。
百般忍辱徒呼負，
斯人瀝¹⁶淚蒼天何？

36.

無限滄桑感，
羈身此樓中。
青山飛不去，
綠水阻英雄。
率爾投筆去，
徒勞反無功。
慎言誠在我，
無語怨東風。

阮題

---

15 余本作「如」
16 原作「磨」

37.

My grief, like dense clouds, cannot be dispersed.

Whether deliberating or being melancholy and bored,

    I constantly pace to and fro.

Wang Can ascended the tower, but who pitied his sorrow?[23]

Lord Yu, who left his country, could only wail to himself.[24]

38.

Poem by One Named Huie, from Heungshan, Consoling Himself

Over a hundred poems are on the walls.

Looking at them, they are all pining at the delayed progress.

What can one sad person say to another?

Unfortunate travelers everywhere wish to commiserate.

Gain or lose, how is one to know what is predestined?

Rich or poor, who is to say it is not the will of Heaven?

Why should one complain if he is detained and imprisoned here?

From ancient times, heroes often were the first ones to face adversity.

---

23 Wang Can (177–217) was an official during a politically chaotic period. While a refugee in Jingzhou (in present-day Hubei), he composed the verse "Denglou fu" (Ascending the tower), describing his own unfortunate circumstances and thoughts of home.

24 Yu Xin (513–581) was an official of the Liang dynasty (502–57). He was sent as an envoy to the northern state of Western Wei (535–57) and was subsequently detained there. Later, he served the succeeding Northern Zhou dynasty (557–81). In his later years, he composed a verse in the *fu* form, "Ai Jiangnan" (Bewailing Jiangnan), reflecting his longing for his native south and describing the rise and fall of the Liang dynasty.

37.

愁似濃雲撥不開，
思量愁悶輒徘徊。
登樓王粲誰憐苦？
去國庾郎只自哀。

38.

香山許生自慰題

壁上題詩過百篇，
看來皆是嘆迍邅。
愁人曷向愁人訴，
蹇客偏思蹇客憐。
得失豈知原有命，
富貧誰謂不由天。
此間困處何須怨，
自由英雄每厄先。

39.

The male eagle is also easy to tame.

One must be able to bend before one can stretch.

China experienced calamities for a thousand years.

Confucius was surrounded in Chen for seven days.[25]

Great men exhibit quality;

Scholars take pride in being themselves.

Gains and losses are entangled in my bosom.

My restlessness elicits self-awakening.

40.

Halfway up the hill on Island, in the building upstairs,

The imprisoned one has been separated from his people summer to autumn.

Three times I dreamed of returning to the native village.

My intestines are agitated in their nine turns by the false Westerner.

I have run into hard times and am uselessly depressed.

There are many obstacles in life, but who will commiserate with me?

If at a later time I am allowed to land on the American shore,

I will toss all the miseries of this jail to the flowing current.

---

25 When Confucius (551–479 BCE) and his disciples were on
the road between Chen and Cai (both in present-day Henan),
officials of these states feared that he would be appointed an
official in the powerful neighboring state of Chu (in present-
day Hubei), which posed a perpetual threat to the smaller
states. Therefore, to prevent Confucius from proceeding on
to Chu, officials ordered troops to surround them and cut off
their food supplies for several days.

39.

雄鷹亦易馴，
能屈始能伸。
也歷千年劫，
曾困七日陳。
偉人多本色，
名士樂天真。
得失縈懷抱，
心猿證悟[17]禪。

40.

埃崙山半樓上樓，
囚困離人夏至[18]秋。
夢繞三匀歸故里，
腸迴九曲偽西歐。
時運不濟[19]空自悶，
命途多阻共誰憂？
倘得他時登美岸，
畢拋牢慘付水流。

---

17 余本作「吳」
18 余本作「自」
19 余本作「齊」

41.

After leaping into prison, I cannot come out.

From endless sorrows, tears and blood streak.

The *jingwei* bird carries gravel to fill its old grudge.[26]

The migrating wild goose complains to the moon, mourning his harried life.

When Ziqing was in distant lands, who pitied and inquired after him?[27]

When Ruan Ji reached the end of the road, he shed futile tears.[28]

The scented grass and hidden orchids complain of withering and falling.

When may I be allowed to soar at my own pleasing?

    By Lee Gengbo of Toishan

42.

There are tens of thousands of poems composed on these walls.

They are all cries of complaint and sadness.

The day I am rid of this prison and attain success,

I must remember that this chapter once existed.

In my daily needs, I must be frugal.

Needless extravagance leads youth to ruin.

All my compatriots should please be mindful.

Once you have some small gains, return home early.

    By one from Heungshan

---

26 According to a folktale, the daughter of the legendary Yandi was drowned while playing in the Eastern Sea. Her soul changed into a bird called a *jingwei*, which, resenting the fact that the ocean had taken her life, carried pebbles from the Western Mountains in her beak and dropped them into the ocean, hoping to fill it up.

27 Another name for Su Wu (140–60 BCE), who, during the Western Han dynasty (206 BCE–24 CE), was sent by the Chinese government as envoy to the Xiongnu, a nomadic people north of the Chinese empire. Su Wu was detained there for nineteen years but refused to renounce his loyalty to the Han emperor.

28 Ruan Ji (210–263), a scholar during the period of the Three Kingdoms (220–80), enjoyed drinking and visiting mountains and streams. Often, when he reached the end of the road, he would cry bitterly before turning back.

41.

牢籠躍入出無能，
無任傷悲血淚橫。
精衛啣砂填夙恨，
征鴻訴月哀頻生。
子卿絕域誰憐問？
阮籍途窮空哭行。
芳草幽蘭怨凋落，
那時方得任升騰？

　　台邑李鏡波題

42.

壁牆題詠萬千千，
盡皆怨語及愁言。
若卸此牢升騰日，
要憶當年有個編。
日用所需宜省儉，
無為奢侈誤青年。
幸我同胞牢緊念，
得些微利早回旋。

　　香山題

43.

Imprisoned in the wooden building day after day,

My freedom withheld; how can I bear to talk about it?

I look to see who is happy, but they only sit quietly.

I am anxious and depressed and cannot fall asleep.

The days are long and the bottle constantly empty; my sad mood, even so, is not dispelled.

Nights are long and the pillow cold; who can pity my loneliness?

After experiencing such loneliness and sorrow,

Why not just return home and learn to plow the fields?

44.

Inscription about a Wooden Building[29]

A building does not have to be tall; if it has windows, it will be bright.

Island is not far, Angel Island.

Alas, this wooden building disrupts my traveling schedule.

Paint on the four walls is green,

And green is the grass that surrounds.

It is noisy because of the many country folk,

And there are watchmen guarding during the night.

To exert influence, one can use a square-holed elder brother.[30]

There are children who disturb the ears,

But there are no incoherent sounds that cause fatigue.

I gaze to the south at the hospital

And look to the west at the army camp.[31]

This author says, "What happiness is there in this?"

---

29 This composition imitates the style of "Loushi Ming" (Inscription about a humble house) by Liu Yuxi (772–842).

30 Money. The ancient Chinese coin had a square hole in the center.

31 The writer here appears to be confused about his directions. The long axis of the barracks building runs roughly in an east-west direction. From the windows, he could see the hospital to the north and the Fort McDowell buildings to the east, but no buildings to the south.

43.

囚困木屋天復天，
自由束縛豈堪言？
舉目誰歡惟靜坐，
關心自悶不成眠。
日永樽空愁莫解，
夜長枕冷清[20]誰憐？
參透箇中孤苦味，
何如歸去學耕田？

44.

木屋銘

樓不在高，有窗則明；
島不在遠，煙治埃崙。
嗟此木屋，阻我行程。
四壁油漆綠，
週圍草色青。
喧嘩多鄉里，
守夜有巡丁。
可以施運動，孔方兄。
有孩子之亂耳，
無呫嗶之勞形。
南望醫 生房，
西瞭陸軍營。
作者云，「何樂之有？」

---

20 原作「倩」

83

45.

Imprisoned in this wooden building, I am always sad and bored.

I remember since I left my native village, it has been several full moons.

The family at home is leaning on the door, urgently looking for letters.

Whom can I count on to tell them I am well?

Prisoners in this wooden building constantly suffer sadness and boredom.

I remember the hardships I had to endure when I was coming here.

I cannot prophesy on which day I will cross the barrier.[32]

The years and months are easily spent in vain.

    Composed by an old man from Toishan

46.

I went east to Asia; I went west to Europe.

From south, I come to North America, where the harsh exclusion laws cause me worry.

Allowing you to enter the place of imprisonment,

Even if you don't shed tears, you will lower your head.

47.

Pacing back and forth, I leaned on the windowsill and gazed.

The revolving sun and moon waxed and waned, changing again and again.

I think about my brothers a lot, but we cannot see one another.

The deep, clear water casts reflections as waves toss in sympathy.

    Composed in the early spring of the Jiwei year (1919) by Guk of Heungshan

---

32 Admission into the United States.

45.

困囚木屋常愁悶；
憶別家鄉月幾圓。
家人倚望音書切；
憑誰傳語報平安？

木屋監囚愁悶多；
記憶來時歷苦楚。
過關未卜是何日；
空令歲月易蹉跎。

　　台山氏翁題

46.

東走亞兮西走歐；
南來北美苛禁愁。
任君入到困囚地；
若不流涕也低頭。

47.

徘徊瞻眺倚窗邊，
日月盈昃轉改旋。
孔懷兄弟難遇望，
淵澄取映浪拋憐。

　　己未年孟春香山谷

48.

The cool wind and bright moon make for a pitiful night.

The desolate feeling is aggravated by my solitary body under the quilt in the
wooden building;

The traveler thinks of his native village, where he once kept company with a willow.

You, my dear, had no intention of traveling because of your fondness for the
banana plant by the window.

Su'e[33] does not know the suffering among mankind.

The whites are intent on imprisoning sojourners from Dongya.[34]

It is unlike living in the village, plowing and studying.

A leisurely life with firewood and rice, one is content using a basket and gourd.[35]

49.

Each day, my sorrow increases as I stay on Island.

My face, as well, grows sallow and my body, thin.

My detention and mistreatment have not yet ended.

I am afraid my petition will be denied and I, sent back.

By Chan

50.

Quietly keeping my feelings to myself, I feel depressed.

My colleagues and I together call helplessly to Heaven.

When do we whip our horses to cross the pass at Tong Guan?[36]

Let me first wave the whip of Zu Ti.[37]

---

33 Better known as Chang'e, the Moon Goddess, she was married to an expert archer Houyi. As a reward for shooting down nine suns that threatened to destroy the earth, the Heavenly Gods gave Houyi the elixir of immortality.

34 Village in Chungshan District.

35 Yan Hui (521–490 BCE), the poorest of Confucius's disciples, ate very simply and yet was content.

36 Tong Guan is a strategic pass in Shaanxi. The rugged terrain there makes it easy to defend against attackers.

37 Zu Ti (266–321) was a general during the Western Jin dynasty (256–316). When non-Chinese people seized control of the Yellow River Valley in the fourth century and the Chinese court had to retreat to the south, Zu Ti swore to recover the lost territory. One of his friends, also a general, once said, "I sleep with my weapon awaiting the dawn. My ambition is to kill the barbarian enemy, but I am always afraid that Zu will crack the whip before me." Thus, the reference means to try hard and compete to be first.

48.
風清月朗可憐宵；
木屋孤衾倍寂寥。
客有鄉思眼伴柳；
卿無旅意戀窗蕉。
素娥未曉人間苦；
白種偏囚東椏[21]僑。
不若村民耕與讀；
優悠柴米樂簞瓢。

49.
埃崙居處日添愁；
面亦黃兮身亦瘦。
留難[22]磋磨猶未了；
最怕批消[23]打回頭。

　　陳題

50.
默默含情意黯然，
吾儕同喚奈何天。
幾時策馬潼關渡，
許我先揚祖逖鞭。

21　中山縣村名，方本作「東亞」
22　舊金山週報作「留連」
23　舊金山週報作「拋消」

51.

I have been imprisoned on Island for seven weeks.

In addition, I do not know when I can land.

It is only because the road of life has many twists and turns

That one experiences such bitterness and sorrow.

52.

Even though it is said that drifting is a man's lot,

Why am I imprisoned when I am not guilty?

Giving repentance and regrets to Heaven, I reprimand myself daily.

I ask the blue heaven, does it know of my plight?

53.

When I think about it, it is really miserable.

For what reason does the blue heaven today

Imprison this humble person in a wooden building?

With no trace of tidings, it is really distressing

51.

埃崙被困七星期；
上岸何時也未知。
祇為命運多曲蹇；
纔受是中苦與愁。

52.

漂泊雖云男兒事；
奈何無罪入囚途。
如天懺恨天天數；
問句蒼天知有無。

53.

自己想來真苦楚；
蒼天今日因如何，
困我鄙人在木樓？
音信無跡實難過。

54.

I came to the United States because I was poor.

How was I to know fate would be so perverse as to imprison me?

News and letters do not reach me, and I can only fantasize.

I hear no news, so who sympathizes with me?

55.

I have been in the wooden building for more than ten days.

My eyes have seen people being sent back.

Witnessing that scene makes one sad.

Spending more than five thousand golden coins,

I drifted alone to this place.

If I am unlucky enough to be deported, my parents will be grieved.

The interest piles one on top of another.

I do not know yet when it will be completely repaid to the creditor.

56.

I raise my brush to write a poem to tell my dear wife,

Last night at the third watch I sighed at being apart.

The message you gave with tender thoughts is still with me;

I do not know what day I can return home.

54.

我為家貧來美境；
誰知命蹇困監牢。
音信莫達空思想；
消息無聞孰可憐。

55.

來到木屋十日餘；[24]
眼見有人撥回去。
令人見景亦生悲；
耗費金錢[25]五千餘。
孤身飄流到此處；
不幸撥回父母悲。
啯啲[26]利息重重疊；
未知何日還清主。[27]

56.

舉筆寫詩我卿知；
昨夜三更嘆別離。
情濃囑語今猶在；
未知何日得旋歸。

24　余本作「十餘日」
25　余本作「刀」
26　余本作「哥的」
27　余本作「了」

57.

The silvery red skirt is half covered with dust.[38]

A flickering lamp keeps this body company.

I am like pear blossoms that have already fallen;

Pity the bare branches during the late spring.

58.

Xishi[39] always lived in golden houses;

Only the dirt walls and bamboo-matted window are left for me.

I send a verbal message to the twin swallows between the rafters:

Is there a good room looming on the horizon?

59.

A drifting duckweed, I arrived a traveler to this place.

As I ascend the building, I have painful recollections of my native village.

It is because of poverty at home that I am detained here.

It has led to my humiliation, which is truly heartbreaking.

---

38 Fleeing in troubled times.

39 A famous beauty of the state of Yue during the Spring and Autumn Period (770–476 BCE), Xishi was sent by King Goujian of Yue as a gift to King Fucha (495–477 BCE) of Wu to divert his attention from state affairs. The Yue state was then able to mobilize its forces to attack Wu and avenge a previous humiliating defeat. Xishi is used here as an oblique reference to Westerners or Americans, since *xi* is the character for "west" and Xishi is a beauty, or *meiren*, the term for "American."

57.
銀紅衫子半蒙塵；
一盞殘燈伴此身。
卻似梨花經已落；
可憐零落舊春時。

58.
西施盡住黃金屋；
泥壁篷窗獨剩儂。
寄語樑間雙燕子；
天涯可有好房櫳。

59.
萍飄作客到此方；
登樓感慨思故鄉。
為著家貧流[28]落此；
致令受辱實心傷。

28　余本作「留」

60.

Random Thoughts While Staying in the Building

For days I have been without freedom on Island.

In reduced circumstances now, I mingle with the prisoners.

Grievances fill my belly; I rely on poetry to express them.

A pile of clods bloats my chest, and I wash it down with wine.

Because my country is weak, I have become aware of the laws of growth and decay.

In pursuit of wealth, I have come to understand the principles of expansion and diminution.

When I am idle, I have this wild dream

That I have gained the Western barbarian's consent to enter America.

61.

Bored and filled with a hundred feelings, I am imprisoned in the building.

Seeing the surroundings stirs one who is sad. How can one stop the tears?

I recall the ship starting off for the land of America.

Looking back, the moon has repeated a cycle.

60.

居樓偶感

日處埃崙不自由；
蕭然身世混監囚。
牢騷滿腹憑詩寫；
塊壘撐胸借酒浮。
理悟盈虛因國弱；
道參消長為富求。
閒來別有疏狂想；
得允西奴登美洲。

61.

無聊百感困監樓；
觸景愁人淚怎收？
曾記動輪來美境；
迄今回溯月返流。

62.

Wandering footloose here and there, I reminisce about old journeys;

Old acquaintances, living or now dead, each has made his important contribution.

I am, in this life, unfortunately, of Chinese descent;

Enduring humiliation, nursing a grievance, now I am a prisoner of Chu.[40]

63.

Having not yet crossed the Yellow River, my heart is not at peace;

After crossing the Yellow River, a double stream of tears flows.

64.

I pray that the day you again enter the cycle of life,

You'll not be a chap with a worthless life from a poor family.[41]

---

40   A prisoner or a person in difficult straits.
41   This is said to be a commentary written on the wall the day
      after a detainee had hanged himself.

62.

浪跡江湖憶舊遊；
故人生死各千秋。
今生不幸為華裔；
忍辱含仇做楚囚。

63.

未過黃河心不息；
過了黃河雙淚流。

64.

祝君再渡巡環日；
莫做貧家賤命郎。[29]

---

29 據說有一同胞懸樑棄世，翌日即有人寫下以上兩句。

The Weak Shall Conquer 圖強雪恥

Poems 65–90

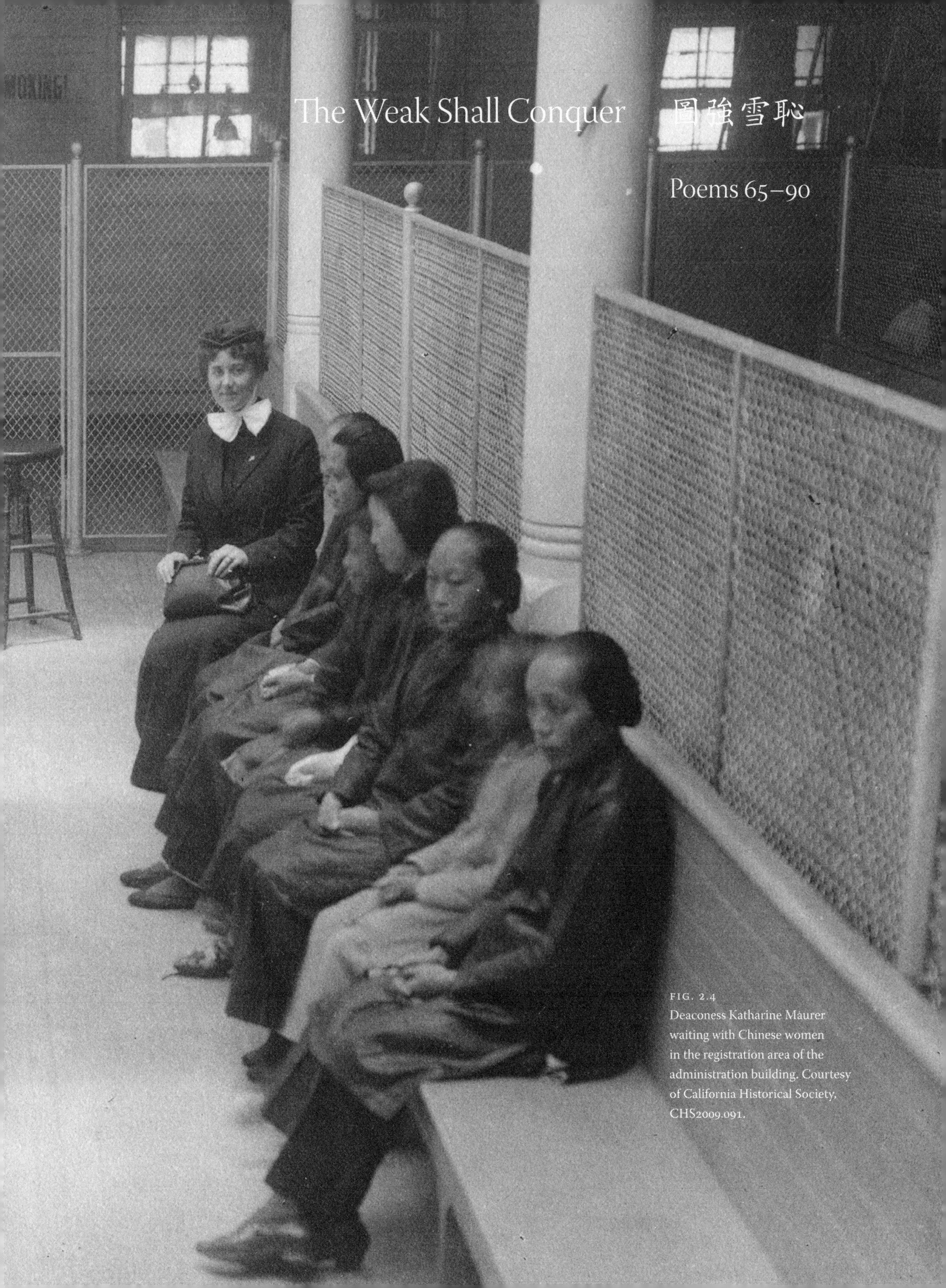

FIG. 2.4
Deaconess Katharine Maurer waiting with Chinese women in the registration area of the administration building. Courtesy of California Historical Society, CHS2009.091.

65.

For what reason must I sit in jail?

It is only because my country is weak and my family poor.

My parents wait at the door, but there is no news.

My wife and child wrap themselves in quilts, sighing with loneliness.

Even if my petition is approved and I can enter the country,

When can I return to the Mountains of Tang[42] with a full load?

From ancient times, those who venture out usually become worthless.

How many people ever return from battles?

66.

Leaving behind my writing brush and removing my sword, I came to America.

Who was to know two streams of tears would flow upon arriving here?

If there comes a day when I will have attained my ambition and become successful,

I will certainly behead the barbarians and spare not a single blade of grass.

---

42 Cantonese colloquial name for China. "Tang" refers to the
    Tang dynasty, during which China's military might and cul-
    tural influence were at their height.

65.

為乜來由要坐監？
祇緣國弱與家貧。
椿萱[30]倚門無消息，
妻兒擁被歎孤單。
縱然批准能上埠，
何日滿載返唐山？
自古出門多變賤。
從來征戰幾人還？

66.

留筆除劍到美洲，
誰知到此淚雙流？
倘若得志成功日，
定斬胡人草不留。

30　舊金山週報作「楦」

67.

I am a member of the Wong clan from Heung City.[43]

I threw away my writing brush and pushed forward, journeying to the capital of the U.S.

I bought an oar and arrived in the land of Gold Mountain.[44]

Who was to know they would banish me to Island?

If my country had contrived to make herself strong, this never would have happened.

Then when the ship had docked, we could have gone directly ashore.

> Dawn of the 24th, in the thirteenth year of the Republic (1924)
> Idle brushstrokes of a wanderer from the Town of Iron[45]

68.

Just now the five nationalities in China have become one family,[46]

But the powers still have not yet recognized our China.

Primarily because foreign debts were piling up,

The foreigners pushed to control finances and to seize power.

69.

The commandant at Nanking[47] sent a cable

And urged the people to transmit funds to the Relief Office.

I hope my compatriots will give all they can

To prevent the loss of our country—a praiseworthy cause.

> Self-governing Association

---

43 Shekki, the administrative center of Heungshan District.
44 Cantonese colloquial name for California.
45 Shekki in Heungshan District.

46 After the 1911 Revolution, five different ethnic groups were recognized in China: Han, Manchu, Mongolian, Muslim, and Tibetan.
47 Briefly the capital of the provisional government of the Republic of China after the 1911 Revolution; also the capital of the Nationalist government from 1927 to 1949.

67.

黃家子弟本香城，
挺身投筆赴美京。
買棹[31]到了金山地，
誰知撥我過埃崙。
我國圖強無比樣，
船泊岸邊直可登。

　　民國十三廿肆晨
　　逍遙子鐵城閒筆

68.

方今五族為一家，
列強未認我中華。
究因外債頻頻隔，
逼監財政把權拿。

69.

南京留守曾電報；
提倡民款達濟處。
仰望同胞捐盡力；
得免淪亡足慰贊。

　　自治會

31　原作「掉」

70.

Being idle in the wooden building, I opened a window.

The morning breeze and bright moon lingered together.

I reminisce about the native village far away, cut off by clouds and mountains.

On the little island, the wailing of cold, wild geese can be faintly heard.

The hero who has lost his way can talk meaninglessly of the sword.

The poet at the end of the road can only ascend a tower.

One should know that when the country is weak, the people's spirit dies.

Why else do we come to this place to be imprisoned?

71.

Twice I have passed through the blue ocean, experienced the wind and dust of journey.

Confinement in the wooden building has pained me doubly.

With a weak country, we must all join together in urgent effort.

It depends on all of us together to roll back the wild wave.[48]

72.

I lean on the railing and lift my head to look at the cloudy sky.

All the mountains and rivers are dark.

Eastern Mongolia is lost, and the date of her return is uncertain.[49]

The recovery of the Central Plains[50] depends on the youth.

Only the tongue of Changshan can slay the villainous.[51]

To kill the bandit, we must wave the whip of Zu Ti.[52]

I am ashamed to be curled up like a worm on Island.

I grieve for my native land, but what else can I say?

---

48 To make an effort to restore declining fortunes, a quotation from an essay by Han Yu (768–824), a scholar-official during the Tang dynasty (618–907).

49 Part of the territory of the northeastern provinces of China (Manchuria), which was lost to Japan in 1931–32.

50 The lower Yellow River Valley, where Chinese civilization had its beginnings.

51 Changshan refers to Yan Gaoqing (d. 756), a Tang dynasty (618–917) official. During the An Lushan Rebellion (755–60), Yan led an army to fight the rebels. He was defeated and captured. All during his execution, he continued to revile the enemy.

52 See n. 37.

70.

木屋閒來把窗開，
曉風明月共徘徊。
故鄉遠憶雲山斷，
小島微聞寒雁哀。
失路英雄空說劍，
窮途騷士且登台。
應知國弱人心死，
何事囚困此處來？

71.

兩經滄海歷風塵，
木屋羈留倍痛深。
國弱巫³²當齊努力，
狂瀾待挽仗同群。

72.

憑欄翹首望雲天，
一片山河盡黯然。
東蒙失陷歸無日，
中原恢復賴青年。
誅奸惟有常山舌，
殺賊須揚祖逖鞭。
憶我埃崙如蜷伏，
傷心故國復何言。

73.

I have ten thousand hopes that the revolutionary armies will complete their victory
And help make the mining enterprises successful in the ancestral land.
They will build many battleships and come to the U.S. territory,
Vowing never to stop till the white men are completely annihilated.

By someone from Fayuan[53]

74.

The dragon out of water is humiliated by ants;
The fierce tiger that is caged is baited by a child.
As long as I am imprisoned, how can I dare strive for supremacy?
An advantageous position for revenge will surely come one day.

---

53   A district in the Pearl River Delta region.

73.
萬望革軍成功竣，
維持祖國礦務通。
造多戰艦來美境，
滅盡白人誓不容。

　　花邑人題

74.
蛟龍失水螻蟻欺，
猛虎遭囚小兒戲。
被困安敢與爭雄，
得勢復仇定有期。

FIG. 2.5
Poem 74 was found on the second
floor of the men's barracks. It was
carved backward, or in reverse,
possibly so that detainees could
make rubbings or copies of
the poem to keep. Courtesy of
Architectural Resources Group.

75.

I left the village well behind me, bade farewell to my father and mother.

Now I gaze at distant clouds and mountains, my sleeves drenched by tears.

The wandering son longed to be wealthy like Taozhu.[54]

Who would have known I would be imprisoned on Island?

I beat my breast when I think of China and cry bitterly like Ruan Ji.[55]

Our country's wealth is being drained by foreigners, causing us to suffer
   national humiliations.

My fellow countrymen, have foresight, plan to be resolute.

And vow to conquer America and avenge previous wrongs!

   By a wanderer from Heungshan

76.

If the land of the Flowery Flag is occupied by us in turn,

The wooden building will be left for the angel's revenge.

---

54 See n. 10.
55 See n. 28.

75.

抛離鄉井別椿萱，

遠盼雲山袂盈珠。

遊子志欲陶朱富，

誰知被圄埃崙間？

榷[33]膚中華囊阮籍，

利權外溢國恥兼。

同胞知機圖奮志，

誓奪美國報前仇。

　香山遊子氏書

76.

花旗旗其轉吾人佔[34]據，

木樓樓留與天使還仇。

33　原作「撫」
34　原作「占」

77.

If you have but one breath left, do not be discouraged from your purpose.

I respectfully exhort my brothers, who are all talents of Chu.[56]

Having a sense of shame, one can eradicate shame.

Only by wielding the lance can one avoid death by the lance.

Do not say that we have not the means to level the ugly barbarians.

I am searching for a method that will turn destiny back.

One hundred thousand men sharpen their swords,

Swearing to behead the Loulan[57] and open the grasslands and fallow fields.

78.

The low building with three beams merely shelters the body.

It is unbearable to relate the stories accumulated on the Island slopes.

Wait till the day I become successful and fulfill my wish!

I will show no mercy when I level the immigration station![58]

By one from Toishan

---

56 It is said that during the Spring and Autumn period (770–476 BCE), raw materials were produced in the state of Chu but were used by the state of Jin, meaning that native talent was used in a foreign land.

57 Loulan was a state during the Western Han dynasty (206 BCE–24 CE) in what is now Xinjiang. Its king was simultaneously a vassal to both the Han emperor and the Xiongnu ruler. In 77 BCE, the Han emperor ordered the assassination of the Loulan king, who had exhibited an unfriendly attitude toward the Chinese. Thereafter, Loulan came under Han rule.

58 Literally, "the customs house." Before 1891, Chinese admissions and departures were processed at the San Francisco Customs House. The first characters of the Chinese lines form the sentence "Island awaits leveling."

77.

尚存一息志無灰，
敬勖同堂眾楚材。
知恥便能將恥雪，
揮戈方可免戈裁。
莫道無謀芟醜虜，
思求有術把天回。
男兒十萬橫磨劍，
誓斬樓蘭闢草萊。

78.

埃屋三椽聊保身，
崙麓積愫不堪陳。
待得飛騰順遂日，
剷除稅關不論仁。

　　台山人題

79.

We are as one, fellow sufferers with mutual sympathy.

Just like Confucius when he was surrounded in the state of Chen.[59]

Secretly, I praise your reliance on the strength of righteousness

To trample the barbarians, rather than letting others do it.

　　By Sun, using the same rhyme words as another poem[60]

80.

The five-colored flag of China flies all over the globe;[61]

　　the nations under heaven all lose heart.[62]

Ten thousand armies punish the foreign lands;

　　the states of Europe all tremble with fear.

81.

Today, we brothers are imprisoned in a jail;

　　it is only because of our ancestral land.

If our countrymen want freedom in the future,

　　then they must make an effort.

---

59 See n. 25.

60 This poem uses the same rhyme words as poem 78.

61 The Chinese flag from 1912 to 1927 had five horizontal
　　colored stripes representing the different ethnic groups in
　　China.

62 Literally, "to lose their gall bladders." The Chinese believe
　　that courage resides in the gall bladder.

79.

同病相憐如一身；
恰似仲尼困在陳。
私維君心仗義力；
足戮胡奴弗讓仁。

　辛和

80.

五旗飄寰球，天下諸邦皆喪膽；
萬軍誅異域，歐洲各國盡寒心。

81.

今日兄弟困牢籠，祇為祖國；
他日同胞欲自由，務須努力。

82.

I bemoan the ancient attitude of disparaging military matters and esteeming civil affairs.

It is a pity that I come too late to support the righteous and extirpate the villainous.

Locked up here, I indeed understand that it is because my country is weak.

Sleeping with awls[63] should spur us to develop our country's strength.

By Han Wei of the Town of Iron

83.

Random Thoughts on the Island

Drifting alone in the ocean, autumn suddenly passed.

I have just gone through ten thousand calamities; still I am a prisoner from Chu.[64]

When Wu Zixu played his flute, he thought of erasing his grievances.[65]

When Su Ziqing held his tasseled staff, he vowed he would one day avenge his wrongs.[66]

When Jiyun shot an arrow at the enemy, he was not doing it to meddle.[67]

When Goujian slept on firewood, he had a reason.[68]

My inflamed liver and bowels are prepared to take life lightly and engage in a life-and-death struggle.

Will the blue heavens allow me to fulfill this ambition or not?

By someone from Toishan who helps sprouts grow[69]

---

63 See n. 4.

64 See n. 40.

65 See n. 18.

66 See n. 27.

67 Nan Jiyun (d. 757). During the An Lushan Rebellion, the rebel army surrounded Suiyang (in present-day Henan). Nan was one of the defenders of the besieged city and shot the enemy general in the left eye with one arrow.

68 Goujian was king of the state of Yue (in present-day Zhejiang). In 494 BCE, he was ignominiously defeated by King Fucha's armies from the state of Wu. Yue recovered, and, two decades later, in 476 BCE, he returned to defeat Wu. It was alleged that King Goujian slept on firewood and tasted gall bladder in order not to forget the bitterness and humiliation of his defeat. Fan Li (Taozhugong) was one of his important ministers (see n. 10).

69 An allusion to *Mencius*, the Confucian classic. A man pulled at his rice plants to help them grow but ended up killing them all. The author is being self-deprecating, suggesting he couldn't leave well enough alone and ended up in prison. The signature may also suggest one who attempts to nurture the younger generation.

82.

輕武重文嗟古風；
挽正鋤[35]奸惜來遲。
羈此儼知因國弱；
眠錐應勵振邦雄。

　　鐵城漢維題

83.

埃崙偶感

飄零湖海倏經秋；
萬劫繞過作楚囚。
伍子吹簫懷雪恨；
蘇卿持節誓報仇。
霽雲射矢非多事；
勾踐臥薪卻有由。
激[36]烈肝腸輕一決；
蒼天諾否此志酬？

　　台山助苗長者題

35　原作「推」
36　余本作「擊」

84.

Traces Left by One from Yingyang[70]

In my lonely drifting life, I experienced great changes.

It is very sad for the innocent to be imprisoned in the wooden building.

I send words to you gentlemen that you should make plans to eradicate this grievance.

While you are enjoying yourselves, in particular, remember our grudge here.

85.

Being imprisoned in this wooden shack is precisely the cause of my worry.

It is like sitting in jail for committing a crime.

The hundred different abuses are really difficult to endure.

My only hope is that my compatriots will avenge this grievance.

---

70 Yingyang, a district in Henan, is said to be the place of origin
     for the Jang or Jung clan.

84.

滎陽遺蹟

飄零身世感滄桑；
淒絕無辜困木樓。
寄語諸君謀雪恨；
樂中尤記個中仇。

85.

木樓被困正堪憂；
儼然犯罪坐監牢。
百般苛待真難受；
惟望同胞雪此仇。

86.

I especially advise my compatriots not to worry.
We need only remember our confinement in the wooden building.
One day after we have united to make our nation strong,
We will then reciprocate in kind to America.

87.

I strongly advise my countrymen not to worry,
Even though you are imprisoned in a wooden building.
Someday after China rises and changes,
She will be adept at using bombs to obliterate America.

88.

For the sake of the mouth, I rushed about and must tolerate humiliation.
I gritted my teeth, clutched the brush, and recorded the circumstances.
The day my compatriots become prosperous and return to China,
They should once more outfit battleships to punish America.

86.
特勸同胞不可憂；
只須記取困木樓。
他日合群興邦後；
自將個樣還美洲。

87.
特勸同胞不可憂；
雖然被困在木樓。
他日中華興轉後；
擅用炸彈滅美洲。

88.
為口奔馳須忍辱；
咬牙秉筆錄情由。
同胞發達回唐日；
再整戰艦伐美洲。

89.

Japan swallows China.[71]

All my compatriots must unite to regulate our homes.

When our homes are regulated, then the state becomes properly governed.[72]

When we become prosperous and strong, we will annihilate the dwarves.[73]

90.

My family was poor, so I was going to Lüsong.[74]

Who would have known this would be a prison even for those just passing through?

One cannot bear to ask about the loneliness in the wooden building.

It is all because of a militarily weak nation with an empty national treasury.

I leave word with you gentlemen that you should all endeavor together.

Do not forget the national humiliations; arouse yourselves to be heroic.

---

71 The original poem has seven characters per line, but the first two characters of lines 1 and 3 are illegible.

72 This comes from "The Great Learning," a chapter in the *Book of Rites*, incorporated as one of Confucius's Four Books. The text is as follows: "Things being investigated, knowledge become complete. Then knowledge being complete, their thoughts were sincere. Their thoughts being sincere, their hearts were then rectified. Their hearts being rectified, their persons were cultivated. Their persons being cultivated, their families were regulated. Their families being regulated, their states were rightly governed. Their states being rightly governed, the entire Kingdom was made tranquil and happy."

73 A derogatory term for the Japanese.

74 "Lüsong" refers to Mexico. Chinese first came into contact with the Spanish on the island of Luzon in the Philippines. Because of the close connection of Mexico, another Spanish-speaking region, with the Manila trade, Mexico became known as Da Lüsong (Big Luzon), while the Philippines became Xiao Lüsong (Little Luzon). During the exclusion era, many Chinese illegally entered the United States from Mexico.

89.

口口日本吞中華；
同胞合力思齊家；
口口齊家次治國；
他日富強滅倭奴。

90.

家道貧窮走呂宋；
誰知借路亦牢籠？
木樓淒涼不堪問；
皆困兵弱國庫空。
寄語諸君齊發奮；
勿忘國恥振英雄。

FIG. 2.6
Medical examination in the
hospital building. Courtesy of
National Archives, Washington,
D.C.

About Westerners　　折磨時日

Poems 91–112

91.

I am distressed that we Chinese are detained in this wooden building.

It is actually racial barriers that cause difficulties on Yingtai Island.[75]

Even while they are tyrannical, they still claim to be humanitarian.

I should regret my taking the risks of coming in the first place.

92.

I thoroughly hate the barbarians because they do not respect justice.

They continually promulgate harsh laws to show off their prowess.

They oppress the overseas Chinese and also violate treaties.

They examine for hookworms[76] and practice hundreds of despotic acts.

93.

The savage doctors examine for hookworms.

I could not go ashore because fate was not kind.

Why should a young man take his life so lightly?

To whom should I cry out for redress of these terrible wrongs?

75　An island in Nan Hai (Southern Lake), west of the Forbidden City in Beijing. Emperor Guangxu (1875–1908) was imprisoned there by Empress Dowager Cixi in 1898 after a coup d'état aimed at halting his reform programs.

76　Only applicants from Asian countries were examined for hookworms. During the early years, infestation with the parasite was cause for deportation. Later, patients were allowed to undergo medical treatment at the immigration hospital at their own expense.

91.

傷我華僑留木屋，
實因種界厄瀛臺。
摧殘尚說持人道，
應悔當初冒險來。

92.

詳恨番奴不奉公，
頻施苛例逞英雄。
凌虐華僑兼背約，
百般專制驗勾蟲。

93.

狼醫要驗勾蟲症；
不能登陸運不靈。
青年何苦輕生命；
冤沉二字向誰鳴？

94.

It is indeed pitiable, the harsh treatment of our fellow countrymen.

The doctor extracting blood caused us the greatest anguish.

Our stomachs are full of grievances, but to whom can we tell them?

We can but pace to and fro, scratch our heads, and question the blue heavens.

95.

I cannot bear to describe the harsh treatment by the doctors.

Being stabbed for blood samples and examined for hookworms was even more pitiful.[77]

After taking the medicine, I also drank liquid,[78]

Like a dumb person eating the *huanglian*.[79]

---

77 As part of the bacteriological exam, blood was drawn from the ears and feces were examined for traces of threadworms and hookworms.

78 Thymol or chloroform was usually administered to loosen the worms from the intestinal walls so that they could be expelled.

79 "Coptis teeta," a bitter herb. This phrase refers to a victim who cannot voice his complaints to anyone.

94.
刻薄同胞實可憐，
醫生剌血最心酸。
冤情滿腹憑誰訴？
徘徊搔首問蒼天。

95.
醫生苛待不堪言，
勾蟲剌血更心酸。
食了藥膏又食水，
猶如啞佬食黃連。

96.

When I began reflecting, I became sad and composed a poem.

It was because my family was poor that I left for the country of the Flowery Flag.

I only hoped that when I arrived it would be easy to go ashore.

Who was to know the barbarians would change the regulations?

They stab the ear to test the blood, and in addition they examine the excrement.

If there is even a shadow of hookworms, one must be transferred to undergo a cure.

They took several dozen foreign dollars.[80]

Imprisoned in the hospital, I was miserable with grief and sorrow.

I do not know when I will be cured.

If I should escape one day, I need to return to my aspirations.

I will leave this place once and for all and not depend on it,

Thus avoiding humiliation and oppression by the devils.

My fellow villagers seeing this should take heed and remember;

I write my wild words to let those after me know.

97.

Abandoning books and inkstone, I drifted across the sea.

The intention was to make a humble person like myself famous.

It was difficult to foresee that I would be faced with imprisonment on arrival.

Still awaiting fulfillment of my ambition, I will long feel aggrieved.

It is enough to cause one to sigh at coming here and being lodged like duckweed.

After sacrificing a huge sum of money, I am now being disemboweled by the devils.

In this journey, I deeply wish to fulfill my ambition.

If not, it will be in vain that my heart breaks in confinement.

---

80 Patients had to pay for their own medical treatment at the
    immigration hospital.

96.
想起愁來題首詩。
因為家窮走花旗。
只望到來登岸易；
誰知番人轉例規？
刺耳驗血兼驗屎；
影有勾蟲要調治。
取得洋蚨數十餘；
困在醫房苦愁悲。
未知何日得痊癒。
若得脫身要念志，
一排[37]走清唔向倚，
免至凌辱受鬼欺。
梓里一看宜謹記；
寫我狂言留後知。

97.
棄書荒硯來飄洋；
意欲把我素心揚。
難料到此遭囹圄；
壯志待酬抱恨長。
堪嘆來此如萍寄；
犧牲巨款受鬼劏。[38]
此行深願酬我志；
否則囚困苦斷腸。

---

37 余本作「派」
38 余本作「膛」

98.

Half of my life has been spent running here and there searching for fame.

I ask myself when I will be satisfied.

All medicine was useless when I contracted a fever.

I did not see a doctor, but still I was afraid.

I think the gods in heaven surely protected me.

I did not need an alchemist's crucible,[81] and the sickness subsided by itself.

From now on, when I hear a storm brewing in the Milky Way,

I will gaze the distance of one thousand *li* and resolve to rise to the heights of the *peng*.[82]

99.

I clasped hands in parting with my brothers and classmates.

Because of the mouth,[83] I hastened to cross the American ocean.

How was I to know that the Western barbarians had lost their hearts and reason?

With a hundred kinds of oppressive laws, they mistreat us Chinese.

It is still not enough after being interrogated and investigated several times;

We also have to have our chests examined while naked.

Our countrymen suffer this treatment

All because our country's power cannot yet expand.

If there comes a day when China will be united,

I will surely cut out the heart and bowels of the Western barbarian.

---

81 One of the dreams of ancient Chinese alchemists was to discover the pill of immortality. In one experiment, cinnabar and other chemicals were heated in a crucible, hence the term "cinnabar crucible."

82 A giant, mythical bird, the roc is reputed to fly ten thousand *li*. Thus, the journey of the *peng* indicates a promising future.

83 To feed oneself, to make a living.

98.

半生逐逐為求名，
借問何時可愜情？
藥石無靈成瘧疾，
岐黃未遇卻心驚。
蒼天想必神能佑，
丹鼎無需[39]病自平。
從此聞飆雲漢起，
行看萬里奮鵬程。

99.

握別兄弟與同窗；
為口奔馳涉美洋。
豈知西奴心理喪；
百般苛例虐我唐。
數次審查猶未了，
還須裸體驗胸膛。
我們同胞遭至此，
皆因國勢未能張。
倘得中華一統日，
定割西奴心與腸。

100.

Fifth Day of the Tenth Moon, Xinhai Year,[84]
  Effusion After Moving to Another Room

I arrived in the wooden building one week ago.

Whenever someone mentions switching rooms, it distresses me excessively.

Gathering all my baggage together, I hurriedly run.

Who would ever know the misery of it all?

101.

The barbarian issued orders to change rooms.

Running up and down, my breath grew short.

It was like warfare, when people's minds are bewildered.

The scene resembled a stampede set off by beacon smoke.[85]

102.

I have lingered here three days, moving again and again.

It is difficult to compare this to the peacefulness at home.

Life need not be so demeaning.

Rushing about so much, smoke came out of my mouth.

  By someone from Heungshan

---

84 The year 1911, when the Chinese Revolution toppled the Qing
    dynasty.

85 In ancient China, towers stocked with firewood were erected
    at strategic points along the frontier. A fire was lit when an
    invasion occurred, and people seeing the smoke would recog-
    nize that a state of war existed.

100.
辛亥十月初五
搬房有感而作

到來木屋一星期；
提起搬房我極悲。
執齊行李忙忙走；
其中苦楚有誰知？

101.
蠻夷發令把房遷，
上下奔馳氣絕然。
恰似干戈人心亂，
聲勢猶如走烽煙。

102.
駐足三天遷復遷，
難比家居咁安然。
人生何苦如斯賤，
馳得勞勞口吐煙。

　　香山人題

103.

I hastened here for the sake of my stomach and landed promptly in jail.

Imprisoned, I am melancholy; even when I eat, my heart is troubled.

They treat us Chinese badly and feed us yellowed greens.[86]

My weak physique cannot take it; I am truly miserable.

104.

Since my imprisonment here, the moon has once again waxed full.

I still do not know when I will be interrogated.

Family poverty forced me to come and endure hardships.

It is difficult to pour out all the anger and grief in my heart.

If I could land after only one interrogation,

It would be a slight mitigation of the barbarians' hundred oppressions.

If I could fulfill my lifelong wish,

Even a little suffering would not matter.

105.

Although I had read through four or five loads of poetry and history,[87]

I had only one blue shirt[88] when I became old.

The American woman[89] asked what age I was;

 Fifty years ago, it was twenty-three.

---

86 Salted cabbage.

87 Literally, two of the Confucian classics, *Shi Jing* (poetry) and
    Shu Jing (history). In ancient times, books were written on
    bamboo slivers; hence, each book was very bulky.

88 This is derived from *qingyi*, or "blue clothing," which custom-
    arily was worn by the lower social classes in China.

89 The Chinese characters for *jiaren* literally mean "beautiful
    woman," a synonym for *meiren*, which is a homophone for
    "Americans."

103.

為口奔馳馳到監，
困愁愁食亦心煩。
薄待華人黃菜餐，
弱質難當實為難。

104.

此間囚困月重圓；
審問何時尚未知。
家窮逼我來受苦；
難盡心中憤與悲。
若得一審能上埠；
稍滅蠻夷百般欺。
倘能遂我平生願；
雖受苦楚亦唔拘。

105.

讀罷詩書四五擔；
老來方得一青衫；
佳人問我年多少；
五十年前二十三。

106.

The young children do not yet know worry.

Arriving at Gold Mountain, they were imprisoned in the wooden building.

Not understanding the sad and miserable situation before their eyes,

They still want to play all day like calves.

107.

The barbarians' cruelty is overwhelming.

Confident of their might, they oppress us Chinese.

All our compatriots meet with such treatment.

It is as if we were criminals locked in a jail cell.

108.

I bowed farewell to my close friends and went abroad.

How was I to know the barbarians would imprison me?

From antiquity, users of brute force have had no sense of justice.

Are there any clever schemes to escape this prison?

If I am deported and sent back to China one day,

Then several months' efforts will have been thrown into the water.

What a pity that Feng Tang aged so easily.[90]

Why was it most difficult for Li Guang to win honors?[91]

    Heungshan

---

90 Feng Tang was a capable official serving King Wen (179–157 BCE) of the Han dynasty (206BCE–220 CE). Later, when King Wu (149–87 BCE) was seeking men of talent, Feng was recommended, but by that time, he was more than ninety years old. His son was appointed in his stead.

91 Li Guang (d. 119 BCE) was a general who served King Wu of the Han dynasty. He was renowned for his many victories over the Xiongnu nomads but was never given a noble title.

106.

少年子弟未知愁，
來到金山困木樓。
不悟[40]眼前悲苦境，
還要終日戲如牛。

107.

番奴狠毒[41]不可當；
倚國豪強虐我唐。
大眾同胞遭至此；
猶如罪犯鎖監房。

108.

揖別知己出外洋；
豈知胡虜困我身？
自古強權無公禮；
有何妙策出牢籠。
一旦撥回歸去國；
數月工程付水中。
可惜馮唐[42]容易老；
何其李廣最難封？

　　香山

40　粵海春秋作「晤」
41　余本作「狠狽」
42　余本作「庚」

109.

Random Feelings

My parents are old; my family is poor.

Cold weather comes; hot weather goes.

Heartless white devils,

Sadness and anger fill my heart.

   By Lee Gengbo of Toishan

110.

A thousand sorrows and a ten-thousand-fold hatred burn between my brows.

Hoping to step ashore on the American continent is the most difficult of difficulties.

The barbarians imprison me in this place.

Even a martyr or a hero would change countenance.

109.
偶感

親老家貧；
寒來暑往。
無情白鬼；
悲憤填膺。

　　台邑李鏡波題

110.
千愁萬恨燃眉間；
望登美洲難上難。
番奴把我囚困此；
列士英雄亦失顏。

111.

This unworthy one with the group is grief-stricken.

Who will transmit the news of death back to the village?

I mourn your having ridden the crane to return to the dark regions.[92]

A traveler arrived in America on a ship.

Tears enveloped the lonely soul as the cuckoo uttered its mournful cry.

Sorrow has led me to dream of traveling to the Terrace of Yang.[93]

It is a pity that medicine was wrongly prescribed.

The corpse was nearly cremated to ashes.

112.

Shocking news, truly sad, reached my ears.

We mourn you. When will they wrap your corpse for return?

You cannot close your eyes. On whom are you depending to voice your complaints?

If you had foresight, you should have regretted coming here.

Now you will be forever sad and forever resentful.

Thinking of the village, one can only futilely face the Terrace for Gazing Homeward.[94]

Before you could fulfill your lofty goals, you were buried beneath clay and earth.

I know that even death could not destroy your ambition.

---

92 Death. In Chinese mythology, cranes are connected with immortality.

93 King Huai of Chu (328–299 BCE) met a female immortal in a dream and had sexual relations with her. She was found every morning and evening at the foot of the Terrace of Yang, which has come to be used as an allusion to a place where men and women meet for sex.

94 During the political turmoil in China at the end of the Western Jin dynasty (265–316), two princesses fled to a distant region for safety and ended up marrying commoners in a village. They were often unhappy and longed for their old homes. Their fellow villagers then built a terrace from which they could gaze in the direction of their home.

111.

忝屬同群事感哀。

訃音誰遞故鄉回？

痛君騎鶴歸冥去；

有客乘槎赴美來。

淚鎖孤魂悲杜宇；

愁牽旅夢到陽台。

可憐藥石施醫誤；

險被焚屍一炬灰。

112.

噩耗傳聞實可哀，

弔君何日裹屍回？

無能瞑目憑誰訴？

有識應知悔此來。

千古含愁千古恨，

思鄉空對望鄉臺。

未酬壯志埋壤土，

知爾雄心⁴³死不灰。⁴⁴

---

43 佘本作「志」
44 佘本作「恢」

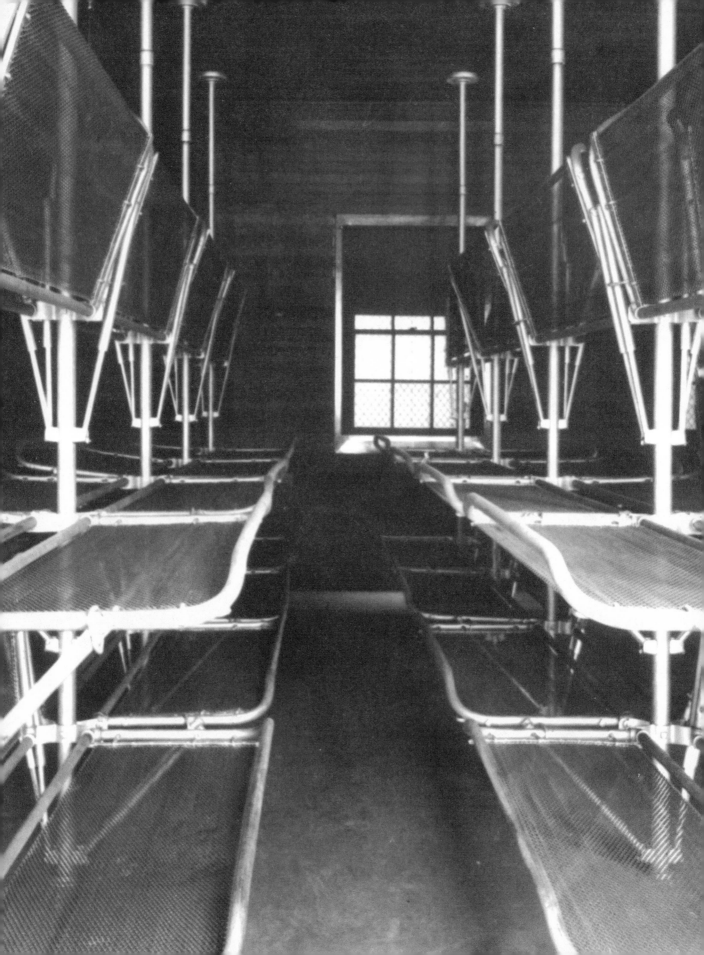

Deportees and Transients 寄語梓里

Poems 113–135

113.

As a traveler weathering wind and dust, I ran east and west,

But I never expected now to wind up in a prison.

Because my plan was leaked, I am now in difficult straits on the mountain.

How will I devise a strategy so that the hidden dragon can emerge?[95]

Wu Zixu, who endured and hid, was able to redress his grievance.[96]

Sun Bin endured humiliation and was successful in avenging his wrongs.[97]

I am now being deported and sent back to my country.

Someday when we become rich and strong, we will annihilate this barbaric nation.

114.

On a long voyage I traveled across the sea.

Feeding on wind and sleeping on dew, I tasted hardships.

Even though Su Wu was detained among the barbarians, he would one day return home.[98]

When he encountered a snowstorm, Wengong sighed, thinking of bygone years.[99]

In days of old, heroes underwent many ordeals.

I am, in the end, a man whose goal is unfulfilled.

Let this be an expression of the torment that fills my belly.

Leave this as a memento to encourage fellow souls.

   13th day of the third month in the sixth year of the Republic (March 13, 1917)

---

95 From the *Book of Changes* (Yi jing). This is symbolic of a sage who is concealed and not yet in prominence.

96 See n. 18.

97 Sun Bin and Pang Juan (d. 341 BCE) studied together under the same teacher during the Warring States period. After completion of their studies, Pang was the first to be appointed to an official post in the state of Wei (in present-day Shanxi). Later, when Sun followed, hoping to get an appointment as well, Pang became apprehensive that Sun would prove to be more capable. He falsely accused Sun of conspiring with the neighboring state of Qi (in present-day Shandong). As a result, Sun was punished—his kneecaps were cut off so that he could no longer walk. Subsequently, he served the state of Qi and in 341 BCE led an army against Wei. Pang was defeated and committed suicide in shame. Sun Bin is known for his book of military tactics.

98 See n. 27.

99 The posthumous title of Han Yu (768–824), a scholar-official during the Tang dynasty. In 819, he fell into disfavor when he memorialized the throne against the elaborate ceremonies planned to honor an alleged bone of Buddha. For this, he was exiled to Chaozhou in Guangdong, then an undeveloped region of jungles and swamps. On his way south, he bade farewell to his grandnephew at a snowy mountain pass, Lan Guan, in Shanxi, and composed a poem to express his feelings.

113.

風塵作客走西東；
不料今時到監中。
因洩機謀山中困；
何籌韜略出潛龍。[45]
子胥忍藏能雪恨；
孫臏忍辱復仇功。
我今撥回歸國去；
他日富強滅番邦。

114.

梯航遠涉歷重洋，
風餐露宿[46]苦自嘗。
蘇武淪胡歸有日，
文公遇雪嘆當年。
自古英雄多磨折，[47]
到底男兒志未伸。
滿腹苦衷聊代表，
留為紀念勵同魂。

中華民國六年三月十三日

45　余本作「籠」
46　原作「宿露」
47　原作「攝」

115.

Barred from landing, I really am to be pitied.

My heart trembles at being deported and sent back home.

I cannot face the elders east of the river.[100]

I came to seek wealth but instead reaped poverty.

116.

A member of the Lee household was ready to leave.

In the last month of summer, I arrived in America on a ship.

After crossing the ocean, the ship docked, and I waited to go on shore.

Because of the records, the innocent was imprisoned in a wooden building.

Reflecting on the event, my heart is vexed and depressed.

I composed a poem to rid myself of sadness and worry.

At present, my application for admission has not yet been dismissed.

As I record the cause of my situation, it really provokes my anger.

Sitting here, uselessly delayed for long years and months,

I am like a pigeon in a cage.

> Composed as a gift by an overseas Chinese,
> a mountain monk from the Town of Iron

---

100 At the end of the Qin dynasty in the third century BCE,
Xiang Yu (232–202 BCE) led eight thousand young stalwarts
from the region east of the Yangzi River (in present-day
Jiangsu) to vie for the rule of China. He was ultimately
defeated by Liu Bang, who subsequently became the first
emperor of the Han dynasty. After losing nearly all his men,
Xiang Yu chose to commit suicide rather than return in
defeat to face the elders of his native region.

115.

阻攔上埠實堪憐，
撥回歸家也心驚。
無面見江東父老，
只望求富反求貧。

116.

李宅人員把身抽；
季夏乘船到美洲。
海過舟灣候上岸；
紀錄無辜困木樓。
念及事情心厭悶；
詩[48]章題首解愁憂。
目下未曾批消案；
錄記情由實可嬲。
在坐虛延長歲月；
此處如籠一隻鳩。

華僑口鐵城山僧題贈

---

48 原作「書」

117.

Lim, upon arriving in America,

Was arrested, put in the wooden building,

And made a prisoner.

I have already been here for one autumn.

The Americans refused me admission.

I was ordered to be deported.

When the news was told,

I was frightened and troubled about returning to my country.

We Chinese of a weak nation

Can only sigh at the lack of freedom.

    Written by a Taoist from the Town of Iron

118.

When a newcomer arrives in America,[101]

He will surely be arrested and put in the wooden building,

Like a major criminal.

I have already been here one autumn.

The Americans refused me admission;

I have been barred and ordered to be deported.

Alongside the ship, the waves are huge.

Returning to the motherland is truly distressing.

We Chinese of a weak nation

Sigh bitterly at the lack of freedom.

The day our nation becomes strong,

I swear we will cut off the barbarians' heads.

101　This poem is very similar to poem 117 except that it has
　　two additional lines and each line has five instead of four
　　characters.

117.

林到美洲，
逮[49]入木樓。
成為囚犯，
來此一秋。
美人不准，
批撥回頭。
消息報告，
回國驚憂。
國弱華人，
嘆不自由。

　　鐵城道人題

118.

新客到美洲；
必逮[50]入木樓。
儼如大犯樣；
在此經一秋。
美國人不准；
批消撥回頭。
船中波浪大；
回國實堪憂。
國弱我華人；
苦嘆不自由。
我國豪強日；
誓斬胡人頭。

49　原作「隸」
50　余本作「隸」

119.

Crude Poem Inspired by the Landscape

The ocean encircles a lone peak.

Rough terrain surrounds this prison.

There are few birds flying over the cold hills.

The wild goose messenger[102] cannot find its way.

I have been detained and obstacles have been put in my way for half a year.

Melancholy and hate gather on my face.

Now that I must return to my country,

I have toiled like the *jingwei* bird in vain.[103]

120.

For two months I was imprisoned; my slippers never moved forward.[104]

I came on the *Manchuria* and will return on the *Mongolia*.

But if I could make the trip to Nanyang,[105] I would.

Why should America be the only place to seek a living?

121.

For half a year after I had been refused entry, I heard no news.

Who was to know that today I would be deported and sent back to Tang?[106]

On the ship, I will have to endure the waves; teardrops fall.

On a clear night, thinking it over three times, the bitterness is difficult to bear.

---

102 Mail service.
103 See n. 26.
104 No progress had been made.
105 Southeast Asia.
106 In reference to "Mountains of Tang," the Cantonese collo-
     quial name for China.

119.

感景拙詠

滄海圍孤峰，
崎嶇困牢籠。
鳥疏寒山緻，
鴻使莫尋蹤。
留難經半載，
愁恨積滿容。
今將歸國去，
空勞精衛功。

120.

乙月被囚履不前，
滿州輪來蒙古旋。
但得南洋登程日，
求活何須美利堅？

121.

批消半載無消息；
誰知今日撥回唐？
船中揾浪珠淚落；
清夜三思苦難堪。

122.

Again I crossed the ocean to come to America.

I only hope this time I can fulfill my ambition.

Who was to know that Heaven would not will it?

Stubbornly, it refused my entry and caused my imprisonment in the wooden building.

123.

I leave word for my compatriots not to worry too much.

They mistreat us, but we need not grieve.

Han Xin was straddled by a bully's trousers yet became a general.[107]

Goujian endured humiliation and ultimately avenged his wrong.[108]

King Wen was imprisoned at Youli and yet destroyed King Zhou.[109]

Even though fate was perverse to Jiang Taigong, still he was appointed a marquis.[110]

Since the days of old, such has been the fate of heroes.

With extreme misfortune comes the composure to await an opportunity for revenge.

124.

This is a message to those who live here not to worry excessively.

Instead, you must cast your idle worries into the flowing stream.

Experiencing a little ordeal is not hardship.

Napoleon was once a prisoner on an island.

---

107 When Han Xin (d. 196 BCE) was a poor youth, a local bully tried to humiliate him by ordering him to crawl between his legs. Han obediently complied and became a laughingstock. Later, he rose to become an important general serving the first emperor of the Han dynasty and was made a marquis.

108 See n. 68.

109 See n. 19.

110 Also known as Lü Shang or Taigongwang, Jiang was an important minister serving King Wen and King Wu of Zhou. According to legend, his talents were not recognized until he was seventy, when King Wen found him fishing on the Wei River. The king had him tutor his son, who later became King Wu. After helping King Wu conquer the Shang state, Jiang was made the marquis of Qi (in present-day Shandong).

122.
再歷重洋到美洲；
只望是番把志酬。
豈知天不為我便；
偏教批消困木樓。

123.
寄語同胞勿過憂，
苛待吾儕毋庸愁。
韓信受胯為大將，
勾踐忍辱終報仇。
文王囚羑而滅紂，
姜公運斗亦封侯。
自古英雄多如是，
否極泰來待復仇。

124.
寄語同居勿過憂，
且把閒愁付水流。
小受折磨非是苦，
破崙[51]曾被島中囚。

---

51 余本作「埃崙」

125.

Bidding farewell to the wooden building, I return to Hong Kong.[111]

Henceforward, I will arouse my country and flaunt my aspirations.

I'll tell my compatriots to inform their fellow villagers.

If they possess even a small surplus of food and clothing,

    they should not drift across the ocean.

126.

For half a year on Island, we experienced both the bitter and the sweet.

We part now only as I am being deported.

I leave words to my fellow villagers that when they land,

I expect them to always remember the time they spent here.

127.

Away from home and living in the wooden building, I am secretly grieved.

Splendor fades with the turn of an eye, so be not too earnest.

I leave words with those who will come to Island in the future.

You should raise your head and observe the people.

---

111 The poet here uses the poetic name of Xiangjiang (Fragrant River) rather than the conventional Xianggang (Fragrant Harbor).

125.
木樓永別返香江，
從此興邦志氣揚。
告我同胞談梓里，
稍餘衣食莫飄洋。

126.
埃崙半載同甘苦；
我今撥回始別離，
寄語同鄉上埠日；
務望時記是中朝。

127.
旅居木屋暗傷神；
轉眼韶光莫認真。
寄語埃崙將來者；
翹頭應望是中人。

128.

May I advise you not to sneak across the barrier?

Green waters surround a green hill on four sides.

Ascending to a high place, one does not see the shore.

To cross the green waters is the most difficult of difficulties.

Life is worth worrying about, and you should restrain yourselves.

Do not treat these words as idle words.

Why not let them send you back to China?

You will find some work and eke out a couple of meals.

129.

The road is far for the traveler; ten thousand *li* are difficult.

May I advise you not to sneak across the border?

The difficult and dangerous conditions are not worth your inquiries.

These are not idle words.

   Twelfth year of the Republic (1923)

128.
勸君切勿來偷關，
四圍綠水繞青山。
登高遠望無涯岸，
欲渡綠水難上難。

生命堪虞君自重，
斯言不是作為閒。
盍任撥回歸國去？
覓些[52]營生捱兩[53]餐。

129.
路遠行人萬里難；
勸君切勿來偷關。
艱險情形堪莫問；
斯言不是作為閒。

　　民國十二年

52　余本作「此」
53　余本作「二」

130.

I entered the land of the Flowery Flag by way of Lüsong.[112]

Conditions at the border were strict, and I was not clever.

In the wooden jail, I was imprisoned for days.

Now I am to be deported in the steel vessel *Persia*.

When Ruan Ji reached the end of the road, who took pity on his weeping?[113]

In a distant land, Li Ling sadly sighed in vain.[114]

There is nothing that can be done about misfortune caused by tyranny.

Fate is unlucky and times are perverse; therefore, I suffer these ordeals.

131.

I abandoned my native village to earn a living.

I endured all the wind and frost to seek fame.

I passed this land to get to Cuba.[115]

Who was to know they would dispatch me to a prison on a mountain?

---

112 Mexico.

113 See n. 28.

114 Li Ling (d. 74 BCE), a Han general, led an army of foot soldiers against the Xiongnu. After fighting against great odds, he was forced to surrender. The Han emperor subsequently executed his mother, younger brother, wife, and children. Li Ling was the grandson of Li Guang (d. 119 BCE), another famous general who fought the Xiongnu.

115 Angel Island was also used as a detention facility for transients on their way to and from Cuba, Mexico, and other Latin American countries.

130.

假道呂宋走花旗，
關情嚴密不知機。
監牢木屋囚困日，
波斯鐵船被撥期。

窮途阮籍誰憐哭？
絕域李陵空嘆愁。
無可奈何事制厄，
命蹇時乖受此磨。

131.

拋離家鄉作營謀，
風霜捱盡為名求。
路經此地來古巴，
誰知撥我入山囚？

132.

People from Dowmoon[116] are going to Tahiti,

Having been in the wooden building for more than ten days.

From Tahiti, there are people returning to the Mountains of Tang.

How were they to know this would be such a callous city?

There are people returning, and there are people leaving.

Having wasted more than three hundred silver dollars,

If I do not get to this city, I will be unhappy.

If I return home, my parents would be extremely grief-torn.

Unpaid interest would be piled one on top of another,

Not knowing when it would be repaid to the lender.

133.

I did not expect to be drifting like duckweed to Mexico City.[117]

I had been all over the world in three years.

Copper cash did not know me, but that did me no harm.

I was tired of listening to the fusillades of rifles and cannons,[118]

So I risked stealing across the barrier to live in the United States.

Who was to know that today I would be punished with imprisonment?

116 Dowmoon District is in the Pearl River Delta region and was
    formerly part of Chungshan District (see map on p. 5).
117 The preceding four lines are largely illegible but appear to
    state that he had to leave his wife and child to go to Mexico
    because his family was poor.
118 Battles in the Mexican Revolution (1910–20).

132.
斗門人往大溪地，
來到木屋十餘日。
溪地有人回唐山，
誰知[54]此埠極難為。
有人回來有人去，
使枉[55]洋銀三百餘。
不到此埠心不忿，
回家父母苦極悲。
留下利息重重疊，
未知何日還他主？

133.
家徒壁立口口留；
握別妻身口口舟。
破浪乘風登墨口；
口口口口口口流。
不料浮萍至墨京；
寰球遍地已三年，
青蚨不識無傷我。
悶聽鎗林砲雨聲；
故冒偷關來居美；
誰知今日受囚刑？

---

54 原作「至」
55 原作「汪」

134.

In January, I started to leave for Mexico.

Passage reservations delayed me until mid-autumn.

I had wholeheartedly counted on a quick landing at the city,

But the year's almost ending, and I am still here in this building.

> Last third of the last month of the seventh year of the Republic (1918)
> Longdu,[119] Heungshan

135.

Detained in this wooden house for several tens of days,

It is all because of the Mexican exclusion law that implicates me.[120]

It's a pity heroes have no way of exercising their prowess.

I can only await the word so that I can snap Zu's whip.[121]

From now on, I am departing far from this building.

All of my fellow villagers are rejoicing with me.

Don't say that everything within is Western style.

Even if it is built of jade, it has turned into a cage.

---

119 An area in Heungshan District from which many immigrants originated.

120 In 1921, the Mexican government revised its treaty with China to ban the immigration of Chinese laborers, and in 1931, an expulsion order forced hundreds of Chinese Mexicans to leave their homes in Sonora and Sinaloa and cross the border into the United States. Many were detained on Angel Island while waiting to be deported to China.

121 In reference to Zu Ti (see n. 37).

134.

元月動程赴墨洲；
船位阻延到中秋。
一心指望頻登埠；
年關將及在此樓。

　民國七年尾月下浣
　香山隆都

135.

木屋拘留幾十天，
所因墨例致牽連。
可惜英雄無用武，
只聽音來策祖鞭。

從今遠別此樓中，
各位鄉君眾歡同。
莫道其間皆西式，
設成玉砌變如籠。

FIG. 2.8
Poem 135 was found on the walls
of a lavatory room on the first
floor of the detention barracks.
Photograph by Mak Takahashi.
Courtesy of Philip P. Choy.

FIG. 2.9
Detention building and stairs
leading to the dining hall in the
administration building, c. 1910.
Courtesy of California State Parks,
2014.

Detention in the *Muk Uk* 木屋拘囚序

TRANSLATED BY MARLON K. HOM

My mind often recalls Su Wu, who, in maintaining his unyielding loyalty to the

    Han dynasty, would rather endure the biting snow on the freezing frontier;[1]

And the King of Yue, who, in reminding himself to seek revenge against the

    state of Wu, would sleep on firewood and lick the bitter gall bladder.[2]

Our ancestors have met adversities;

They have overcome hardships;

Their trials and tribulations are duly recognized in the history books.

Showing their might before the barbarians,

    Calming the anxiety within themselves—

That would resolve my lifelong yet unfilled ambitions.

And yet,

My generation is indeed unlucky;

Our lives have been most unfortunate.

We drift like tumbleweed in a foreign country

And suffer the fate of detention as in Youli.[3]

A *muk uk* is a wooden building. This poem, which was written by a Chinese detainee and first published in *Chinese World* newspaper on March 16, 1910, is translated from *Xinning Zazhi* 28 (1911): 76–78. *Chinese World* deleted fifteen lines critical of the Qing government from the poem. There are also minor textual differences between the two versions. An earlier version of this translation was published in Yung, Chang, and Lai, *Chinese American Voices*, 118–24.

1   During the Western Han dynasty, Su Wu (140–60 BCE) was sent by the Chinese government as envoy to the Xiongnu, a nomadic people north of the Chinese empire. He was detained there for nineteen years but refused to renounce his loyalty to the Han emperor.

2   Goujian was king of the state of Yue (in present-day Zhejiang). In 494 BCE, he was ignominiously defeated by King Fucha's armies from the state of Wu. Two decades later, in 476 BCE, Yue recovered and returned to defeat Wu. It was alleged that King Goujian slept on firewood and tasted gall bladder in order not to forget the bitterness and humiliation of his defeat.

3   King Wen (ca. 12th century BCE), founder of the Zhou state, was held captive at Youli because the last Shang king regarded him as a potential threat to Shang rule. His son, King Wu (1134–1115 BCE), later defeated the Shang and established the Zhou dynasty.

嘗思齧雪餐毡，蘇武守漢朝之節；
臥薪嘗胆，越王報吳國之讎。
古人坎坷屢遇，
艱辛備嘗。
卒克著名於史冊。

振威於蠻夷，以解私懷之憂，
而慰畢生之願也。
獨我等時運不濟，
命途多舛。
蓬飄外國，
永遭羑里之囚。

When we bade farewell to our village home,

We were in tears because of survival's desperation.

When we arrived in the American territory,

We stared in vain at the vast ocean.

Our ship docked

And we were transferred to a solitary island.

Ten *li* [4] from the city,

My feet stand on this lonely hill.

The *muk uk* is three stories high,

Built as firmly as the Great Wall.

Room after room are but jails,

And the North Gate firmly locked.

Here—

Several hundreds of my countrymen are like fish caught in a net;

Half a thousand Yellow Race are like birds trapped in a mesh.

As we lift our heads and look afar,

The barbarian reed pipes add all the more to our anguish and grief.

As we cock our ears and try to listen,

The horses' neighing further worsens our solitude and sorrow.

---

4   One *li* is approximately one-third of a mile.

離別故鄉，
頻洒窮途之淚。
躬到美域，
徒觀海水之汪洋。
船泊碼頭，
轉撥埃崙之孤島。
離埠十里，
托足孤峯。
三層木屋，
堅如萬里長城。
幾座監牢，
長扃北門管鑰。

同胞數百，難期漏網之魚；
黃種半千，恍若密羅之雀。
有時舉頭而眺，
胡笳互動，益增惆悵之悲。
或者傾耳而聽，
牧馬悲鳴，翻惹淒涼之感。

During the day, we endure a meal of crackers and cheese,

   Just like Yan Hui eating rice and water;[5]

At night, we wrap ourselves in a single blanket,

   Just like Min Qian wearing clothes made of rush.[6]

We wash in the morning in salty tidal water;

We drink murky water to quench our thirst.[7]

In this newly open facility,

Neither land nor water is in harmony with us.

Drinking the water makes many cough;

Eating the meal causes many to have sore throats.

A hundred ailments come about;

Our pain and suffering are beyond words!

At times, the barbarians would become angry with us;

They kick and punch us severely.

By chance, in their sudden cruel moment,

They would point their guns at us.

They scrutinize us like Prince Qin inspecting his soldiers;[8]

They trap us with schemes like Han Xin's multiple levels of encirclement.[9]

Brothers cannot share words, separated by faraway mountains;

Relatives cannot comfort one another, divided by the distant horizon.[10]

Inside this room—

   Neither Heaven nor Earth answers my cries.

Outside this prison,

   A hundred birds chirp in grief in the mournful woods.

   A thousand animals run in fright among gloomy clouds and mist.

This is indeed living with nature, amidst trees, rocks, deer, and wild boars!

---

5   Yan Hui (521–490 BCE), the poorest of Confucius's disciples, ate very simply and yet was content.

6   Min Ziqian (536–487 BCE), or Min Sun, one of Confucius's disciples, was treated cruelly by his stepmother when he was young. She used to clothe him in rushes, which did not keep out the winter cold.

7   At the time, the immigration station did not have any fresh-water tanks. Drinking water came from a spring, which at one point contained traces of fecal contamination.

8   Li Shimin was a general before he became the second emperor of the Tang dynasty.

9   Han Xin (d. 196 BCE) was an important general who served the first emperor of the Han dynasty.

10   Chinese detainees were not allowed visitors for fear of collusion before the immigration interrogation.

日餐醬酪，步顏子之簞瓢；
夜蓋單毡，同閔騫之蘆服。
清晨盥洗，盡是鹹潮；
終日飲滋，無非濁水。
矧遐荒新闢，
水土欠和。
飲焉而咳嗽者甚繁，
啜焉而喉痛者不少。
病端百出，
苦楚難云。

間有偶觸胡怒，
拳脚交加。
忽起狼心，
鎗頭向指。
人數目算，泰王之點兵尚存；
戎馬重圍，韓信之妙計猶在。
兄弟莫通一語，相隔關山；
親朋欲慰寸衷，相離天壤。
處此間也，欲籲天而天無聞。
入此室也，欲叫地而地不應。
且也樹木陰翳於囚外，百鳥悲啼。
雲霞垂覆於山前，千獸駭走。
正所謂與木石居，與鹿豕遊者矣。

Alas! Heaven!

So desolate is this sight;

It is disheartening indeed.

Sorrow and hardship have led me to this place;

What more can I say about life?

Worse yet,

A healthy person would become ill after repeated medical examinations;

A private inspection would render a clothed person naked.

Let me ask you, the barbarians:

Why are you treating us in such an extreme way?

I grieve for my fellow countrymen;

There is really nothing we can do!

All the tall bamboo from Zhongnan Mountain cannot bear our words of
frustration.[11]

All the water in the Eastern Sea will not cleanse our sense of humiliation.

Perhaps, we can be—

Like Emperor Min of Jin, who didn't reject the shame of wearing blue
garb and serving wine,[12]

Like Li Ling, who pounded his chest in agony for his Han army
surrendering to the Huns.[13]

Our ancestors have encountered such misfortune—

Why does our present generation endure the same?

In a moment of desperation,

What more can one say?

In waiting with concealed weapons for the right moment to arrive—

It is nothing but pure fantasy.

---

11   This idea is taken from a proverb, which alludes to crimes so numerous that they will not fit on slips made from all the bamboo in the Zhongnan Mountains. The ancient Chinese often wrote on bamboo slips.

12   In 316, King Min of the Jin dynasty was captured by the Xiongnu and forced to perform such humiliating acts as serving wine to the victors.

13   Li Ling (d. 74 BCE), a Han general, led an army of foot soldiers against the Xiongnu. After fighting against great odds, he was forced to surrender.

嗟！嗟！

觸景生情，

荒涼滿目。

愁誰遣此；

命也何如？

尤有慘者，診脉數回，無病宛然有病；

驗身數次，裹身一若裸身。

借問昊天，使我奚至此極？

哀哉吾輩，然亦無如之何。

雖削南山之高竹，寫不盡離騷之詞。

竭東海之波流，洗不淨羞慙之狀。

然或者，狄庭行酒，晉愍不辭青衣之羞；

漢軍降奴，李陵曾作椎心之訴。

古人如此，

今人獨不忍乎？

夫事窮勢迫，亦復何言？

藏器待時，徒空想像。

Alas,

Such tyranny of the White Race!

Such tragedy of the Yellow Souls!

Like a homeless dog forced into a confining cage,

Like a trapped pig held in a bamboo cage,

Our spirits are lost in this wintry prison;

   We are worse than horses and cattle.

Our tears shed on an icy day,

   We are less than the birds and fowl.

In my exile to the ocean's end,

I have found enjoyment in reading newspapers.

It is said that

My old country, my native soil—

   Split apart like pea pods,

   Cut up like melons.

I mourn that

My motherland, my native culture—

   Swallowed by wolves,

   Digested by the tigers.

It is my wish:

Someone like Chen She will drop the plows on the field,[14]

Someone like Tian Heng will raise the righteous banner[15]

And pick up the weapons—

Leveling the state of Qin,

Wiping out the state of Wu.

---

14 Chen She (d. 208 BCE) led the first large-scale peasant rebellion recorded in Chinese history, against the Qin imperial government in 209 BCE. His forces soon expanded from nine hundred to several tens of thousands as he proclaimed himself a royal sovereign. However, he was defeated by a Qin army and subsequently assassinated by his chariot driver, who chose to surrender to the foe.

15 Tian Heng (d. 202 BCE) was a descendant of the nobility in the state of Qi, which was absorbed into the Qin empire. Toward the end of the Qin dynasty, he and his cousin led many former soldiers of Qi in a revolt to reestablish the state of Qi. He was defeated by the Han and fled with five hundred followers to an island. Soon afterward, the Han emperor summoned him to Luoyang, where he killed himself. When his followers on the island heard the news, they all committed suicide.

嗚呼！
白種強權，
黃魂受慘。
比喪家之狗，強入牢籠；
追入笠之豚，嚴加鎖鑰。
魂消雪窖，眞犬馬之不如。
淚洒冰天，傷禽鳥之不若也。

但我躬既竄海曲，
性品悅看報章。
稱說舊鄉故土，豆剖瓜分；
哀憐舉國斯文，狼犿虎噬。

所望陳涉之徒，輟耕隴畝。
田橫之客，早建義旗。
稱干比戈，
掃秦川為平壤。
仗矛秉鉞，
蕩吳國作丘荒。

Just take a look at China today:

We the Han people must take over.

Otherwise—

We will be butchered;

We will be enslaved;

We will be subjugated.

There is a difference between the true ruler and the imposter.[16]

How can we bear witness:

Four hundred million Chinese people, again, enslaved by other nations?

Five thousand years of civilization, like in India, obliterated?[17]

We are filled with grief.

How can we suppress our cries?

16 These lines, which critique the inept rule of the Qing govern-
   ment in power at the time, were not included when *Chinese
   World* published the poem.
17 During this period, when China was threatened by foreign
   powers, Chinese patriots often used the example of India,
   which was then ruled by the British, to alert their country-
   men to the threat foreign aggression posed to China's sover-
   eignty.

請看今日之域中，
定是漢家之天下。
不然，任人肉我，
甘為婢膝奴顏，
捨己從人，
不分偽朝正統。

將見四百兆之華民，重為萬國之奴隸；
五千年之歷史，化為印度之危亡。
良可慨也，
尚忍言哉？

FIG. 2.10
Ellis Island Immigration Station,
c. 1920. The building marked with
a triangle is where the Chinese
poetry was found. Courtesy of
Harry H. Laughlin Papers, Special
Collections Department, Pickler
Memorial Library, Truman State
University.

Poems from Ellis Island

TRANSLATED BY CHARLES EGAN

1.

Thinking of home, my tears begin to flow;

I wonder, when I can ever be free of worry?

Parents, uncles, wives, and children scattered;

Our houses and rooms completely leveled.

Luckily I landed in the Flowery Flag,

Thinking I would be safe and free of sadness.

Who knew that I'd be seized by immigration officials?

They threw me in detention, ignoring my protests.

How can I gain relief from these oppressive laws?

I await the time of our victory, for then we can be free.

I hope compatriots will join together, pool their strength,

Donate funds, and return home to kill our enemies.[1]

Then, when I'm reunited with my parents, wife, and children,

With laughter I'll describe my journey to the West.[2]

2.

Though imprisonment is bitter, my life will be long;

When I landed from the ship, I feared bodily harm.

I urge you: don't be afraid of immigration laws—

It's certain we'll be freed to go home in peace.

---

1   Japan invaded China in 1937, sparking the Sino-Japanese War.

2   *Journey to the West* (Xiyou ji) is a favorite novel among the Chinese, who often entertained one another with narrations of scenes during their leisure time.

1.

思念故鄉眼淚流，
不知何日可無憂。
父母伯叔妻兒散，
樓房屋宇變成溝。
命大如天花旗到，
以為安寧可無愁。
誰知移民將我捕，
不由分說入拘留。
何能解決苛條例，
待期勝利可自由。
亦望同群齊合力，
捐輸回國殺我仇。
得見父母妻兒會，
笑口吟吟講西遊。

2.

長監苦困壽命長，
去船恐有身受傷。
勸君莫怕移民例，
定有安然放我歸。

3.

A girl just sixteen, of dazzling beauty,

A pair of jade arms, and a pillow for a thousand heads.

The dot of rouge on her lips has been tasted by countless men;

Each night, her bridal bower welcomes a new bridegroom.[3]

4.

A thousand days at home are easy;

Half a day abroad is hard.

---

3   This poem was inscribed below several sketches of a sexual
     nature. It is not an original poem but rather is a muddled ver-
     sion of a well-known poem from the popular novel *Emperor
     Qianlong Travels to the South* (Qianlong xia Jiangnan).

3.
二八佳人巧樣貌，
一雙玉手千人枕。
伴點脂唇萬客帛，
洞房晚晚換新郎。

4.
在家千日好，
出外半天難。

FIG. 2.11

This two-story building at the corner of Ontario and Dalls Streets in Victoria, B.C., was used as an immigration and detention center from 1908 to 1958. Chinese immigrants who were detained there called the building *chu jai uk* (pigpen), a term that originated from the Chinese coolie trade in the early nineteenth century. In his article "A 'Prison' for Chinese Immigrants," David Chuenyan Lai describes the building as a virtual prison, with brick walls that were 20 inches thick and barred windows. The first floor housed a reception room without any windows and a dining room for one hundred people; the second floor was partitioned by concrete walls into prison cells that opened into a central corridor; and the basement had a large kitchen that had all its openings covered with iron screens and bars. The building was demolished in 1977.
Photo by David Chuenyan Lai.

Poems from Victoria, B.C.

TRANSLATED BY DAVID CHUENYAN LAI
AND CHARLES EGAN

FIG. 2.12
A piece of the wall with the poem
"My Wife's Admonishment"
written on it that was rescued by
David Chuenyan Lai in 1977.
Photo by David Chuenyan Lai.

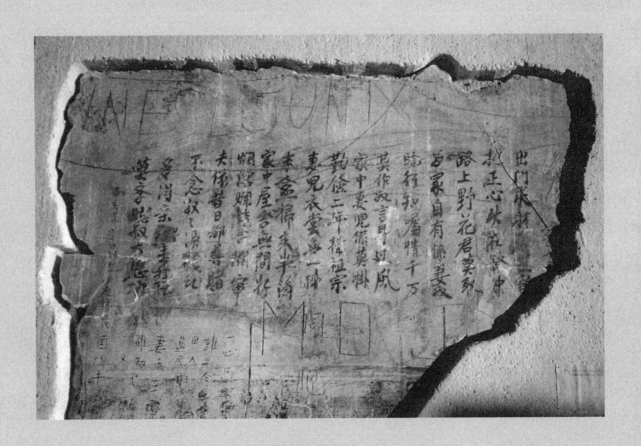

1.

Because I covet riches, I'm locked up in this cage;

Coming here, my ship was tossed by countless waves.

If only I did not need to labor for money,

I would already have returned home to China.

2.

My heart filled with resentment, I cannot sleep;

Thinking of the foreign slaves,[1] my anger soars to heaven.

They cast me into jail and subjected me to anguish—

Who will console me even if I cry until dawn?

    March 26, eighth year of the Republic (1919)

3.

Sitting alone in the customs office,

How could my heart not ache?

Had my family not been poor,

I would not have traveled far away from home.

It was my elder brother who urged me

To embark on a voyage to this shore.

The black devil[2] here is unjust—

He forces the Chinese to clean the floor.

Two meals a day are provided,

But I wonder, when will I be homeward bound?

    Lee from Ning District[3] September 4, 1911

---

1   A pejorative used to describe those considered inferior—
here, Westerners.

2   A pejorative to refer to those of African descent—here,
presumably, an African Canadian working at the immigration
station directed the detainees to sweep the floors.

3   Sunning District, an old name for Toishan.

1.

窮想金錢困牢籠，
遍舟頑頡浪萬重。
若非勤為天財就，
會向中華家下還。

2.

心心懷恨不成眠，
提起番奴怒沖天。
將我監房來受苦，
五更嘆盡有誰憐。

　　己未八年三月廿六日

3.

獨坐稅關中，
心內起不痛。
亦因家道貧，
遠遊不近親。
兄弟來到叫，
只得上埠行。
黑鬼無道理，
唐人要掃地。
每日食兩餐，
何時轉回返。

　　辛亥年七月十二日李字題寧邑

4.

My Wife's Admonishment

We are poor, so you're leaving home to seek wealth;

Keep hold of propriety while on this journey.

Never pick wildflowers along the road,[4]

For you have your own wife at home!

Before you depart, I admonish you a thousand times;

Don't let my words just whistle past your ears.

Don't worry about us, be diligent and frugal,

And two years hence return to sweep the ancestors' tombs.

Your wife and children haven't a thing to wear;

Not half a cup of rice can be scooped from the pot.

Our house and rooms are dilapidated;

Our housewares are worn, and the curtains torn.

In the past, you did nothing but gamble;

You never thought of me and my flowing tears.

You are fortunate your elder brother has paid the taxes—

Always remember your great debt to him![5]

　　Lee from Ning District arrived July 12, 1911

4　To engage in romantic/sexual affairs while away from home.
5　Because two characters in the last couplet have been rubbed out, the translation is tentative.

4.
妻囑情

出門求財為家窮，
把正心頭在路中。
路上野花君莫取，
為家自有係妻奴。
臨行知囑情千萬，
莫作奴言耳過風。
家中妻兒係莫掛，
勤儉二年掃祖宗。
妻兒衣裳無一件，
米盒掃來無半筒。
家中屋舍無間好，
爛溶爛揸穿爛帘。
夫係昔日都尋賭，
不念奴奴淚飄飄。
多得親兄來打稅，
莫學忘叔大恩公。

　　辛亥七月十二日到李字題寧邑

5.

I have always yearned to reach Gold Mountain—
Unexpectedly, I found only poverty and hardship.
I was detained in a cell, and tears rolled down my cheeks.
My wife at home is longing for my letter—
Who can foretell when I will be able to return home?

    Eighth year of the Republic (1919)

6.

NOTICE

Fellow countrymen, quickly read the following:

Having amassed several hundred dollars,
I left my native home for a foreign land.
To my surprise, I was thrown into a prison cell!
Alas, there is nowhere for me to go from here.
I can see neither the world outside nor my dear parents—
When I think of it, my tears stream down.
To whom can I confide my bitter sorrow?
All I can do is etch a few lines on this wall.

    By someone from Sunwui District

5.

一心只望來金山，
誰知金山窮艱難。
困人監房眼淚流成行，
妻子在家望信番，
誰知三冬二秋轉回唐。
民國八年口月

6.

示告
同胞快看

即日修得數百金，
拋別鄉間往番邦。
誰知把我入監房，
且看此地無路往。
不見天地及高堂，
自思自想淚成行。
此等苦楚向誰講，
只達數言在此房。

新會人作

7.

People said the West was so wonderful—

Yet I suffered wind and frost for forty years.

White-haired now, I'm returning to my old village;

Bitter tears stream down, wetting my lapels.[6]

8.

En Route to Canada in 1921,

  Imprisoned in the Vancouver Immigration Jail

"The Gentleman is content in poverty"[7]—but he need not be poor;

Why then, has it been my fate to be imprisoned in a cage?

Though China is vast, for me there wasn't room to stick an awl,[8]

So I rode the waves to the ends of the earth and now cry bloody tears.

Making a living forces a man to wander east and west,

So I abandoned family and country to seek out Old Tao.[9]

When will I break free of this little cage,

Beat my wings toward heaven, and soar ten thousand miles?

  By Chi Chan[10]

---

6 Among the wall poems David Chuenyan Lai transcribed at the Victoria immigration building was a half-decipherable fragment. Years later, he saw the complete poem in a magazine article by Huang Zhongji about popular Hakka songs from Toishan. The complete text is translated here. See David Chuenyan Lai, "Zhuzai wu nei," and Huang Zhongi, "Xiang lang ge."

7 Quoted from the *Analects* of Confucius: "The Gentleman is content in poverty, while the small man is swept away by it."

8 To not even have enough space to press the point of an awl—a metaphor for dire poverty.

9 Also known as Taozhugong, a wealthy merchant who lived during the fifth century BCE. His name symbolizes wealth.

10 Chi Chan is a pen name. Chinese text transcribed by Him Mark Lai from *Taishan Huaqiao Gongzuo Baogao Zhoukan*, November 1929.

7.

人話外洋那樣好，
風霜捱盡四十秋。
至今白髮回故里，
辛酸淚水隨襟流。

8.
民十赴加困于雲埠移民監

君子固窮未必窮，
何期遭際困囚籠。
中華偌大無容錐，
浪走天涯血淚紅。

生計逼人西復東，
家邦拋棄志陶翁。
何時衝破樊籠去，
奮翮雲霄萬里縱。

　　次塵

9.

I wanted so much to come to Gold Mountain. Due to poverty, I deserted
my parents, wife, and children. I remember all the advice they gave at
my departure, and how they managed to raise more than a thousand
dollars to help me on my way. I have now safely arrived, but for some
reason, the authorities here have examined my eyes and all sorts of
things. They forced me to strip off my shirt and pants and to lay bare my
body. I have suffered a hundred kinds of torture and humiliation because
China is weak and I am poor. Thinking of my parents, I say to my fellow
countrymen—return home and help make our mother country strong
and rich!

9.

一心走金山者，棄父母與妻兒，只因家貧。憶昔臨
行，父母妻兒叮囑。千方萬計成仟餘，資助。乃得
安然上岸。何意事生，驗眼多端，脫衫除褲，露身，
百般刑辱，皆因國弱家貧。追憶父母，勸同胞，回
頭返鄉，興祖國。

ORAL HISTORIES

Speaking for Themselves: Oral Histories of Chinese Immigrants on Angel Island

JUDY YUNG

FIG. 3.1A–L
Certificates of identity issued to Chinese immigrants whose stories are included in this section. Beginning in 1909, all Chinese residents in the United States were required to hold a certificate of identity as proof of their legal entry and lawful right to remain in the country. After 1940, these certificates were replaced by alien registration receipt cards, or "green cards." Courtesy of National Archives, San Francisco.

THE BEAUTY OF ORAL HISTORY, WHICH CAN BE DEFINED AS spoken testimony about the past, is that it allows ordinary folks to speak for themselves, fill gaps in the historical record, and also validate their lives. At the beginning of our efforts in the 1970s to preserve the poems and document the history of Chinese immigrants on Angel Island, Him Mark Lai, Genny Lim, and I knew that oral histories would be essential to fulfilling that goal, since there was so little written or published about the subject in English or Chinese at the time. Our task was made more urgent by the fact that most of the former detainees were then in their seventies and eighties, and many had already passed on. It was made more difficult by the reluctance of our subjects, many of whom had come to this country illegally as paper sons and daughters, to be interviewed.

We knew that practically every Chinese person who immigrated to the United States between 1910 and 1940 must have spent time on Angel Island. So finding former detainees to interview was no problem, but getting them to tell us their stories proved difficult. Who would want to admit that they were illegal immigrants? Who would want to dredge up bad memories about their interrogation and imprisonment on Angel Island? We decided to begin our research project by interviewing our families and the acquaintances whom we knew well. Then we branched out to relatives of close friends and referrals from community organizations like Self-Help for the Elderly, the Chinese YMCA, and the Chinatown Branch Library.

We convinced many former detainees to let us interview them by saying (and we really meant it) that their children and grandchildren, if not the rest of America, needed to hear their stories and to learn from their immigration experiences, good and bad. We also promised them anonymity, which we honored by using pseudonyms in the transcripts and our book. Being "insiders"—we were all children of former detainees, Cantonese speakers, and members of the Chinese American community—had its advantages. It helped us gain the trust and cooperation of our informants and establish rapport with them during the interview. Our respective genders also helped open doors and facilitate interviews with both men and women.

Since we were all busy with full-time jobs during the weekdays, we could conduct interviews only on weekends. Nevertheless, we still managed to record forty interviews between 1976 and 1978, with eight female and twenty-four male detainees, two immigrant inspectors, two interpreters, one maintenance worker's wife, and three Chinese community workers who used to visit detainees in the men's barracks. The interviews generally took 90 to 120 minutes and were conducted in the Cantonese dialect in interviewees' homes. By promising anonymity, we were able to obtain verbal permission to record the interviews on cassette tapes. Aware of their reluctance to be interviewed and their fear of the law, we did not follow protocol and ask for written consent. Nor did we ask to see old family pictures and documents or try to photograph interviewees for the record.

What did we want to know? We developed a list of questions arranged by topic and in chronological order as a guide for the interviews. All informants were basically asked the same questions, covering their family backgrounds and education in China, why and how they immigrated to the United States, details about their detention on Angel Island, their lives after they were released from Angel Island, and their personal reflections on the impact of exclusion and Angel Island on their lives. (See interview questions on pp. 201–2. We were so afraid of offending our interviewees or causing them undue stress with intrusive questions that we often failed to ask follow-up questions or pursue sensitive topics such as interrogations, sexual or physical abuse if any, or conflicts in the barracks. Following Chinese decorum, we listened respectfully to our elders, not daring to challenge anything they told us or be too aggressive in our line of questioning. We always ended the interview with the open-ended question "Is there anything else you want to tell us about Angel Island?" But very few took the initiative to tell us anything more.

Ten years later, after I returned to the University of California, Berkeley, for graduate school, I applied for and received a small grant from the California Department of Parks and Recreation that allowed me to transcribe all of our past Angel Island interviews and conduct twenty more interviews with former Chinese detainees. By then, our book *Island* had been published, the immigration site had been restored, and the "dirty secret" of illegal immigration had been aired in public without any damage to the reputation of individuals or the Chinese community as a whole. On the contrary, the exposé had called attention to the wrongs that had been committed against Chinese immigrants on Angel Island and paid tribute to their courage and perseverance in the face of adversity. I had no trouble finding former detainees to interview through the visitors' logbook at Angel Island and through my contacts in the Chinese American community.

For this second round of interviews, I used the same list of questions, but I was able to pursue other topics, such as poetry in the women's dormitory, suicides and attempted escapes, sanitary conditions, solitary confinement and other forms of punishment, riots and protests, and basically how race, class, and gender discrimination had shaped the detainees' lives on Angel Island and afterward. This time I was able to get signed consents, photographs and documents, and permission to use real names and photographs in future publications. I translated and transcribed all of the taped interviews and deposited them in the Asian American Studies Library at UC Berkeley, the California Department of Parks and Recreation in Sacramento, and the Angel Island Immigration Station Foundation in San Francisco as part of the public record and for use by other researchers. Combined with eight interviews that Felicia Lowe conducted in 1984–86 for her film *Carved in Silence*, the collection became known as the Angel Island Oral History Project.

For the first edition of *Island*, we chose to publish only excerpts from the various interviews to complement the poems. While this choice allowed us to tell a composite story of their immigration experience on Angel Island, it prevented us from telling anyone's entire story and the full impact of racial exclusion on his or her life. In this second edition of *Island*, the following twenty stories out of our oral history collection and a few other sources are presented in full, from beginning to end. The thirteen male detainees, five female detainees, one immigrant inspector, and one interpreter represent the diversity in gender, detention time, and perspectives, including that of the applicant/prisoner and the employee/law enforcer.

Compelling stories include those by Soto Shee, who attempted to commit suicide by hanging herself in the women's bathroom; Lee Puey You, who literally cried a bowlful of tears while detained on Angel Island for twenty months before being deported; Smiley Jann, who transcribed close to one hundred poems on the walls and whose essay of indignation was published in a Shanghai journal as early as 1935; and Mock Ging Sing and Koon T. Lau, who both poignantly recalled their tearful parting from their grandmothers in China and the mental anguish they suffered while detained on Angel Island.

Other interviews were selected for the rich details and new revelations they offer about the Angel Island experience. Genny Lim's story of her transpacific grandfather and father, which is based on a close reading of their immigration files, helps us understand the complexities and intricacies of legal cases involving claims of birthright citizenship. Likewise, the stories of Him Mark Lai's father, who was among the first to be processed through Angel Island in 1910, and my own father, who was detained for five weeks in 1921, shed light on how immigrants were able to circumvent the exclusion laws by claiming merchant status. The *sun hei* (venting or moaning in sorrow) stories told by Law Shee Low, Mrs. Wong, and Lee Puey You provide a deeper understanding of how women's experiences of life on Angel Island were different from men's as well as the different strategies women employed to cope with their confinement.

In most cases, our interviewees had painted a negative picture of the staff who were responsible for enforcing the immigration laws and policies on Angel Island. Yet interviews with interpreter Edwar Lee and immigrant inspector Emery Sims about the operations of the immigration station, their respective jobs, and their encounters with Chinese detainees show them to have been conscientious employees sympathetic to the plight of the Chinese. So complicated and tricky was the immigration process for Chinese applicants that even real sons sometimes failed the interrogation and were deported, as in the case of Lee Show Nam. Having been detained on Angel Island for eighteen months, he was able to share many details about the Self-governing Association and the goings-on in the men's barracks. The story by Xie Chuang, excerpted from his autobiography, provides a rare portrait and political analysis of a Communist who was arrested, detained on Angel Island for more than a year, and deported because of his political beliefs. During his long stay on Angel Island, he organized a food riot in the dining hall, and he recalled a suicide poem that was carved on the walls but is no longer visible today.

The subjects speak for themselves and in their own words, but in order to ensure a narrative flow and minimize interruptions, I have eliminated the questions and any redundancies and false starts in the interviews and rearranged segments of interviews for clarity and organization. I chose to use Cantonese instead of standard pinyin romanization in order to better reflect the speakers' identity and dialect. I have also added editorial notes to provide essential biographical information, historical context, and meaning for the stories, as well as footnotes to clarify cultural and historical references.

Whenever possible, I corroborated and amplified the stories with information from immigration case files stored at the National Archives at San Francisco. These records, which were not made available to researchers until the late 1980s, document every Chinese applicant for admission or readmission to the United States during the exclusion era. The files include transcripts of interrogations, visas and notarized affidavits, business records, letters, legal briefs, and photographs that, together, provide a fuller and more accurate picture of the immigration process and outcome than that given by our interviewees. They also show how meticulous and thorough many of the immigrant inspectors were in their investigations as well as their rationales for admitting or excluding an applicant. Some summary judgments go on for pages, listing all the discrepancies between the testimonies of the applicant and the witnesses.

Sad to say, almost all of the people we interviewed have since died. Of the twenty profiles in this book, only Mock Ging Sing and Lee Show Nam are still alive. Thus I asked family members to assist by answering questions, filling gaps, reviewing stories for errors, and providing photographs. For example, Mrs. Wong had refused to tell us anything about her life in the United States after Angel Island. It wasn't until I got my hands on her immigration file at the National Archives after her death in 1989 that I realized she had to return to China with her entire family in the 1930s. Fortunately, I found her son James through my community network, and he was willing to explain why she had to leave, how she fared in China during the Sino-Japanese War, and how she managed to come back to the United States in 1958. Similarly, I came to know the full tragic story of Lee Puey You, the woman who cried a bowlful of tears, only after she died in 1996 and two of her daughters shared her alien file with me.

Remarkably enough, detailed experiences occurring forty to seventy years past ring clear and true today. In some cases, descriptions of people and events have been blurred or dulled with the passage of time. Because of the communication barrier between detainees and immigration authorities, some actions and events have also been misconstrued. But overall, the oral histories give a fairly consistent and accurate picture of daily life for Chinese immigrants on Angel Island over time. We have arranged the twenty stories chronologically by the year that each person was at Angel Island, beginning with Lai Bing, who was among the first group to be processed in 1910, and ending with Lee Puey You, who witnessed the fire that shut down the immigration station in 1940.

ANGEL ISLAND ORAL HISTORY PROJECT—INTERVIEW QUESTIONS

Background information

1   Where and when were you born?

2   How large was your family? What did your family do for a living?

3   How much schooling did you have? What did you do for a living? Marriage?

4   Why and how did you come to the United States?

5   What were your expectations of America?

6   How did you prepare to come to America? Using what immigration status? Did you know about Angel Island before you came?

The Voyage

1   How old were you when you left for the U.S.? Who accompanied you on the voyage? How much did it cost and how did you pay for it? What did you take with you?

2   What were the route and procedures you followed on the voyage beginning with departure from your family?

3   What were the conditions on the ship coming to America? What were the eating and sleeping arrangements? How crowded was the ship? What other passengers were there? How did you pass the time? What were your thoughts and feelings at the time?

4   How long did the voyage take? Did you encounter any problems along the way?

Detention at Angel Island

1   When did you arrive? Where did you first land? What happened after you landed? How were you transported to Angel Island?

2   Describe your first impressions of Angel Island. How were you processed and treated upon arrival (including initial questioning and physical examination)?

3   Describe your living quarters. How many people? What furnishings and provisions? Toilet facilities? General sanitary conditions? Comforts and amenities? Privacy? What did it lack?

4   Describe the people with whom you stayed. Age? Birthplace? Socioeconomic status? Literacy? Length of detention? Transients? Deportees? General mood? Interactions? How often did new arrivals come and detainees leave?

5   Describe your daily life there. Schedule? Meals? Activities and pastimes, including exercise? Rules, regulations, and privileges? Contact with outsiders (guards/matrons, missionaries/social workers, visitors)? How did the staff treat you? Who did the cleaning and laundry? What happened if you became sick? Was there thievery? Who cut your hair? Shopping?

6   Was there any poetry on the walls? Did you write any or see anyone else write on the wall? What did you think about the poems?

7   Did you see anyone passing coaching notes? How was it done?

8   Do you recall any extraordinary events while you were there (suicide, punishment or solitary confinement, protests or riots, special entertainment, etc.)?

9   Describe the interrogation process. How long before you were called for interrogation? Where was it held? Who was there? How were you treated? What did they ask? How many times were you interrogated and for how long? Did you have to sign anything? How well did you do? How did you feel about it?

10 How long before you were given the results? Did you pass or not? How did you feel about the results? If you failed, why? Did you appeal? How? What was the final outcome?

11 What was the total time you spent on Angel Island? How did you feel about your stay there? What helped to make it bearable for you?

12 How do you think the detention experience has affected you? Do you think it was justifiable? What is most unforgettable about Angel Island for you?

After Angel Island

1   Where did you go and with whom after your release from Angel Island?

2   Briefly describe your family, work, and social life after Angel Island.

3   Have you ever returned to Angel Island? How did you feel about returning?

4   What do you think is the legacy or the lessons of Angel Island for future generations of Chinese Americans and for all Americans?

5   Is there anything else you want to tell us about Angel Island?

Lim Kam On and Lim Tai Go:
The Transpacific Fathers

GENNY LIM

LIM KAM ON

G RANDFATHER LIM KAM ON CARVED OUT HIS FORTUNE IN TWO
countries, the United States and China. According to his immigration
file, he claimed U.S. birthright on May 14, 1878, the fourth year of
Kwong Sui (Guangxu), and his birthplace as 741 Commercial Street
in San Francisco. He also claimed that he was brought to China in 1881 at
the age of three and returned as a bachelor on the *Siberia*, May 15, 1903,
a day after his twenty-fifth birthday. With no written records to prove or
disprove his native homebirth by a midwife, his application to land was im-
mediately refused the following day after testimony before Inspector John
Lynch and Interpreter C. Richards. He was held in detention at the Pacific
Mail Steamship Company shed awaiting deportation under the Chinese
Exclusion Act, on grounds that he was "not a member of any of the classes
of Chinese persons who are permitted by law to come, to be, and to remain
in the United States."[1]

Lim Kam On's case, not unlike those of other paper son Chinese im-
migrants, relied on false claims to U.S. citizenship in order to circumvent
the Chinese Exclusion Act. I believe that Grandfather was born in Chew
Kai village, Toishan District, and that he was already married with a family
when he first came to the United States in 1903. By claiming U.S. birthright,
he hoped to be admitted into the country. When Kam On was denied entry
and imprisoned in the detention shed awaiting deportation, he had Lee Wat
file a petition for a writ of habeas corpus in the federal district court, alleging
that he was entitled to land and was being unlawfully detained.[2]

The case was heard before the Honorable E. H. Heacock (The Referee),
with T. C. West acting as attorney for Lim Kam On, D. F. McKinlay as
attorney for the United States, and R. H. Jones (The Interpreter) in San
Francisco's U.S. district court on June 30, 1903. Similar to the immigration
interrogations at Angel Island, Kam On was asked ninety-four questions
and cross-examined along with two witnesses—Lim Jeung, a distant uncle

1   *In the Matter of Lim Kam On
    on Habeas Corpus*, file 12968,
    Admiralty Files, U.S. District
    Court for the Northern
    District of California, RG 21,
    NARA-SF; file 12017/4862
    (Lim Kam On), Return
    Certificate Application Case
    Files of Chinese Departing,
    RG 85, NARA-SF.

2   A writ of habeas corpus
    requires the person
    detaining the petitioner to
    demonstrate to the court that
    the confinement is lawful.
    Until *Ju Toy v. United States*
    (1905) prohibited Chinese
    from appealing their cases
    to the court, many Chinese
    immigrants used this legal
    route to resist exclusion
    and gain admission into the
    country. Between 1882 and
    1905, the federal district
    courts and state circuit
    courts heard more than
    9,600 Chinese habeas corpus
    cases. Over 50 percent of the
    cases were overturned. See
    Erika Lee, *At America's Gates*,
    47–48.

and business partner, and Chew Yee, a family friend. Lim Jeung was asked fifty-five questions and Chew Yee, twenty-eight questions, mostly to verify that Kam On had been born in the United States and that they had indeed seen him at his home in Chew Kai village. Detailed questions were asked about Lim's birth date, descriptions of his home in China, and their specific encounters with the boy and his family.

Q. Did Lim Jung ever eat in your house when you were there except on holidays?

A. My remembrance is that it was always on holidays.

THE REFEREE. Well, you want to remember. We do not want it indefinite. Was it on other days than holidays?

A. Well, it was after the passing of the New Year, not on the New Year days, but one of the days of the New Year.

MR. MCKINLAY. Well, how many times do you remember of his eating in your house?

A. Two or three times.

MR. MCKINLAY. Does he say "two" or "three"?

THE INTERPRETER. Just as I gave it.

MR. MCKINLAY. Was it just three times?

A. My remembrance is three times. . . .

Q. How long did he stay that evening he came to your house, the night before he left?

A. Just a short period.

Q. Well, what do you mean by a short period?

A. Not half an hour.

Q. Did anybody go outside of the house with him when he left?

THE INTERPRETER. There is where the difficulty comes about "outside."

THE REFEREE. Change it then. Did anybody go to the door with him?

A. I escorted him.

Q. Where to?

A. Just to the door; just on the inside I stood.

Q. Nobody went outside the door with him?

A. No.

Seemingly satisfied that Lim's answers agreed with those of the witnesses, Heacock ruled that Lim was born in San Francisco on May 14, 1878, and recommended his release from the Pacific Mail Steamship shed, where he had been detained for two and a half months, on July 1, 1903. Once this judgment was made, it would be cited as proof of U.S. citizenship every time Grandfather applied for a departure certificate or returned from a trip to China. As a returning U.S. citizen, he would land at the port of San Francisco and not have to go to Angel Island.

Immigration records show that Grandfather made a total of three trips to China. He departed for China on December 10, 1907, and was readmitted to the United States as a native on May 10, 1909. On his application for a return certificate on December 29, 1914, he gave his residence as 314

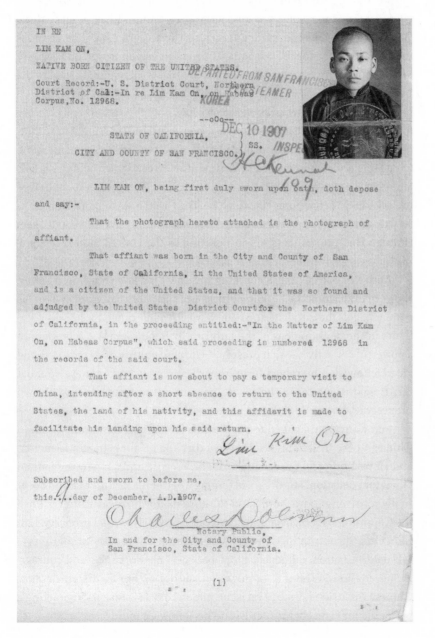

FIG. 3.2
Affidavit filed by Lim Kam On attesting to his native U.S. citizenship before he departed for China in 1907. Courtesy of National Archives, San Francisco.

First Street, Marysville, California. His application was approved, and he departed on January 30, 1915, and returned on July 24, 1916, this time with his eldest son, Lim You Len, and was landed on the same day. By this time, Kam On was thirty-six years old and reported that he was married to Lew Shee, a woman with bound feet who lived in China with four sons and one daughter, ages seventeen, fifteen, thirteen, seven, and eleven. (The seven-year-old was my father, Lim Tai Go.) Lim Kam On was a prosperous businessman residing in Marysville and a partner in the King Fung How Company in Hong Kong. On January 3, 1921, Grandfather, at forty-three years of age, filed a request for a return certificate, granting him a temporary visit to China for the last time. The request was approved on February 8, 1921, but there was no further record of him ever having returned to the United States.

Lim Kam On's immigration file provides only the skeleton of a history for a man who, by all accounts, was a successful businessman, entrepreneur, visionary, philanthropist, and pioneer. Grandfather's general store, King Fung and Company at 534 Washington Street, which sold dry goods and Chinese staples, was a busy community hub. There was a second store on Jackson Street, Quong Hi, which he likely held a stake in, that sold lottery tickets until they were outlawed. He was said to have helped villagers through the legal process of immigrating to the United States, in some instances, by claiming them as relatives.

Active in both Chinese communities in China and the United States, Kam On undertook the building of a school and a railroad extension to his rural village, Chew Kai, in Toishan. While in San Francisco, he was a key figure in the development of the Lim Family Benevolent Association into a powerful collective, which preserved Chinese culture and traditions and aided fellow clan members from its earliest days, when Chinese couldn't testify against whites in the courts, become naturalized citizens, or own property under the Alien Land Law of 1913.

Lim Kam On managed to support his family and community both in China and the United States. He ran a thriving business in San Francisco and Hong Kong and eventually brought his wife and sons to the United States for education. His dream of forging a better life in America and eventually returning to his homeland to retire in comfort was fulfilled, until the Communists took over and confiscated privately owned property. Lim Kam On's life exemplified the classic virtues of Cantonese immigrants— self-determination, diligence, effort, patience, perseverance, and courage. He never allowed the U.S. immigration authority, nor its discriminatory Chinese exclusion laws and racist attitudes, to defeat his goal of making a better life for himself, his family, and his fellow Chinese.

Father said he was the first in San Francisco Chinatown to own a LaSalle, the marque Cadillac of its day. Pop, like any true American, loved cars. A dapper man with a slicked-down pompadour parted on the side, Pop had a necktie collection that rivaled any stylish English gentleman's. He cut a dashing figure on the dance floor with his smooth foxtrot, cha-cha, and rumba. If grandfather Lim Kam On was a man who had carved out a home in two countries, father Tai Go, or Din Tun, as his cronies knew him, was a man who had carved out his identity from two cultures.

In sharp contrast to his stern, no-nonsense, taskmaster father, Pop had a dignified reserve and warm, easygoing manner. A loyal friend and devoted father, he loved Cantonese opera as much as big-band swing music—especially the popular Stan Kenton and Ernie Hechsher bands, which he'd heard live at the Fairmont Hotel as a janitor and bellboy. Despite his love of Western culture, he was a traditional modernist—open to the new yet deeply committed to preserving the old. He embraced Chinese values and philosophy but often criticized the backward, superstitious attitudes and beliefs he felt many stubborn Chinese held. A compelling orator and respected elder of the Lim Family Association, it was in fact, exactly to the theme of family tradition and community that Edward Lim, or Lim Tai Go, a father of seven, who had struggled to rise from working as a janitor, waiter, cook, and store clerk to being a retired clothing contractor, dedicated his last breath. Just as Father ended his welcome speech at the 1976 Annual Lim Family Association Spring Banquet in Sun Hung Heung Restaurant and uttered the words, "Xie-xie!" (Thank you!), he collapsed and never regained consciousness. He had suffered a sudden heart attack and died shortly afterward.

Father's convoluted paper history, not unlike those of many paper sons of his generation, belies his secret, real life. I believe my father was born in Chew Kai village, Toishan District, in 1907. Lim Kam On became Tai Go's adopted father when Kam On took Tai Go's mother as his second wife. When Kam On departed for the United States with the boy in 1915, leaving the mother behind in Macao, little did Father know that he would never see her again. It was rumored that his mother had died tragically in a theater fire, though in those early days, no conclusive forensic evidence was ever taken or found. Kam On, whose first and second wives were deceased, took Lew Shee, his third wife, to the United States, claiming her as his first and only wife.

My father's immigration file, however, presents another story.[3] In 1921, when he and his two alleged native brothers applied for a temporary leave to visit China to pursue their education, Lim Tai Go claimed he was born at

3   File 22619/7-28 (Lim Tai Go), Return Certificate Application Case Files of Chinese Departing, RG 85, NARA-SF.

FIG. 3.3
Left to right: Lim Kam On holding
his young son with Lim Tai Go
(at center) and his real mother in
China, c. 1912. Courtesy of Genny
Lim.

208 Alice Street in Oakland, California, on November 4, in the thirty-third
year of Kwong Sui, or 1907, although he mistakenly claimed the year to be
1906—a discrepancy the immigrant inspector was quick to seize upon. He
said his mother was Wong Shee and that his father, Lim Quong Yuen, had
worked as a cigar maker in Oakland. He had two younger brothers who
were also born at home. In 1914, the family moved to 627 Commercial
Street (Standard Cigar Company), where his father worked. Lim Quong
Yuen, however, became sick and returned to China in 1917. After he left,
the family moved to 649 Kearny Street, then to 534 Washington Street, a
few days before their hearing.

When asked if he ever attended school, Tai Go replied that he was nine
when he started at the Oriental Public School in 1915 and was still attending
the sixth grade, with Miss Howard as his teacher, at the time of the hearing.

He also attended the Chung Wah Chinese School. However, an investigation of school records by Inspector Mayerson showed that Lim Tai Go was born in China and that his parent or guardian was named Lim Yuen Hone at the time of his entry to the Oriental Public School on July 26, 1915. The father's name, Lim Quong Yuen, was also not listed in the school records for Tai Go's brother Lim Chew Yuen.

In an effort to verify Lim Tai Go's claim of U.S. birth, Inspector James Butler cross-examined him, his stepmother, Wong Shee, brothers Lim Hong Gock and Lim Chew Yuen, and guardian Lim Hong Ying about his birth, family background, past residences, and schooling. Ultimately, Wong Shee's

FIG. 3.4
Affidavit by Wong Shee attesting to her son Lim Tai Go's birth in the United States. Courtesy of National Archives, San Francisco.

209

confusion over her date of marriage and the birth date of her son Lim Hong Gock, Hong Gock's conflicting answers about their various residences, Lim Tai Go's confusion over the exact year of his birth, and Inspector Butler's suspicion of witness Lim Hong Ying, who had testified as a witness in fifteen other cases, created an overall unfavorable impression. Butler concluded, "The cases of these applicants are not bona fide, that these applicants do not bear the claimed relationship to one another and furthermore that they were not born in the United States."

Following this decision, another witness, Cheow Yee, foreman of the Standard Cigar Company for more than twenty years, testified on behalf of the family on March 17, 1922, saying that he was present at the parents' marriage in Oakland and that he was also present at the birthday feasts of each of the sons in Oakland. Moreover, he verified that the family had moved to the site of the Standard Cigar Company in 1914 and that all the sons attended Chung Wah Chinese School in San Francisco. Their father, Lim Quong Yuen, had worked at the cigar factory in East Oakland and at 627 Commercial Street before he departed for China. But Butler was still not convinced that the three boys were native-born citizens and refused to approve their application for a return certificate.

The family then took the appeal route and retained attorney Oliver Stidger to file an appeal on behalf of the three boys with the Immigration Bureau in Washington, D.C., on March 24, 1922. Assistant Commissioner-General of Immigration I. F. Wixson sustained the appeals of Lim Tai Go, Lim Hong Gock, and Lim Chew Yuen on May 15, 1922, and Lim Tai Go's return certificate was finally approved on May 23, 1922. Father left the United States for China on July 6, 1922, and returned on October 1, 1923, accompanied by his brother, Lim Chew Yuen. He claimed a wife, Chin Shee, of natural feet, in China and also reported one son and no daughter. I believe my father was reporting a fictitious wife and son in China at this time in order to help others come to the United States later as paper sons. He did not marry my mother, Kwong Shee, until sometime after 1927 during his second visit to China. As my mother told me in an oral history interview, "When your father returned to China at the age of eighteen, he wasn't married but reported he had been. He just picked any name. He said he was married to a Chin, so I used the name Chin Lin Sun to come in 1938. My real surname is Kwong."[4]

Father made three more trips to China. He departed on November 4, 1927, and returned on June 6, 1931, using the aliases Lim Din Wah and Edward Lim. He was working as a waiter at 534 Washington Street, and reported wife Chin Shee was still living in China with their three sons. He departed again for China on August 24, 1934, and returned on July 3, 1935.

4   Lin Sun Lim interview.

Tai Go's fourth and final application to leave the United States indicated that he was living at 1106 Powell Street in San Francisco and working as a store clerk at 534 Washington Street (King Fung and Company). His address in China was his father's Wah Fung Company on Connaught Road West in Hong Kong.

Tai Go departed on June 8, 1940, and returned from this last trip to China on February 8, 1941. He reported six children—four sons and two daughters—and gave his wife's full name as Chin Lin Sun. In actuality, father had five daughters, three of whom were born in the United States, and two sons, both born in the United States. It's likely he reported more sons than daughters so that he could keep paper son slots open for potential male immigrants to the United States. However, father never sold those slots,

FIG. 3.5
Lim Tai Go's family. Left to right: Cecilia, Lin Sun Lim holding Genny, Betty, Ronald, Lim Tai Go, and Doreen, 1947. Courtesy of Genny Lim.

probably due to fear of getting caught. This misrepresentation prevented him from bringing his two oldest China-born daughters to the United States at the worst possible time. The Second Sino-Japanese War had erupted, and Japanese soldiers were invading the southern villages of China, so the young girls had to flee to the hills and hide for several days with only a box of crackers for food. Many years later, they would immigrate as adults to the United States.

Another footnote to Father's transpacific saga was that the origins and whereabouts of his real father were unknown. In spite of the patchwork paper identities, dates, names, and places that formed Father's composite background, he managed to surmount the legal challenges to his birthright and citizenship imposed by the Chinese Exclusion Act. To make a home in the world for his wife and family, he had to shuttle back and forth between the United States and China to care for both his China- and American-born children, crossing the Pacific seven times to reunite with loved ones in both countries. With tremendous fortitude, wisdom, courage, and pride, he withstood the vicissitudes of war and the poverty of the Depression and sacrificed his own dream of one day retiring and going home to China, as did his father before him, in order to guarantee his seven children better lives as bona fide American citizens.

Lai Bing: Paper Son of a Merchant

HIM MARK LAI

M Y FATHER, MAAK YUK BING, ENTERED THE UNITED STATES as a "paper son" using the surname Lai, but he was born a member of the Maak family in Congxia, Nanhai District. During his youth, there were approximately eight thousand inhabitants in the area, of which three thousand had the surname Maak. A number of people from Congxia became merchants in nearby Guangzhou and Hong Kong. Others emigrated to Southeast Asia, where they made their living as craftsmen— cobblers, mechanics, and tailors. Few went to the United States. So far as I know, my father was the only male from his village to settle in San Francisco.

My great-grandfather Maak Ding was a tenant farmer who rented eight to ten *mu* (about 1.5 acres) of land belonging to the clan temple in order to cultivate mulberry leaves and pond fish.[1] His son, Jeung Jee, my grandfather, worked as a handloom operator weaving silk textiles at a small factory in Dasha village, about two miles away. He lived and boarded at the factory while his wife, who wove bamboo ware in her spare time to supplement the family income, stayed in the home village with their two sons and one daughter.[2] If all went well, Maak Ding could clear several hundred Chinese dollars annually. Adding to his son's ten to twenty dollars' earnings per month and his daughter-in-law's income, the family was self-sufficient. However, any adverse turn of events could easily upset their modest situation.

One wintry afternoon, when my father was about ten years old, Maak Ding lowered the water level in his fishpond, intending to harvest the fish the next day. Suddenly that night, the weather dipped below freezing. By the next morning all the fish had died. Since dead fish had little market value, this turn of events was a major disaster. He couldn't pay his rent on the land or repay the debts he had incurred at the beginning of the growing season. Maak Ding died the following year. His death, no doubt, was hastened by the catastrophic blow to his livelihood. His son, Jeung Jee, was forced to return to the village.

This story is excerpted from *Him Mark Lai: Autobiography of a Chinese American Historian*, which was published posthumously in 2011. The author chose to transliterate Chinese words in the pinyin system.

1 The right to use the ancestral field was subject to a bid every two or three years, with the land assigned to the highest bidder. Typically, 30 percent of the crop went to the clan's coffers, while 70 percent was kept by the sharecropper. The income from the ancestral lands was supposed to be used to support charitable activities for the entire clan.

2 Nanhai was a region with highly developed handicraft industries. Weaving bamboo ware was an important cottage industry in the area.

Life had become increasingly difficult, when a fellow villager named Maak Tou returned home from Singapore for a visit in 1907 or 1908. He was a tailor in that Southeast Asian city who made enough money to return to the village for visits every two to three years. To the poverty-stricken family of Maak Jee, Singapore appeared to be a place with better economic opportunities. The family scraped together the ten to twenty Chinese dollars needed for passage, and when Maak Tou returned to Singapore, Maak Jee asked him to take his eldest son, Yuk Bing, my father, with him. Five days later, they reached their destination, and Bing soon found himself working as a tailor's apprentice, learning to operate a sewing machine. He was sixteen years old at the time.

At this point, another person, who drastically changed the course of my father's life, entered the picture. His mother, Hing Oi, had come from the Lai clan in the neighboring village of Xiajiao. She had an older widowed sister, Yoen Oi, whose husband had passed away within a year of their marriage. Of sturdy peasant stock and not hobbled by bound feet, she had gone to the provincial capital of Guangzhou to find work. Soon afterward, possibly in the 1880s, she followed a fellow clansman who was on his way to do business in New York. Landing in California, she chose to stay in San Francisco, where she found work as a *dai kam* (a bride escort) and served as a hairdresser for the women in Chinatown, including the numerous prostitutes. She also did needlework and sewed buttons on garments. Lai Yoen Oi lived in San Francisco for more than two decades, returning home only once for a short visit during that period. Thrifty and shrewd, she accumulated a sum of money from her earnings and retired to Guangzhou shortly before the 1906 San Francisco earthquake.

In spite of the persecution of the Chinese in California at that time, Lai Yoen Oi felt that economic opportunities there were far better than in China, and she had aided three cousins to come to the United States. Soon after the 1906 earthquake, one of these cousins, Lai Poon, returned to China for a visit. He had only one son. In those days the Chinese were reluctant to let their only sons, who were the guardians of the ancestral tablets, leave the native village to go overseas. Yoen Oi felt that the slot for someone to enter the United States should not be wasted, however. Since her sister Hing Oi's oldest son, my father, was already old enough to work, she thought, "Why not send Bing to the United States as the son of Lai Poon, the merchant?"[3]

In 1909, the preparations were completed for Father to come to the United States. The eighteen-year-old son of Maak Jee was now known as Lai Bing, the minor son of Lai Poon, partner in Tuck Chong and Company, a dry goods and clothing store at No. 10 Sullivan Alley, San Francisco. His "mother" was now Du Shee. Apparently no money changed hands for the

3 At this time, native-born Chinese Americans were admitted, but their children were not. Thus it was easier to enter the United States as one of the exempted classes than as a derivative citizen. Many people bought bogus partnerships in firms in order to qualify for entry as merchants. That was how Lai Poon was able to come to the United States and later help Maak Yuk Bing immigrate as a merchant's son.

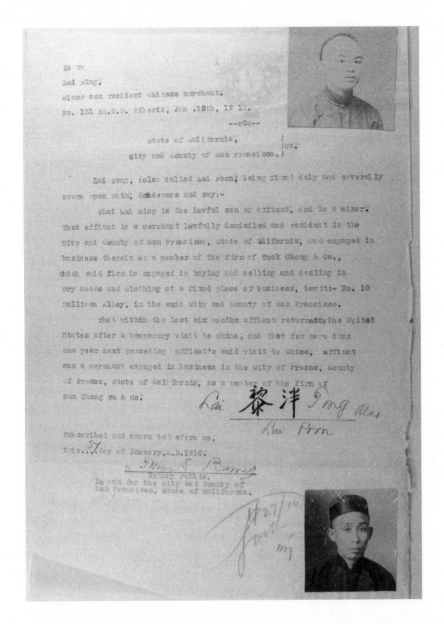

slot, since Lai Yoen Oi had helped Lai Poon come to the United States and
Lai Poon was merely returning the favor. Lai Poon returned earlier to Cali-
fornia to pave the way for them, and on December 18, 1909, Father boarded
the *Siberia* in Hong Kong listed as "Lai Ping," Passenger No. 131, for the
transoceanic voyage.

After a month's voyage, the ship entered the Golden Gate on Thursday,
January 13, 1910. Immediately upon arrival, Father was transferred with
other Chinese passengers to the dilapidated wooden shed at the Pacific
Mail Steamship Company wharf at First and Brannan Streets, where arriv-

ing Chinese were detained to await rulings on their eligibility to land. This wooden shed was scheduled to be abandoned, and Father was among the last group of Chinese to be detained there. On Saturday, January 22, he and more than four hundred Chinese detainees, including eighty-four fellow passengers from the *Siberia*, were ordered transferred to the newly opened Angel Island Immigration Station. Thus my father gained the dubious honor of being part of the first group of Chinese to be processed at the new facility. Two weeks later, he was interrogated, and on Monday, February 7, 1910, he was admitted to the United States.

Editor's note: According to Lai Bing's immigration file, affidavits and interviews with two white witnesses attested to Lai Poon's status as a merchant. Lai Bing was interrogated by Inspector Warner aboard the *Siberia*. He was asked a total of forty-nine questions about his family history, schooling, village layout, and visits that he made to the house of his witness Lai Yuen in Nam Suey village. Next, his father, Lai Poon, was asked a total of 116 questions by Inspector P. F. Montgomery regarding his business in Chinatown, family background, and village life. He had trouble remembering the exact ages of his two sons, and he denied ever going to visit Lai Yuen with his son. Lai Bing was reinterviewed on February 4, 1910. He changed his answer about where Lai Yuen lived but insisted that his father had gone with him once. The inspector persisted, "Your father says he never went to Lai Yuen's house with you at any time and states he doesn't know why you should say so." Lai Bing stuck to his answer, "I went with him all right." Perhaps to prevent adding to the confusion, Lai Poon changed their witness from Lai Yuen to Lai Pooey, saying that Lai Yuen was too busy to come testify. In his summary report, Inspector Montgomery raised his suspicion about Lai Poon's status as a merchant since he never saw him at the Tuck Chong Company during his many visits there for another investigation. "While there are minor contradictions between the father and his alleged son, they are not vital," he wrote. Lai Bing was landed on February 7, 1910.[4]

His brief apprenticeship at a tailor shop in Singapore served Father well. He soon found employment at George Brothers, a manufacturer of apparel for workingmen at 644 Washington Street. Lai Bing was hired as a general helper and did such miscellaneous work as moving bolts of cloth, making buttonholes, and sewing on buttons. He spent a few years working at Lai Poon's garment factory in Fresno, California, and processing apple crops in Sebastopol, California, during World War I.

By the early 1920s, Father had been away from China for more than a decade. He had reached the age of thirty, and it was time for him to get

4   File 22143/3–14 (Lai Bing), Immigration Arrival Investigation Case Files, RG 85, NARA-SF.

married and settle down. In preparation for his return to China, he became a "partner" in the Shun Lee Company, a manufacturer of gentlemen's underwear, clothing, and shirts at 534 Washington Street in San Francisco. He bought passage on the *Hoosier State* and departed in March 1922 as a "merchant" returning to China for a visit.

Editor's note: Before departing for China, Lai Bing retained attorney C. Trumbly to help him file an Application of Chinese Merchant for Preinvestigation of Status. His application was approved after immigration inspectors visited the Shun Lee Company and interviewed two white witnesses and two Chinese business associates who confirmed that Lai Bing was indeed a partner in the business. Lai Bing was also interviewed. "Applicant has appearance of member of exempt class and speaks good English," concluded Inspector H. Schmoldt in his report.[5]

While in Guangzhou, Father made a point of visiting his aunt Lai Yoen Oi to express his appreciation for helping his family while he was absent overseas. She had sent his younger brother to a good school in Guangzhou. Now she suggested that her adopted daughter, Dong Hing Mui, be a prospective bride for Bing.

Dong Hing Mui was the daughter of Dong Wah of Sanshui District, who owned a rice mill in Hong Kong. She was his first-born, and her mother had died during the birth. Perhaps feeling that the child was unlucky, Dong Wah gave her to Lai Yoen Oi when she was about one and a half years old. Although she was raised in the Lai family, Dong Hing Mui retained her family name. As a child she was always crying and restless. But she grew up to be Lai Yoen Oi's favorite. She knew only the rudiments of written Chinese, but Hing Mui was intelligent.

When Dong Hing Mui was a young girl, Yoen Oi had suggested making arrangements for her to go to Gold Mountain for a better future. But Hing Mui had refused to consider leaving home and the idea was shelved. Now she was of marriageable age, and Yoen Oi's nephew, Bing, seemed a good choice because he could take her to the United States as his wife. Bing and Hing Mui agreed to the match, and they were married on May 25, 1922, in a traditional ceremony in Congxia. While still in the village, Father looked for a suitable marital partner for his younger brother. He also used part of his savings to purchase a plot of land and build a brick house in the village.

That year, the political situation in the Guangzhou region was extremely unstable. The Kuomintang (Chinese Nationalist Party), under the leadership of Sun Yat-sen, had established a revolutionary base in Guangzhou in alliance with the warlord Chen Jiongming, who had military control of the

5   Ibid.

FIG. 3.7
Dong Shee and Lai Bing, 1923.
Courtesy of Laura Lai.

area. The fragile alliance between the two factions ruptured, and forces supporting Sun Yat-sen fought with Chen's armies in various localities. Soon after Sun succeeded in forcing Chen to retreat from Guangzhou, warlord armies from Yunnan and Guangxi entered the city and went on a rampage of pillage and rape. Soon the warlords began to jockey with one another for domination. Only after many negotiations was Sun able to bring the situation under control.

Right around this time, Father learned that the United States was about to tighten immigration laws for Asians.[6] So despite the unstable political situation in the Guangzhou region, he decided to return to America with his bride, leaving their brick house in the village in the hands of his older sister and younger brother. In February of 1923, the couple left for Hong Kong just before all public transportation was suspended due to the threatened entry of warlord troops into Guangzhou. The newlyweds had to leave behind much of their baggage and wedding gifts. But shortly before they were to set sail to the United States on April 18, communications were restored between Guangzhou and Hong Kong, and Lai Yoen Oi arrived with their trunks and packages to see them off to America on the *Nile*. Although they probably did not realize it at the time, the couple would never see China again.

Father and his bride arrived in San Francisco on May 14, 1923. They took passage on first class so as to facilitate their entry into America. This strategy succeeded, for Father was admitted readily as a returning merchant and his bride did not have to spend any time on Angel Island. She was admitted as a merchant's wife on May 25.

Editor's note: Another way that Lai Bing tried to expedite the immigration process for Dong Shee was to falsely report that she was five months pregnant and, according to a letter written by his attorney, Edsell & Dye, that she had "suffered extreme nausea during the entire journey from China." Dong Shee was interrogated aboard the *Nile* and asked a total of sixty-five questions about her husband's family and village, her own family, and details of the marriage ceremony. Lai Bing, in turn, was interrogated at Angel Island and asked seventy-nine questions about the same topics. In addition, Ly One, who had been a guest at their wedding in Congxia, was interrogated about Dong Shee's marriage to Lai Bing. There were only a few minor discrepancies between the testimonies of husband and wife. Dong Shee was landed exactly eleven days after her arrival in the United States.[7]

6   Congress was debating the Immigration Act of 1924, which would bar Chinese wives of merchants and U.S. citizens from immigrating to the United States.

7   File 22143/3–15 (Dong Shee), Immigration Arrival Investigation Case Files, RG 85, NARA-SF.

FIG. 3.8
Family portrait, 1940s. Left
to right: Henrietta, William,
Dong Shee, Him Mark, Lai Bing,
Helen, and Lim. Courtesy of
Laura Lai.

The couple made their home in San Francisco Chinatown. My mother soon learned to operate the sewing machine and got a job at George Brothers, where my father worked. She gave birth to all her children at our residence, 1030 Grant Avenue. The same midwife, Leaventon, attended her, for the circumstances of the family were such that Father could not afford to send his wife to a hospital. It was only during the few months around a birth that my thrifty parents allowed themselves the luxury of installing a telephone at home in case of an emergency. As soon as Mother had recovered from the rigors of childbirth, the telephone service would be discontinued.

Father gave me the name Lai Him (etiquette-modesty) when I was born in 1925. After me came Lai Wo (etiquette-harmony), who later became known as William, in 1927. Next came Lai Git (beautiful-chastity) or Henrietta, who came into the world in 1930. She was born with a congenital birth defect, lacking joints in her hips. Two years after Lai Git came the fourth child Lai Ha (beautiful–morning mist), who was born in 1932. She was later given the name Helen. Care for the baby of the family, Lai Lim (etiquette-incorrupt), who arrived in 1934, consumed much of Mother's time. Lai Lim's stomach rejected milk fed to him as delivered by the milkman, and it had to be reboiled before his body would accept it. He was also afflicted with rickets. A younger son, Lai Hoong (etiquette-heroic), was born in 1936, but he expired from an illness after a couple of months. Mother usually controlled her emotions fairly well, but when this baby was taken away in a basket, I saw her cry for the first time, and my parents decided that there were enough children in the family.

Father was always fearful that immigration officers would discover he had entered the country as a paper son. To remind us of our origins, he had deliberately selected middle names for his children using homonyms of the Chinese character for Lai. The sons' names included the character *lai* 禮, meaning "etiquette," while the daughters' names included the character *lai* 麗, meaning "beautiful." He also taught us a concocted story about him being adopted in order to explain the discrepancy in our surnames, should someone ask. Fortunately, Father's immigration status was never questioned by the authorities up to the day he died,[8] but the middle name caused much confusion for those of his sons who did not have Christian names, my youngest brother, Lim, and me. In my case, acquaintances often haven't quite known whether to address me as Lai, Him, Mark, or Him Mark!

8   Lai Bing died in 1976, and Dong Shee in 1987.

Tom Yip Jing:
"To Speak from the Heart"

Editor's note: For a long time I had wanted to know more about my family history and how my father, Tom Yip Jing, immigrated to America in 1921. But each time I asked my father, I was rebuffed with "Children should not know too much." But the perfect opportunity came when I began working with Him Mark Lai and Genny Lim on the first edition of this book in the mid-1970s. My father agreed to be interviewed by Him Mark, while I, his youngest daughter, sat quietly close by listening to his every word.[1]

That afternoon, I learned for the first time that my grandfather Tom Fat Kwong was the first in my father's family to come to the United States. Around 1910, he sneaked across the Mexican border and made his way to the San Francisco Bay area, where he found work with relatives in the flower-growing business. "My father served in World War I," he proudly told Him Mark, "and he was planning to send for his two sons." But one dark night while he was riding home on his bicycle, Grandfather was hit by a truck. He was then thirty-eight years old. According to the family genealogy book, Tom Fat Kwong died on July 1, 1920, and his body was returned to China for burial. Without his remittances to support the family, it was decided that my father, who was the oldest of three children, should go seek his fortune in America. In his straightforward manner of speaking, this is what my father told us.

Life in China was good until my father died and there were no more remittances. It was my two uncles in America who sent for me. They bought papers that said I was Yung Hin Sen of Sin Tung village in Sunwui District and the nineteen-year-old son of a merchant in Stockton. But I was really seventeen at the time. The papers cost $100 per year of age [$1,900], and the agreement was that they pay a deposit and the rest after I was admitted. If I should fail, the deposit would be refunded and all we would lose is the passage money.

1   Tom Yip Jing interview, April 17, 1977.

I came with a "paper brother," Ah Yum. His father and my father were actually brothers. We spent over a month in Hong Kong taking care of all the travel arrangements with the help of Wing Hung Chong, a *Gam Saan jong* [Gold Mountain firm] run by one of our cousins. They helped us fill out the forms at the U.S. consulate and took us to the doctor's office for the physical exam. Only after we were cleared by the doctor could we book passage. Then we had to wait for departure time. All this took about a month, during which time we got room and board at Wing Hung Chong for 50 HK cents a day. We slept on canvas cots that were folded up and put away during the day.

I came by steerage on a Japanese ship [*Persia Maru*]. The fare to San Francisco was $85 at the time and the voyage took about a month. Soon after I arrived, I was taken to Angel Island. The next day, I had to undress and defecate for the doctor. If you had hookworms, you're dead! They would make you take medicine that made you sick for sure. There was a Yee fellow who borrowed some feces from another person and then was found with hookworms. It didn't make any sense! I was ready to give them a $100 bribe if I failed, but fortunately, I had no problem.

The quarters where we stayed were crowded. The beds were stacked three decks and had just enough room for one person to sleep. There was a fenced-in exercise yard. You could go out there and play ball or stay in the barracks and read the newspapers or gamble—*pai gow*, *tien gow*, *sup ng woo*, but no mahjong then. Our clansmen in San Francisco sent us spending money, but we only played for small stakes. Sometimes they would send us food, and when the guard came to deliver the package, they would call out, "Ho sai gai [good luck]!"

At mealtimes, the guard would yell "Chow-chow" and open the doors. Then zoom, everyone would rush downstairs to the dining hall. We always had plenty to eat because our Wong Leung Do people ran the kitchen.[2] The first table by the kitchen was reserved for the six of us from Wong Leung Do. We were served special dishes like steamed spareribs, pork hash, sausage, sometimes duck or chicken. While the others had mush, eggs, and toast for breakfast, we had chicken *jook* [congee]. Whenever the staff wanted to pass coaching notes to a detainee, they would hide it under a plate and signal us with their eyes. We would pocket it, take it upstairs for a small commission, and get it to the right person. We were never caught. We also knew we could always bribe the guards.

Editor's note: According to my father's immigration file, he arrived on June 13, 1921, and was interrogated on July 15.[3] His paper father, Yung Dung, went first. He was asked a total of fifty-four questions about his family background, village life, and contacts with his family.

2   My father was born in Che Pai village, Wong Leung Do, Heungshan (Chungshan) District, in 1905. He said that the village once had eighty to ninety families living there, but 75 percent of the people moved to the United States. The majority settled in the San Francisco Bay area and specialized in growing chrysanthemums. See Him Mark Lai, "Potato King and Film Producer."

Q. Who in the United States has seen your family in China and can testify as to the claimed relationship?

A. Joe Show.

Q. What does he know about your family?

A. I have known him since CR 5 [1916]. In CR 7 [1918], I gave him a letter and a one-pound package of American ginseng to take to my family in China, which he did, as my wife wrote and told me about it.

Q. At the time of the arrival of your witness here on his return trip, he stated he did not take any letters, or anything else, to anyone in China from anyone in the United States on this trip. What have you to say to that?

A. I gave him the stuff to take to my family, and if he did not say it, he must have forgotten it.

My father's paper brother Yung Hin Biew went next and answered all seventy-four questions about his marriage, family background, village life, and schooling without a problem. My father went last and did not do as well. He must not have studied his coaching book as carefully as his paper brother had. He forgot the name of his sister-in-law and the date he cut off his queue.[4] But his answers to many other difficult questions were in agreement with his brother's.

Q. What have you been doing in China?

A. Attending school in the Yong Suie Yin ancestral hall in the home village.

Q. How many outside doors to that hall?

A. One, facing east.

Q. Is the name of the hall over the door?

A. Yes.

Q. Carved, or painted?

A. Painted.

Q. Of what material is the hall built?

A. Brick.

Q. Can you name some of the pupils who attended with you?

A. Yong Ping, Yong On, Yong Fook, Yong Show, Yong Sam, Yong Wah, Yong Him, Yong Yit, my brother and I; that is all.

Q. Any more boys in the village?

A. No, except one named Chin, at home farming.

Q. How many girls in that village?

A. Four.

3   File 20288/3–8 (Yung Hin Sen), Immigration Arrival Investigation Case Files, RG 85, NARA-SF.

4   During the Qing dynasty (1644–1911), all Chinese men were required to wear a queue, or pigtail, as a badge of allegiance to the Manchu government.

FIG. 3.9
Portrait of Tom Yip Jing's paper
family taken after he was landed
in 1921. Left to right: Yung Dung,
Yung Hin Sen Jing (Tom Yip Jing),
and Yung Hin Biew. Courtesy of
National Archives, San Francisco.

Both brothers knew to insist that Joe Show had visited their home in China.
"The two applicants were checked against each other and there are no ma-
terial discrepancies between them," wrote Inspector Jacobsen in the final
report. They were landed that same day. Fifty-six years later, my father de-
scribed the interrogation this way.

The interrogation took about two hours. I had studied the coaching book
day and night before destroying it in Hong Kong, but you never know what
they might ask you. Who counts the number of steps in front of their house
or how many chickens they had? And even if you counted them, who knows
whether your father will give the same answer? I could say twenty, and my
father could say thirty. They interrogated my brother, my father, and me—

that's three people who have to agree. Even real sons could fail. After our interrogation, we went back to the barracks and listened for our names to be called. Finally, I heard the guard yell my name and "Dai Fow [First City]!" That meant I was free to go to San Francisco.

Editor's note: Dad told me in a later interview that after he was landed, he attended English class at Cumberland Presbyterian Church while working as a houseboy for a white American family.

It was an easy job. I made breakfast at 7:00; then I went off to school until 2:00; then I went back to prepare supper and help around the house. The job covered meals and I was able to bunk at a "bachelor room" in Chinatown with ten other men from Wong Leung Do. But I was only making $20 a month. After six months of that, I quit school in order to make more money. I asked around and found a job working for a relative in the flower business—watered the plants, "picked suckers" off the flowers, and stuff like that. It was hard work, morning to night, ten hours a day. After a year of that, I found a better job washing dishes in a Chinatown restaurant. It was still long hours, but I earned $60 a month. From there, I found work as a cook for a white American family in Burlingame. I had to do everything—cook and clean, and no days off. But after dinner was over, I was free to come and go, so I often took the bus to San Francisco Chinatown. The job included room and board and I made $75 a month. I stayed there many years. My last job before I went back to China to get married was as a gardener on a private estate in Menlo Park. I shared the job with Third Uncle and was making $80 a month with room and board and Sundays off.[5]

Editor's note: Although tall and handsome, my father was not a swinging bachelor. When not working, he hung out at Hip Sen Tong, a fraternal organization for immigrants from Wong Leung Do. There, he could catch up with the political news and community gossip, gamble at mahjong or *tien gow,* and smoke the bamboo water pipe. When I asked him why he didn't date and marry one of the local Chinese girls, he replied, "As the saying goes, 'In marriage, a bamboo door should be paired with a bamboo door, a wooden door with a wooden door.' What Chinese girl would want to marry a laborer who makes only $2 a day?"[6] But as a *Gam Saan haak* [guest of Gold Mountain] returning home to get married, he would have no trouble finding a bride.

When my father turned thirty-one in 1937, he decided he had saved enough money to return to China and get married. He retained attorneys White and White to help him apply for a return certificate, and as required

5   Tom Yip Jing interview, November 20, 1986.

6   Ibid.

FIG. 3.10
Jew Law Ying and Tom Yip Jing
with daughter Bak Heong, in
Menlo Park, California, where
Tom worked as a gardener on a
private estate in 1941. Courtesy of
Judy Yung.

7   After a fire destroyed the
    administration building
    in August 1940, the Angel
    Island Immigration Station
    was moved back to the
    mainland.

8   File 40766/11–13 (Jew Law
    Ying), Immigration Arrival
    Investigation Case Files, RG
    85, NARA-SF.

by law, he deposited $1,000 in the bank to ensure that he would be readmitted into the country. Because of strike conditions in San Francisco that year, he departed from the port of Seattle. He took with him presents that Wong See Chan, whose mahjong parlor he had often frequented, asked him to give to her niece Jew Law Ying in Wong Leung Do. This was how he came to be introduced to his wife-to-be. It was basically an arranged marriage, but my mother had a say in the matter. Knowing that Law Ying was from a wealthy background, my father tried to be honest with her. He told her that he was a poor gardener and that she would have to work hard in America. But my mother had always dreamed of going to Gold Mountain, and given the Chinese exclusion laws, marrying a *Gam Saan haak* was the only way she could fulfill her dream.

A few months after they were married in a traditional wedding ceremony, Tom Yip Jing returned to the United States alone to find a way to change his status from laborer to merchant in order to send for his wife. He did so by borrowing $1,000 from an uncle to become a partner in the Far East Company in San Francisco Chinatown. By then, my oldest sister, Bak Heong, had been born in Macao. But because she failed the eye exam and had to be treated for trachoma, my mother and sister were not able to join my father in America until the spring of 1941.

Upon arrival in San Francisco after a monthlong journey by ship, mother and daughter were detained at the temporary immigration station at 801 Silver Avenue for further inspection.[7] According to Jew Law Ying's immigration file, immigration inspectors asked my mother a total of 98 questions, and my father, 102 questions, about their wedding day, their family history, the village where they were married, the house where they lived, and their stay in Hong Kong before my father returned to the United States in 1938.[8] Again, my father had not studied the coaching book as carefully as he should have. He could not remember which direction the head of his village faced and whether my mother's grandparents were living in Macao or Dai Chek Hom village when he first met my mother. But each time the inspector tried to bait him with answers my mother had given, he was quick with a retort.

Q. Is the cooking stove in the north kitchen portable or built in?

A. That kitchen has a stationary double stove and two portable stoves, one large and one small.

Q. How does the smoke escape from the permanent stove or built-in stove?

A. The smoke rises to the ceiling and through the side openings on the roof.

Q. Are you sure that there is a glass covering over the skylight in the north kitchen?

A. Yes.

Q. Your wife states that the north kitchen skylight is not equipped with glass and that the smoke from the stove goes out through that skylight. What do you say to that?

A. If she said that, she must be right, because I was very seldom in the kitchen and paid very little attention to it.

In contrast, my mother answered all the questions with confidence, even volunteering information at times. Her husband was a paper son, but she was really Jew Law Ying, the granddaughter of Chin Lung, the potato king of Stockton, California. She felt she had every right to enter the United States. The ease of both my parents during the interrogation was noted in the summary report, and that, combined with "no discrepancies worthy of mention" in their testimonies, contributed to the final decision to admit Jew Law Ying and Yung Bak Heong into the country.[9]

For the next fifty years, my father struggled to make a living to support his family of six children while living in the shadows of society, always fearful of being detected and deported. While my mother worked in a Chinatown sweatshop, he worked as a ship-fitter in Richmond, California, during World War II, a cook in a Chinese American restaurant downtown, and a janitor at the ritzy Mark Hopkins Hotel from 1949 until he retired in 1970. Although he had planned to return home someday to pay respects to his ancestors, he never did. "If you don't hit it big, what's the point in going home?" he told me.[10]

So distrustful was he of the U.S. government that he chose not to "confess" and adjust his immigration status during the Confession Program in the 1950s. "They were trying to deport the Chinese for coming into the country with false papers," he recalled. "They looked for evidence at the cemeteries and arrested people in the restaurants. Things were getting out

9 For a history of my mother's immigration to the United States, including a comparison between answers in her coaching book, transcripts of the interrogation, and oral history interview, see Yung, *Unbound Voices*, 9–98.

10 Tom Yip Jing interview, November 20, 1986.

FIG. 3.11
Family portrait, 1954. Left to
right: Patricia, Sandra, Jew Law
Ying, Warren, Sharon (Bak
Heong), Tom Yip Jing, Virginia,
and Judy. Courtesy of Judy Yung.

of control and there was nowhere to hide. That's why I told my children never to tell anyone that their real surname is Tom."[11] My father took his paper son secret to his grave. Surrounded by his wife and five daughters as he lay dying of cancer at home, he gave his last will and testament.

Your mother wants me to speak from the heart. What does that mean? It is to talk about my journey from China to America and how I had to work like a mule. It was Third Uncle who told me to come if I had any pioneering spirit to prosper and build a better future. But no matter how hard I worked, I could not succeed. I had little schooling so I was forced to rely on my bare hands and to be a "jack of all trades." Then I had a succession of children in a couple of years to support. In order to meet expenses, I had to sweep floors, wash dishes, and do odd jobs. Just at that time, an employment agency in Chinatown found me a job at Ho Sai Gai Restaurant. Being a good worker, they offered me $115 per month. I started as a dishwasher and advanced to cook. When I got off work there, I went to Cumberland Presbyterian Church to work as a janitor and got a couple of bucks for that. Later, my wife and I went to work in the flower farms while my daughters shelled shrimp in Chinatown. The money was barely enough to pay our expenses. Lucky the rent was cheap—$12 a month for two rooms—and your mom was able to bring work home to sew. We earned a couple of thousand dollars a year and were doing okay.

11   Ibid., April 17, 1977.

As things got better, my wife wanted to save to buy property. But I said how could we make the mortgage payments on two or three hundred dollars a month? I didn't know she was so capable, because just then, my son had a terrible accident and all our money went to pay for his hospital bills. So this building is all due to your mother's work, not mine. We had just enough to make the mortgage payments, but not too much left over. If we could afford tofu, then we couldn't afford salt. We passed each year that way, with this or that daughter helping with a couple of dollars here and there. When I had saved up $3,000, Mommy advised me to put it in the bank for safekeeping. After my daughters started to work and earn their own money, they would give me *lei see* [lucky money] on special occasions, and I was able to add it to the pot. By and by, I was able to accumulate this amount of money [$8,150] to leave you. So that's about it. All my life your daddy has worked and this is all the money I have to show for it, and this building, which you must not sell while your mother is still alive.[12]

Editor's note: My father passed away nine days later, on November 25, 1987. He had always been a hardworking and humble man. But when we asked him if he wanted a marching band at his funeral, a custom reserved for the "big shots" in Chinatown, he smiled and nodded his head. Following his instructions, we laid him to rest at Woodlawn Cemetery with his Chinese name, Tom Yip Jing, and his American name, Yung Hin Sen, inscribed on his gravestone.

12 Tom Yip Jing's last will and testament, November 16, 1987.

Law Shee Low:
"That's How It Was"

Editor's note: Law Yuk Tao (maiden name) was born in Kai Gok village, Heungshan District, in 1903, the third child of seven children. Her father was a doctor and teacher, and the family was doing quite well until fighting broke out among the warlords and banditry became rampant in the emigrant villages of Guangdong. The family succumbed to poverty, and Yuk Tao was married off to Low Gun, a *Gam Saan haak* who was fifteen years her senior. Nine months after their wedding, they sailed for America. Upon arrival, Law Shee Low was detained on Angel Island for ten days before she was admitted into the country as a merchant's wife.

The following story of Law Shee Low's detention at Angel Island and her subsequent hardworking life in America is taken from three interviews that I conducted in 1982, 1988, and 1989 at her home in San Francisco. I found her to be a pragmatic woman and a candid interviewee with a vivid memory for details. Her favorite refrains were "That's how it was" and "Thank heaven!" She believed in making the best of every situation and putting her faith in fate and *tien wong* (heavenly god). Law Shee Low was a survivor, a kind-hearted soul, and a model wife and mother who lived to be ninety-seven years old.[1]

Before the bandits came, the living conditions were not too bad. If you had money, you could stay home and take it easy. If you were poor, you could still farm or hire yourself out as a farmer. Life was very simple. We had a bit of money because my grandfather owned land. We had three generations living under the same roof, and we all got along fine, including my sisters-in-law. Then when I was twelve years old, the bandits came and took everything. They destroyed our farmland and property, and we became poor. There was no calling for doctors, so my father went to the city to be a teacher. But he had a hard time collecting tuition; the students were so

[1] Law Shee Low interviews. An early version of this story was published in Yung, *Unbound Voices*, 211–23.

FIG. 3.12.

Affidavit of Low Gun in support
of his wife's admission to the
United States, June 20, 1921.
Courtesy of National Archives,
San Francisco.

poor. Sometimes they would pay him with clothes, sometimes ten catties of sweet potatoes or ten catties of preserved olives. Every other day, my sister and I would take our baskets and help him lug it all back. After two years of almost no pay, he returned to the village and became a doctor again.

We had many *mui jai* [slave girls] before, at least three at one time. We slowly married them off one at a time. When we became poor, we couldn't afford to replace them. There was no more money for my sister and me to continue with school, so we stayed home and learned to cook and clean house. We were very capable and we learned fast. Every morning, we had to draw water from the well for cooking, for tea, and for washing. I swept the floor, washed the dishes, chopped wood, and tended the garden. We also had to take care of my grandmother and mother because they had

bound feet and it was difficult for them to get around. I would help grandmother with the cooking, and until I became older, I was the one who went to the village marketplace every day to shop. My brothers never helped out. They continued going to school. It was work for girls to do.

My parents decided to marry me off to a *Gam Saan haak* from the next village. We were poor and there was no other way. We had no food to go with rice, not even soy sauce or black bean paste. Times were so bad that some of our neighbors even had to go begging or sell their daughters. My parents thought I would have a better future in Gold Mountain. My husband was thirty-four years old to my eighteen years. His father died when he was seven. He had an uncle who sponsored him to America as his paper son when he was sixteen. There he sewed for a living in order to pay back the debt, but he said he was a salesman in a clothing store. My grandmother didn't like him, but the matchmaker was able to convince my grandfather that it was a good match. I didn't even have the nerve to look at him when he came over to our house for a visit. Oh, we were so stupid then!

We got married on November 14, 1921, in Shekki. My husband became a Christian in America, so we had a Christian ceremony. He got an American minister to perform the ceremony. I wore the traditional Chinese tunic and skirt set but had an American-style veil and carried a bouquet of flowers. My parents didn't object since China was starting to modernize. After the wedding, we lived in this big house in Shekki that we rented from a clansman for $8 a month. There was his sister (a grass widow who had a nervous breakdown because she never heard from her husband in America), her mother-in-law, and some *mui jai*. They gave us part of the house to live in until we left for America in August of 1922.

The voyage by sea took about a month. We traveled in second class—six people to a room. Men and women were segregated. I was only seasick one day and one night when the ocean got turbulent. When we arrived in San Francisco, my husband didn't have to stay at Angel Island, but I did. Unfortunately, he forgot to give me some papers and so they kept me on the ship. All the other Chinese passengers got off, then the Japanese women got off. There was this young kid, a son of a friend of mine, who didn't have his papers either. The two of us had to wait almost half a day, standing throughout, because there were no chairs. Fortunately, we arrived during the daytime and it was nice weather. But we were beginning to worry that they would not take us to Angel Island. The kid was only nine years old and skinny. He began to cry. I was young then and able to bear it all.

Upon arrival, we didn't have to take a full physical examination, just give a stool sample. They gave us each a basin, and fortunately, I was able to defecate and pass the exam. Those found with hookworm had to go to the hospital. Liver fluke was considered incurable. There was a young bride who had it and was deported. After that, we were told to leave our luggage in the storage shed by the pier and just take what we needed. We would be allowed to retrieve things later. I put some clothes in a bag and took some bedding— a comforter, blanket, and two pillows—that my husband had given me. The kid was to stay with us in the women's barracks, but his father hadn't given him anything to take except a big towel for washing. So he helped me lug the bag and bedding up the stairs into this big room. There were about six or seven women there and four double-deck bunk beds, all with springs but no bedding. I took the top bunk and gave one of the pillows and the blanket to the kid. Later when I left, he returned my things to me. I often wonder what happened to him.

Life at Angel Island was like being in prison. Every morning we would all get up at 6:00, and they would let us out for meals and then lock us up again when we came back; the same at lunch and dinnertime. We always ate after the men were done. The food was terrible! The bean sprouts were cooked so badly you wanted to throw up when you saw it. It was the same food all the time, either bean sprouts or Chinese cabbage. The food was steamed to death—smelled bad and tasted bad. The vegetables were old, and the fatty beef was of poor quality. They must have thought we were pigs! There was rice, but it was cold. I just took a few spoonfuls and left. Not even a drop of tea, and you know how we Chinese love to drink tea. Whenever my husband sent me food—dim sum, cantaloupes, and Chinese sausages—I would share it with everyone. The old, white lady we called Ma [Deaconess Katharine Maurer] delivered the packages to us. They would call out my name and search it for any hidden coaching notes. The kid's father never sent him anything good to eat. That was sad because he didn't like the food either. He stuck with me the whole time I was there.

There was nothing much to do. Ma was a good person, brought us needlework to keep us busy, but we didn't know how. She was willing to teach us, but we weren't in the mood. Once a week, a matron would take us for a walk around the island. I never went. Mostly, we just sat there and waited out the days, staring out the window. We hardly even chatted. No arguments, no jokes. Everyone was just worried about not being able to land. There were a few women who had been there for a long time, like these two women who had been there for over three months. They didn't cry, didn't seem to care. They even sang sometimes and joked with the janitor. Whenever the matron offered to take us out for walks, just the two would go. The younger woman was very nice and helped us dress our hair. They had little going for themselves, but they managed to struggle on. There was also a young woman who was seven months pregnant. She had come with a pimp and was deported. There were all kinds of cases—it was frightening. Later, when they told us that people had hanged themselves in the bathroom, we were afraid to go to the bathroom alone. Even when we went to bathe, we made sure we had company.

One woman who was in her fifties was questioned all day and then later deported, which scared all of us. She told us they asked her about the number of chickens, the neighbors, and the direction the house faced. How would I know all that? I was scared. Later, when I was called for the interrogation, one woman told me to drink a few mouthfuls of cold water to stop the fear, so that's what I did. There was an inspector, a Chinese interpreter who was very nice, and a white lady taking notes. The white inspector asked me when did I marry, what was my surname, my age, and that was about it. When the interpreter asked me whether I had visited my husband's ancestral home on my wedding day, I said no because I was afraid he was going to ask me which direction the house faced, like the woman had said, and I wouldn't know. Evidently, my husband had said yes. So when they asked me again, this time in the presence of my husband, and I said no again, my husband yelled, "*Choi!* You went there. Why don't you say so?" The immigration officer objected by hitting the table with his hand and scared me to death. So I quickly said, "Oh, I forgot. I did pass by in the wedding sedan chair but I didn't go in." When they asked me to sign my name in Chinese, I didn't know that they had decided to land me. On the way back to the barracks, I thought for sure I was going to be deported, so I cried and cried. Then I heard them call me to get ready to leave on the four o'clock boat for San Francisco. So I quickly changed my clothes and the others happily helped me pack. Only the kid was sad to see me go. I just hope the other ladies took care of him.

Editor's note: According to Law Shee Low's immigration file, she and her husband were each asked fifty questions about their family background, their wedding, living quarters in Shekki, and their journey from Shekki to

Hong Kong on their way to America. Because of a few discrepancies in their testimonies, they were both recalled for questioning, which gave Law Shee Low the opportunity to correct her answers.

ALLEGED HUSBAND RECALLED

Q. Why didn't the minister give you a marriage certificate?

A. He did give me one, but I lost it moving so much.

Q. Was your wife ever in your home village of Lum Bin Tong?

A. Yes, once.

Q. When was that?

A. Shortly before we left Shekki for Hongkong.

RECALL OF ALLEGED WIFE

Q. Did you get a marriage certificate from the white man, Lom Jip?

A. No.

Q. Do you know if your husband got one?

A. I do not know.

Q. You stated you had never visited your husband's home village, is that correct?

A. I visited there once.

Q. When was it you visited that village?

A. This year, I don't remember when.[2]

The following is how Law Shee Low described her life in America after she was released from Angel Island.

When I got here, lots of people had no work. We were so poor we just had pickled vegetables with rice for dinner. We rented a room on Stockton Street for $11 a month. We did everything in that one room: sleep, eat, and sit. We had a small three-ring burner for cooking. There was no icebox, and my husband had to shop for every meal. We did not use canned goods and things like that. We ate only Chinese food. There was no hot water, and we would all hand wash our clothes. We used to dry them on the roof or in the hallways. That's what happens when you are poor. It was the same for all my neighbors. We were all poor together.

My husband worked as a cook in a restaurant twelve hours a day for $60 a month. His earnings barely covered the rent and food. I wanted to learn how to sew, so my husband bought me an old-fashioned sewing machine, and when he got off work from the restaurant, he would teach me how to sew. At first, a Low clansman brought me things to sew. Someone else showed me how to do the seams and how to gather. This one teacher I

2 File 21412/4–3 (Law Shee), Immigration Arrival Investigation Case Files, RG 85, NARA-SF.

had—a Mr. Wong from a neighboring village—specialized in baby clothes with beautiful decorations, embroidered pockets and all. He taught me well, and I made over two dozen pieces a day. The pay was over a dollar a dozen. I did that for ten years or so. It wasn't much, but it helped to cover some of the food and rent. I just gave it all to my husband since he did the shopping. In those days, we had only two meals a day. My husband might help make the rice, but I always did the cooking.

I had a total of eleven children—seven daughters and one son survived. They were all born at home. Who had money for the hospital? Sometimes one of the neighbors would help me. If not, I managed myself. That's the way it was. I lost two sons at childbirth. Another died when he was three. We didn't have any money, and he had pneumonia. Their father sent him to the public hospital and he got worse. He kept losing weight, so we brought him back to Chinese Hospital. He died soon after. He was a good boy. I cried for a few years; it was so tragic.

When I first went out to sew, I put my daughter who was a few months old in a basket. But after a few weeks of that, I came back to sewing at home. It was much easier. At home, I could work and take care of the children. There were jobs for women in the cannery and fruit orchards, but I couldn't do that because of the kids. Besides, it wasn't proper. Proper Chinese ladies should always stay home and take care of the housework, children, and husband. It was a pity, but that's the way life was for us ladies then. It was the same for all my neighbors. We were all good, obedient, and diligent wives. All sewed; all had six or seven children. We did not go out and waste our husbands' money. Every now and then, my husband would buy me some material and I would make clothes for the kids and myself. As for shoes, since I didn't go out, one pair of shoes would last me ten years. I just tried to send money home to China whenever there was money to spare.

During the Depression, we were so poor we wanted to die. My husband lost all of our savings in a restaurant business in Oakland. Then he went to Suisun to pick fruit. When there was no more work, he found a job at a restaurant in Vallejo. He just made $40 a month at this restaurant. He gave me $20 and kept $20 for himself. I sewed at home and made another $30 or $40. So we struggled on. Then business got slow at the restaurant, and he quit and came back. We got two machines and we both sewed at home. He would help with the easier pieces, and I would do the harder ones. When things got worse and we had no money for rent or food, their father got in line for milk and relief money from the federal government.

I sewed at home until my youngest daughter was five. By that time, they didn't allow us to sew at home anymore. So I sewed in the factories for another twenty, thirty years, until I was sixty-five and able to retire. I would

FIG. 3.14
Law Shee Low with her children,
1954. Left to right, front row:
Victor, Maxine, Nancy, and Emily;
back row: Edna, Ruby, Law Shee
Low, Pearl, and Bessie. Courtesy of
Victor Low.

stop work to go shopping at 12:00 noon. Then after I prepared the food, I would go back and sew. I always came home at 5:00 to cook dinner. At 6:00, we had dinner. Then I usually brought home some odds and ends to finish. At one point, I also babysat one of my granddaughters for a few hours. Between the children and sewing, I never had a free moment. Thank heaven I had good health and was able to go on like that for years!

Fortunately, all the children turned out well. They never gave me any trouble. They went to school, came home and ate, then went to bed. They even took care of their own weddings. We didn't have any money to help them. But they understood my situation and have always been good to me. My oldest daughter was sick for a long time, and my husband had a heart condition for quite a few years before he died in 1956. My sewing money barely covered the rent. Fortunately, my children all pitched in to pay for the food, my rent, the electricity, insurance, everything; and they give me spending money. For the last ten years I've been able to send money home to China. They asked me whom I wanted to live with, but I decided living here by myself was more convenient. You know, they were worth all the hardships and struggles.

Mrs. Wong: "Had I Known It Was Like This, I Would Never Have Come!"

Editor's note: Mrs. Wong was the first and oldest woman we interviewed for *Island.* A petite and energetic lady at eighty-seven, she used to come to the Chinatown Branch Library, where I worked, whenever there was a special program for Chinese seniors—tea parties, musical performances, storytelling, and films. When I found out that she had been detained on Angel Island for more than two weeks in 1923, I got her permission to record an interview with her. Because we promised to keep her identity anonymous, we never bothered to ask for her full name. We knew her only as Mrs. Wong.

Genny Lim and I conducted the interview in Mrs. Wong's one-room apartment in a senior housing project. Dressed in a neatly ironed cotton print dress, she sat in her overstuffed chair by a television set that had long since ceased to work. Across from her was a bed and a small table with a Bible, sundry boxes, and papers on top. The sitting room was partitioned off from the kitchen by a portable screen that had photos, calligraphy, and calendars tacked to it. With the sun pouring in through the glass doors behind us, she attentively answered our questions in the Toishan dialect. But she was reluctant when it came to questions about her life after Angel Island. "No point in talking about those things that have no bearing on the topic," she said. Many years later, after I found her immigration file at the National Archives and communicated with her son James, I came to understand why she had chosen to hide certain information from us.[1]

It was James who told me that his mother's full name was Lew Sau Kam. She was born in Wong Woo village, Toishan District, in 1883, the second daughter in a family of six children. James, who grew up in China, imagines that, like other village girls, she probably had to help in the fields, feed the chickens and pigs, and do house chores, while also learning sewing and embroidering, which she did very well. At the age of twenty, she married Wong Ting Cheong of Nom Hong village. According to immigration records, he was a silk and jade merchant in Canton. They had two sons and

[1] File 21811/2–10 (Lew Shee), Immigration Arrival Investigation Case Files, RG 85, NARA-SF; James Poy Wong, e-mail correspondence with Judy Yung, July 10, 2013.

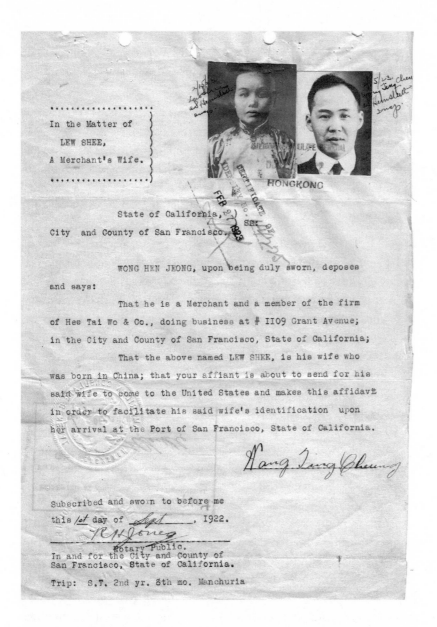

In the Matter of
LEW SHEE,
A Merchant's Wife.

State of California,
City and County of San Francisco.

WONG HEN JEONG, upon being duly sworn, deposes
and says:

That he is a Merchant and a member of the firm
of Hee Tai Wo & Co., doing business at # 1109 Grant Avenue;
in the City and County of San Francisco, State of California;

That the above named LEW SHEE, is his wife who
was born in China; that your affiant is about to send for his
said wife to come to the United States and makes this affidavit
in order to facilitate his said wife's identification upon
her arrival at the Port of San Francisco, State of California.

Wong Ting Cheung

Subscribed and sworn to before me
this 1st day of Sept , 1922.
R H Jones
Notary Public.
In and for the City and County of
San Francisco, State of California.

Trip: S.T. 2nd yr. 8th mo. Manchuria

FIG. 3.15

Affidavit by Wong Hen Jeong (Wong Hing Cheong) dated September 1, 1922, attesting to his status as a merchant and his intention to send for his wife, Lew Shee. Courtesy of National Archives, San Francisco.

one daughter before he left in 1910 for America, where he became a partner and bookkeeper in a meat market in San Francisco Chinatown.[2]

James also told me that his mother was a progressive woman for her time. She refused to have her feet bound as a child, and after she was married, she got permission from her husband to attend a church-sponsored school in Toising for four years. In the process, Mrs. Wong became a devout Christian and learned Chinese well enough to teach in the girls' schoolhouse in Sam Hop. Finally, after a separation of twelve years, her husband was able to send for her as a merchant's wife. On January 5, 1923, she boarded the

2 According to James, his mother had only one son then. Perhaps the couple claimed an extra daughter and son so that they could help others immigrate to the United States as their paper children.

239

Nanking steamer in Hong Kong with her sixteen-year-old son, Wong Poy Yen. This is what she told us about her journey to America.[3]

At the time of my departure, I was thirty-three years old and a schoolteacher in my village. I had just finished the three-day examinations at the end of the school semester. My husband had been in business for over ten years in America. He had an attorney prepare my papers. They had already made our ship reservations, so once I arrived in Hong Kong, it was very easy to continue on to America.

I remember my son and I boarded the ship on the third day of the month. We traveled in first class and stayed in a room with two sets of bunk beds.[4] My son and myself occupied one set of bunks, and another woman with the surname Wong and her son occupied the other. Confined and sea-sick, it was difficult to eat. For breakfast, I had two eggs. I didn't eat lunch. For dinner, I had some vegetables with rice. The woman I shared the room with didn't eat anything the whole time. She was seasick. She wouldn't eat; she wouldn't leave her bed. Later on, I climbed on deck and walked around a bit. Her, she never got out at all, never even left the room.

After a month or so, the ship docked in San Francisco and we were taken straight to Angel Island to be interrogated and examined. Someone came and took us to the women's quarters and pointed out our beds to us. It was a big hall with rows of bunk beds. My son slept on the upper bunk, me on the lower bunk. There were many Japanese. They arrived and left on the launch within twenty-four hours. But us, we were confined inside so long. I kept thinking in my heart, "What a worthless trip coming here! Confined all the time—it's just like being in jail!"

There were all types of women living there. There were prostitutes, bad women too, who stayed at the other end of the room. They didn't come over to our side. Some had been confined there for two or three years. They could see that my son, who was fourteen, was a pretty big boy.[5] They would urge him, "Come over here, come on over, and I'll give you *lei see* [lucky money]." After that, I followed my son everywhere! I went with him to the bathroom—wherever he went, I followed. I didn't dare let him go anywhere alone. Those girls were very bad! I told them off. I said, "Where do you get the nerve to behave in such a way! Huh, how dare you be so brazen!" I scolded them so that they didn't dare do that again.

For meals, we went to the big dining hall. At the sound of the bell, we all went down together, about twenty of us in a group escorted by two guards. The melons were all chopped in pieces and thrown together like pig slop. The pork was in big, big chunks. Everything was thrown into a big bowl that resembled a washtub and left there for you to eat or not as you wished. They

3   Mrs. Wong interview.
4   Mrs. Wong may have con-
     fused first class with second
     class, in which, instead of
     having a private cabin, one
     had to share a cabin with four
     to six people.
5   According to Mrs. Wong's
     immigration file, she was for-
     ty years old and her son was
     sixteen at the time. He must
     have looked much younger
     because boys over the age of
     twelve usually stayed in the
     men's barracks.

just steamed the food until it was like a soupy stew. After looking at it, you'd lose your appetite! There was cabbage, stewed vegetables, pork, and bits of stewed meat of low quality, that kind of thing. Sometimes we would receive roast duck or chicken from relatives in San Francisco. But there was no place to store it, no place to heat it up, so we heated it on top of the radiators for awhile and ate a little of it at a time.

The women had it much better than the men. There was a matron who took us out for a walk around the island once a week. The men were forbidden to leave the building. There was steel wire bracing all the windows, just like a prison. I kept thinking, "Had I known it was like this, I would never have come!"

To pass the time away, you had to occupy yourself any way you could. If you wanted to knit or sew, you could. Some of the ladies who were there for a long time finished a lot of knitting projects. I had some books with me to read. If you didn't have anything, you didn't do anything. That's why in just two weeks I became disgusted and bored with just sitting around. There wasn't anything special about it. Day in, day out, the same kind of thing. Everyone was worried. "When am I going to get in?" Or else, "They're going to deport me!" Everyone had to be patient and tell themselves, "I'm just being delayed; it doesn't matter." Before we came, we never knew it would be so cruel. We were all distraught, but what could you do about it? Everyone just sat around and waited.

I never even bothered to bathe. I kept thinking each day that I would be ready to leave, and as each day went by, I just waited. I didn't eat much, nor move around much, so I never perspired. I had no need to wash my clothes. Even if I did, I couldn't do it. There was no place to hang your laundry. And there was no place for you to write letters. All we had were rows of bunk beds and a narrow path between the beds, just enough room to walk through, and not even a chair. We just sat on the bed, that's all.

Prior to the interrogation, we were not allowed to have any visitors. We could hear the guard saying, "Here they come, here they come!" But they never let you see the witnesses. When it was my turn, the interrogators were very thoughtful at the hearing. The white lady gave me some candy, and by the time I finished eating my candy, the interrogation was over. It didn't take more than ten minutes. They just asked a few questions, nothing much: What is your father's name? What village are you from? How old are you? And so forth. They questioned my husband first, then me, then my son. When my son went in, they noticed the strong resemblance between father and son and said, "There's no need to question him." Our papers were all true, so it was quite easy. After they finished the interrogation, we were able to get on the ferry two days later. For me, it was fast; for others, it was not. Some were very slow, some several months, some several years I even heard them say.

Editor's note: A look at Mrs. Wong's immigration file revealed that the interrogation had indeed gone well for the family. Two Chinese and two white witnesses had attested to her husband's good standing as a bookkeeper at the Hee Tai Wo meat market, "an up-to-date establishment with many white patrons," according to an on-site investigative report. On February 15, 1923, Wong Ting Cheong appeared before the Board of Special Inquiry at Angel Island and was asked more than one hundred questions about his business, family background, village life, the remittances he sent home, and his witnesses. Similar questions were asked of Mrs. Wong on the same day. Her matter-of-fact responses to some of the questions showed that she was an educated woman accustomed to speaking her mind.

Q. What did your husband do before he came to the United States?
A. He was a student; you will have to ask him.
Q. Was he ever in business?
A. I don't know.
Q. Didn't your husband ever tell you what he was doing before he came to the United States?
A. No. The people in China before the Republic [1912] were not as wise as they are today. Nowadays the wives ask their husbands.
Q. Did your husband live right in the home village with you up to the time he came to the United States?
A. Sometimes he came home and sometimes he did not. I don't remember how often he came home.

Mrs. Wong's son Wong Poy Yen later testified that his mother had been a schoolteacher in the village, a fact that apparently impressed the board. "Applicant Lew Shee is evidently a respectable Chinese woman," wrote Inspector Jones in the summary report. He noted that the only detrimental feature in the case was Lew Shee's ignorance of her husband's occupation before he immigrated to the United States. Otherwise, "the testimony is in agreement and contains much that is very favorable to the application." The board recommended that mother and son be admitted into the country.[6]

When we asked Mrs. Wong questions about her life after Angel Island, she was willing to mention only that her husband worked in a meat market on Grant Avenue while she sewed at a garment factory and taught Chinese school for the Congregational Church, of which she had always been a proud member. Quite understandably, she did not tell us that she gave birth

6   File 21811/2–10 (Lew Shee).

to three more sons in America and that the family had fallen on hard times during the Great Depression. In 1934, they decided to return to China for work and so that the three boys could have a good Chinese education. They couldn't even afford the boat fare, and the California Relief Administration ended up covering their passage in third class.

It must have been a difficult journey for Mrs. Wong to return to China penniless and in steerage accommodations when just a decade before she had traveled in second class with high hopes of a new life in America. She did not even know if she could ever return to the United States, as she had burned that bridge behind her by not applying for a return certificate. As she told the immigrant inspector on Angel Island before she left, "I probably will not return to this country because I have no money to pay my passage, but if permitted, I would return with my children." She did, however, apply for return certificates on behalf of her three American-born children.

Upon their return to China, the family settled in Canton, where Wong Ting Cheong found a government job in a paper mill. The boys enrolled in an elite elementary school, and Mrs. Wong was able to lead a leisurely life—reading newspapers and novels, attending church, and visiting relatives in the city and in her village. But the family's fortunes took a drastic turn after war with Japan broke out in 1937. The family split up and ran for cover. "In escaping the fires of war, we fell into the abyss of hopelessness," said James mournfully. The father evacuated with his work unit to Canton Bay, while the mother and children fled to Toising. The war cut off the father's income, and food became scarce. James remembers eating less rice and meat and more sweet potatoes and fermented beans. "My mom held on as long as she could. She knew that if we stayed in China, we would all die." Indeed, Mrs. Wong did later lose her eldest son to starvation caused by a drought in Toishan. In 1941, she borrowed money for the boat fare from a relative in the United States and sent two of her sons, Henry and James, back to America. She kept her youngest son, Lincoln, who was constantly sick with asthma, in China with her. Afterward, she moved back to Canton and relied on her two sons in America to support her through the war years and Communist takeover.

After working their way through college, Henry got a job in aeronautics with the National Aeronautics and Space Administration and James was employed as a structural engineer with the state of California. But not until 1958 could they find a way to bring their mother back to America on a visitor's visa. By then, Lincoln had graduated from medical school and married, but he could not get permission to leave China until 1979. Wong Ting Cheong remained in Hong Kong until he died in 1975 at the age of eighty-seven.

Returning to America when she was seventy-five, Mrs. Wong found it difficult living with any of her children's families in the suburbs. She eventually moved back to the familiar surroundings of Chinatown and spent her remaining years working as a seamstress until her eyes failed her and attending church every Sunday. Mrs. Wong passed away in 1989 at the age of 106. Her son James attributes her longevity to her strong will and religious faith. "Throughout her life, she experienced many calamities and many tears were shed, but she remained standing because of her faith in God."

John Mock, Kitchen Helper:
"Then *Vroom*, They Ate and Were Gone!"

Editor's note: John Mock, aka Mock Chung Nin, was born in Cheuk Suey Hong village, in the Wong Leung Do area of Heungshan District in 1905. He was the oldest of three sons. In 1919, he came to America using the bogus identity of Mok Jun Lum, the eleven-year-old son of merchant Mock Gee Kai. He was accompanied by his paper father, paper mother, and paper brother. (His father was really his grand-uncle, his mother was his aunt, and his brother was a fellow villager.) Seventeen days after their arrival at Angel Island, members of the family were individually interrogated about the family background, the layout of the village and of their house, and the boys' schooling. Finding only a few minor discrepancies between their testimonies, Inspector Franklin recommended that they be landed.[1] Little did Mock know then that he would be returning to the island in a few years to work as a kitchen helper.

Wanting to hear about both his immigration and work experience at Angel Island, Him Mark Lai and I interviewed John Mock at his San Jose home in 1975. We were able to establish a rapport with him right from the start because Mock was Him Mark's sister's father-in-law as well as my father's clansman. In vivid detail and with good humor, he described the working conditions, the food that was served, how the kitchen staff helped get coaching notes to detainees, and a food riot that he himself witnessed.[2]

In those days, the food contractor was white, but the kitchen staff were all Chinese. Eight out of ten workers were Wong Leung Do people. Gai Yuk's father was the head cook at Angel Island and got me the job. As a kitchen helper, I did everything—wash dishes, cut vegetables, wash and steam the rice. The chief cook was paid $100 a month; the assistant cook, $80; and the rest of us got $70. We got up at 4:00 in the morning. The first meal was served at 6:00. We took a one-hour break at 1:00 and then worked until 4:00. If there were a lot of people to feed, we got off at 4:30. In those days, it was

1   File 18703/16—30 (Jew Shee), Immigration Arrival Investigation Case Files, RG 85, NARA-SF. I am indebted to Robert Fong for the biographical information about John Mock.
2   John Mock interview, December 27, 1975.

FIG. 3.17
John Mock's paper family. Left to right: Mock Gee Kai, Jew Shee, Mok Jun Fook, and Mok Jun Lum (John Mock). Courtesy of National Archives, San Francisco.

common to work ten hours a day. Sometimes a ship would arrive at nine o'clock at night and we would have to feed everyone.

Each day I washed rice for two meals—that was fourteen or fifteen bags of rice that weighed fifty pounds each. It was really quite simple. The sink was bigger than a bathtub and made of wood. You dumped the rice into the sink, stirred it around, and then used a basket to drain out the water. Then you took the rice upstairs and asked the cook how much rice to cook. Two woks were used to steam the rice. The wok must've been eight feet wide. It was so large that I had to stand on a *ng ga pei* [Chinese liquor] box to reach it. Each wok cooked 175 pounds of rice. It took four hours. We prepared the rice the day before. The rice cook had to get up at 3:00 in the morning to turn on the steam, so he was paid more. The rice scooper was the size of a shovel. You shoveled the rice into bowls, and the waiters took them out to the dining room. There were at least ten waiters—all *fan gwai* [foreign devils].

We had to cook for whomever passed through—European food, Japanese food, and Chinese food, of course. People from India ate salmon with potato paste. For the Chinese, we served them rice in the morning and evening, and *jook* with some minced pork or tapioca and crackers at lunch. There was always a main dish and a small dish to go with the rice. Main dishes were like beef and potatoes, dried bean curd and pork, vermicelli and pork, dried vegetables and fish, usually sand dabs on Tuesdays and Fridays. The small dish was usually salted fish, fermented bean curd, or bean paste. On Sundays, we served Chinese noodles. Nothing special was served on holidays. The boss was given 17 cents a head per meal. Twenty-five cents in those days could buy you pot roast or beef stew in Chinatown, so he made money on the afternoon meal when we served *jook*. Before the hearing, the steamship company paid for the meals. If you should fail and decide to appeal your case, then you had to pay for your own meals.

The dining hall had thirty-three long tables, which seated six to eight people apiece. When I was working there in the 1920s, there were over seven hundred Chinese inmates, so they had to eat in shifts. Meals were quick—about half an hour each shift. The men ate first. We used two steamers to cook the food. The dishes were placed on the tables before they came down. Two guards would bring the men down, and two others would watch them in the dining hall. Then *vroom*, they ate and were gone! Then the women came down to eat. There were no seconds on dishes, just on rice. Many of the immigrants could eat six or seven bowls of rice at a meal! If that wasn't enough, they could fill up on salted fish or buy snacks at the concession. The white boss had us cook extra dishes to sell, like pork and vegetables or spareribs in black bean sauce. The money was put in a plate and went to the boss. We also steamed or warmed up food that relatives had sent from the city—Chinese sausages, barbecued duck, and other deli food. We would put it out on the cart for people to come and claim.

In between meals, I was assigned to peel potatoes or cut salted fish into chunks. The red potatoes were about two inches in diameter and of the cheapest quality. The Chinese vegetables were at least three or four feet long—what we would call throwaways. We used a long table to chop them up and then soak them in water. We always served the old bread first. It didn't come sliced, so we had to cut it with an electric knife that was sharp enough for the hard bread. No one ever got sick because of the food. They were very diligent about inspecting the kitchen. If they even saw a cockroach, they would fumigate.

We were provided room and board on the island. There were many workers. We Chinese got one house, Westerners had theirs, the hospital staff had theirs, the gardeners had theirs, and so on. The houses were very nice. After work, some of us played Chinese chess; others played musical instruments. Sometimes I would go fishing. At one time, detainees who had already been interrogated were allowed to come to our quarters to chat or play chess. But later, the immigration officers forbade it. We ate better than the detainees. The steamed rice they ate was terrible, so we cooked our own rice. On our days off, we would go to San Francisco to buy food and liquor, which we brought back to share with coworkers.

There were eight of us working there, so one of us was off every day of the week. Newcomers would write their relatives in the city to ask for things. Then the relatives would find us and ask us to take things back to the island. As long as they had the name and manifest number of the detainee, the package would get to the right party. We would drop by Canton Flower Market [owned by Wong Leung Do people] in Chinatown and ask if there was any coaching information to take back to the island. Each time we did

this, we were given $5. We were prepared to be searched upon return. When security got tight, we didn't try to bring in anything. We never got caught. We would press a buzzer, and someone would quickly run down for the message. We only did this for people we knew, such as our clansmen.

While I was there, Chinese detainees staged a food riot one day. The reason was this: There was a Self-governing Association that wanted fair treatment for the Chinese, including better food. Everyone agreed and started throwing dishes around the dining hall. Out of desperation, the immigration people called the Chinese consul general, who sent a representative to explain that the menu was set by an agreement with the American government. It could not be changed by the cooks. But they still thought it was our fault and wanted to beat us up. The white boss then pointed a gun at them and said, "Whoever comes in first, gets it first." No one dared. Good thing there were telephones, and a call was made to Fort McDowell for help. Soldiers came immediately, and everyone was forced back upstairs. Do you know they refused to come down to the dining hall to eat for the next three days? We cooked as usual, but they refused to eat. So the boss closed the food concession that sold sandwiches and crackers, to punish them.

It was very hard work, but I was young then. For example, the stove used coal, which was delivered in large quantities. I had to help carry one-hundred-pound sacks from the dock to the kitchen on the second floor.

Everything was big and heavy. One thing I liked about the job was this: Being over there, we never got caught in the middle of a tong war. There was one worker who was so scared of the tong fights that he never went over to San Francisco even on his day off. After a year or so, he saved enough money to return to his village in China. I left the job after two years, figuring that I could find a job that paid as much in the city.

Editor's note: After he left his job at Angel Island, John Mock worked at a cannery in Mayfield, California, while attending school. He found a better-paying job at Stanford University as a cook for one of the fraternities. After World War II, he became a farmer, growing cauliflowers, tomatoes, and celery in Woodland, California, and, later, chrysanthemums in the San Jose area. He returned to China in 1930 to get married, and in 1950, his only son, Mock Mei Hon (aka Philip Fong), took the same "crooked path" to come to the United States—as the paper son of a clansman. John Mock's wife was not able to join him in America until 1963, a year after he became a naturalized U.S. citizen. An active member of the Bay Area Chrysanthemum Growers Association and Hip Sen Tong, John Mock died in 1980 at the age of seventy-five.[3]

3   John Mock interview, May 3, 1969.

Soto Shee: A Story of Survival and Hope

KATHY ANG

I HAD ALWAYS BEEN INTRIGUED AND FASCINATED BY MY HUS-band's maternal grandmother, Soto Shee. By the time I met her, she was widowed, the matriarch of a large extended family, highly re-vered and respected, independent, strong-willed, and strong-bodied. She was the oldest person I had ever known, living to the ripe old age of ninety-six. I often wondered about all the life experiences she had gone through.

I was especially interested in her immigration story, and I would pepper my mother-in-law, Mabel, for information. Mabel would always tell us that her mother was pregnant with her during the twenty-seven-day journey across the Pacific, that the rough seas caused her to be seasick the entire time, and that it was a miracle that she did not suffer a miscarriage. Later, we would learn through Soto Shee's alien file, obtained from the U.S. Citizen-ship and Immigration Services, that they survived through other miracles as well. It is truly a story of survival and hope.

Born in 1896 in the village of Tai Foo Lay, Yanping District, Soto Shee was the oldest of five children in a well-to-do family. At seventeen, she entered into an arranged marriage with Lim Lee, the son of a U.S. citizen. After they married, Lim Lee came to the United States alone and worked with his father at the Shanghai Restaurant in Auburn, California, and as an officer of the Salvation Army in San Francisco. Five years later, he returned to China to start a family with Soto Shee.

Lim Lee and Soto Shee had the good fortune of having two sons, and Lim Lee decided to take his wife and second son to America in 1924. He was an American citizen, and he expected that his family would be admit-ted to the United States without any problems. Leaving the eldest son with Lim Lee's parents in Hoiping District, Lim Lee, Soto Shee, and their seven-month-old son, Soon Din, embarked for Hong Kong. Baby Soon Din's name, which means "smooth and successful progress," reflected their optimism and expectations for a bright future. From Hong Kong, they boarded the *Shinyo Maru* for San Francisco.

THE FIRST MIRACLE: SURVIVING THE SEA VOYAGE

Their tickets were for steerage class, the cheapest tickets and the worst conditions. This was no luxury cruise. No separate cabins. Instead the family shared the large hull of the ship near the engine room with hundreds of other steerage passengers. Dank, dark, and crowded. Noisy, with no privacy, sleeping in tiered bunks. Limited toilet facilities and stench. Meager food and rationed water. What a contrast to the comfortable life Soto Shee had known in China!

It may have been near impossible for Soto Shee to get adequate nutrition and hydration during that month at sea. Her body demanded that she eat for three. She needed nourishment for (1) her own body, (2) her pregnancy, and (3) extra nutrition to breastfeed Baby Soon Din. Who knows how much she was able to eat, much less keep down, due to seasickness and the nausea and vomiting common in the first trimester of pregnancy? Soto Shee was right. It was a miracle that she did not suffer a miscarriage.

THE SECOND MIRACLE: SURVIVING ANGEL ISLAND

Arriving at Angel Island, they found the sanitary conditions intolerable. Immigration officers had long complained about the unhealthy conditions and fire hazards in the ramshackle buildings. Conditions were so bad that year that the *San Francisco Chronicle* called the structures unfit for human habitation while the Chinese Six Companies made the case to President

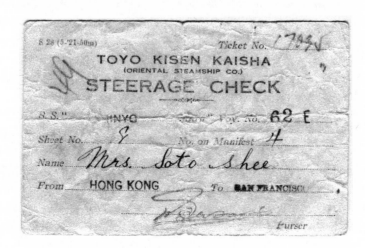

FIG. 3.19
Soto Shee's steerage ticket.
Courtesy of David Ang.

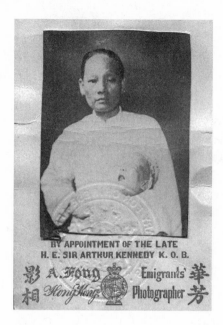

BY APPOINTMENT OF THE LATE
H. E. SIR ARTHUR KENNEDY K. O. B.

影 A.Fong 華
相 HongKong Emigrants' Photographer 芳

Calvin Coolidge and Secretary of Labor J. J. Davis that several detainees had become ill and even died due to the poor conditions at the immigration station. Even years later, there were documented complaints of Chinese immigrants not having toilet paper or soap.

On August 10, 1924, two and a half weeks after their arrival, the unthinkable happened. Soto Shee's infant Soon Din died on Angel Island. The cause of death was gastroenteritis, a condition usually caused by a virus or bacteria, transmitted by contaminated water or food and leading to severe vomiting and diarrhea. Gastroenteritis is highly contagious. Soto Shee was surely at high risk of contracting gastroenteritis herself as she cared for her baby, Soon Din. Gastroenteritis in a pregnant woman could lead to severe dehydration and fever, which would put her fetus at risk of death or a miscarriage. But again, both Soto Shee and Mabel survived.

THE THIRD MIRACLE: SURVIVING THE DESPAIR

Imagine Soto Shee's grief with the death of her baby boy. She was alone, in detention in a foreign country, unable to understand the language and details of her circumstances. She was separated from her husband, who as a returning American citizen was landed in San Francisco the same day that the ship came in. Soon Din's body was taken from her and delivered to his father in San Francisco. Soto Shee was not allowed to leave Angel Island to attend her baby's funeral and burial in San Francisco because she was deemed inadmissible and slated for deportation according to the newly passed Immigration Act of 1924.[1] Had she arrived just one month earlier, she would have been admitted as the wife of a U.S. citizen. Because an appeal was filed on her behalf, Soto Shee was able to postpone her deportation date and stay on Angel Island until her case was reviewed.

Two days after Baby Soon Din's death, the doctor at Angel Island confirmed that Soto Shee was two months pregnant. Her attorney Joseph Fallon pleaded with immigration officials to understand her tragic circumstances. "The mother is pregnant and in a very nervous state of health," he wrote. A request was made that Soto Shee be released on bond from Angel Island to be with her husband in San Francisco. But officials in Washington, D.C., responded that "no unusual hardship exists" and denied the request. In her despair on the night of September 4, 1924, Soto Shee tried to hang herself in the women's lavatory at Angel Island. Fortunately, Matron Grace McKeener, who oversaw the women's barracks, found her and cut her down.[2] Both

1   The Immigration Act of 1924, also known as the National Origins Act, was aimed at restricting immigration from southern and eastern European countries and excluding all aliens ineligible for citizenship, namely Asians. In effect, it stopped any further immigration of the Japanese as well as Chinese wives of merchants and U.S. citizens. A ruling by the U.S. Supreme Court in 1925 allowed wives of merchants to be admitted, while Congress passed an amendment in 1930 allowing wives of U.S. citizens married before July 1, 1924, to be admitted.

2   File 23550/8–4 (Soto Shee), Immigration Arrival Investigation Case Files, NARA-SF.

Soto Shee and Mabel (fetus) were rescued. If McKeener had found them just a few minutes later, it may have been too late. Another miracle. They both survived.

PERSISTENT HOPE

Three months later, Soto Shee was released from Angel Island for temporary admission on $1,000 bond. She gave birth to Mabel on February 26, 1925, at home in San Francisco Chinatown and gave her the Chinese name Mei Ho 美好. Mabel always told us that her parents named her very intentionally. "Mei" as in "Mei Gwok," the Cantonese word for "America" or "Beautiful Country," and "Ho" meaning "good." Somehow, despite this incredibly rocky start, Soto Shee and Lim Lee maintained hope that life would be good for them and for their family in America.

For the next six years, Soto Shee lived with the constant threat of deportation over her. Each year, she had to file papers to postpone deportation and renew her $1,000 bond. Soto Shee and Lim Lee persisted and fought the deportation until the Chinese American Citizens' Alliance finally convinced Congress to amend the immigration law to admit Chinese alien wives of U.S. citizens in 1930.

The family settled in San Francisco Chinatown, where Lim Lee worked as a kitchen helper at the Presidio Golf Club, a street vendor in Chinatown, and later owned and operated the Kay Sun Laundry on Waverly Place. Soto Shee shelled shrimp, sold handicrafts, and kept the laundry running while raising a family of eight children. In the late 1940s, they moved to Marysville and opened the Sing Chong Restaurant, serving Chinese and American food. Soto Shee was the chief cook and worked long hours at the restaurant. A decade later, they sold the restaurant to their daughter Evangeline and son-in-law Wai Lim and retired in San Francisco. Lim Lee died in 1961 at the age of sixty-seven. Soto Shee lived independently to age ninety-six, dearly loved and respected by her eight children, twenty-two grandchildren, and ten great-grandchildren.

FIG. 3. 21
Mabel (sitting in chair) with Lim Lee, Soto Shee, and Baby Henry, 1928. Courtesy of David Ang.

Wong Gung Jue:
A True Chinese Character

PENELOPE WONG

Editor's note: Henry Wong (aka Wong Yen Yi) immigrated to the United States as Wong Gung Jue, the paper son of an American-born Chinese citizen, on August 25, 1927. He was grilled for three days and asked a total of 231 questions about his family background, village life, and voyage to America. The immigrant inspectors found a number of discrepancies between his testimony and that of his alleged father and brother.[1] Slated for deportation, Henry was stuck on Angel Island for more than a year while waiting for a court ruling on his appeal. In 1991, when he returned to Angel Island for a visit, he showed docent Sandra Gin the exact spot on the barracks wall where he remembered writing a poem with a gold-tipped fountain pen that his godfather in Denver, Colorado, had given him. The poem was no longer visible, but as soon as Henry returned home, he rewrote the poem from memory in beautiful calligraphy and sent it to Sandra for safekeeping.[2]

Unfortunately, I did not have the opportunity to interview Henry Wong, the only known surviving Angel Island poet, before he passed away in 2004. The following story by his daughter Penelope was written in consultation with her siblings and in response to my questions about Henry's life before, during, and after his long detention at Angel Island.

Our dad was a man of confounding complexity, contradiction, and contrariness. Straddling two countries he loved—China for its long history and his beloved heritage, America for its brash promises of quick riches and freedom to try-try-try just about anything—Wong Gung Jue was like a character straight out of one of his beloved Peking operas. Still looming large in our memories, he was bigger and louder in life.

To give a chronological account of him just doesn't feel or sit right. He was an oversize personality who could display wisdom and patience in recounting a Chinese story or fact, but just as quickly his mood could change

1   File 26162/4–8 (Wong Gung Jue), Immigration Arrival Investigation Case Files, RG 85, NARA-SF.
2   We are indebted to Sandra Gin for keeping the handwritten poem for more than twenty years and turning it over to the Angel Island Immigration Station Foundation for safekeeping.

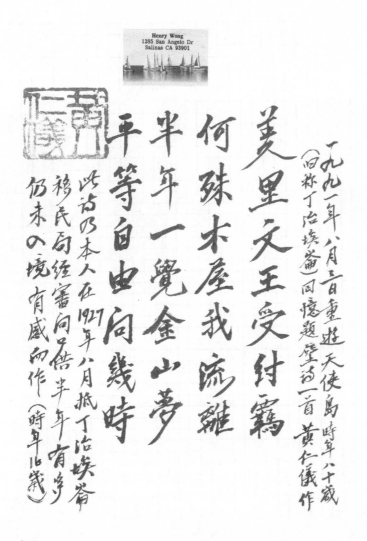

一九九一年八月三日重遊天使島時年八十歲
（回稱丁治埃崙）回憶題壁詩一首 黃仁儀作
美里文王受拘囚
何殊木屋我流離
半年一覺金山夢
平等自由向幾時
此古乃本人在1927年八月抵丁治埃崙
移民局經審向居半年有多
仍未の境有感而作（時年16歲）

FIG. 3.22
Wong Gung Jue (Wong Yen
Yi), 1928. Courtesy of National
Archives, San Francisco.

FIG. 3.23
On August 3, 1991, when I
returned to Angel Island at the
age of eighty, I remembered
the poem I had written on the
wall. "Like King Wen, when he
languished under house arrest / I,
too, am confined in this wooden
prison. / For half a year, I have
gazed at the American Dream.
/ As for 'Equality' and 'Liberty,'
I still ask, 'When?'" I wrote this
poem in August 1927 at the Angel
Island Immigration Station. I had
been interviewed several times
by inspectors during the past
half year and was still awaiting a
decision on admission (written at
age 16 by Wong Yen Yi).

to impatience and noisy indignation if he felt slighted or disrespected by an impertinent someone, something.

All we can do is paint an impressionistic portrait of him. Bits and pieces of the puzzle free-fall into place, as each of my siblings and I remember him. And, as often happens in every family, we realize the "Rashomon" effect (the iconic Japanese film in which different perspectives are reflected) and marvel at what each of us remembers . . . and forgets.

An exquisite calligrapher, scholar, poet, and singer. A tireless teacher and ambassador of Chinese language and culture. A determined impresario of Chinese movies and music. A wacky inventor, craftsman, and builder. (Our home in Salinas sported a small plane's cockpit as a skylight and a painted mural of the Great Wall of China in our front yard.) A man with a self-described "long stomach" who could spend hours feasting on his fa-

FIG. 3.24
Nellie Sue Lee and Henry Wong
on their wedding day, Fresno,
California, 1940. Courtesy of
Penelope Wong.

vorite Cantonese delectables such as fish eyeballs and smoked duck giblets (among other Western-rejected body parts), as well as relish a Carl's Jr. Western Bacon Cheeseburger with extra everything and the Friday night Red Lobster special.

Accomplished at many things cultural, he never achieved the business success he yearned for. As my brother Stan relates: "He trained as a diesel engineer in Oregon, but as a young Chinese male, could not find work in that field largely due to racial prejudice and discriminatory laws in effect throughout America and especially the West Coast during the 1930s."

In 1940 he married our mother, Nellie Sue Lee, who was born in Fresno, California, and the two of them moved from Fresno to fertile Salinas Valley, aptly dubbed the "Salad Bowl of the World." At first they operated a Chinese import store featuring art goods, but then in order to avoid the World War II draft so that he could stay home and support his growing family, he became a truck farmer. While he grew a variety of Asian vegetables (bok choy, winter melon, Chinese broccoli, and mustard greens), the primary cash crop was green onions (which I still can't abide). Even though he wasn't ultimately successful as a farmer (due to untimely weather, lack of cash flow, scale of operation, and his lack of focus), he used his imagination to create a Frankenstein-like contraption from a two-wheeled steel trailer to convey the many aluminum sprinkler pipes required for frequent crop watering. Also applying his engineering training, he later came up with a conveyor belt system to speed the hand processing of those hateful green onions.

In the post-farming years of the 1950s, one of the many ventures he tried was to open a café in the industrial part of Salinas. He spent a fortune on equipment to introduce dim sum to the American masses, but he never built a business plan to accomplish it. But oh, could he sing the praises of that Cantonese delicacy! He could make your stomach growl with his passionate description of what makes the perfect *siu mai* or *fun gor.*

To pin down a straightforward description of him is impossible. Let's start with the basics: his name and date of birth. When my sister, Victoria, and I sat before the cemetery manager to fill out the paperwork for his crypt, we were asked his name. In unison, we each replied *with authority.* Only she said "Gung Jue Wong," and I said "Hon Way Wong." When we saw the puzzled look on the manager's face, we both corrected ourselves by uttering with cocky certainty: "Henry H. W. Wong." The same sitcom response occurred when we were asked his date of birth. I can't recall who said what, but each of us had a different answer. Seeing the manager become concerned, Victoria and I quietly conferred, and, as if trying to win a rousing round of the TV game show *Family Feud*, we compromised on the date that is carved into his crypt stone. If anyone were to ask me the same question as one of those pesky security questions, I probably would fail the test. Just like my father "failed" the Angel Island test when he arrived in San Francisco from Toishan.

Now that we think about it, my father never spoke to us about his Angel Island experience. But as we learn more about what he endured at Angel Island and how he survived by writing poetry and daydreaming about what he would achieve in America, we begin to see how his personality was influenced by that year of captivity, deprivation, and isolation from family and friends. As my sister, Victoria, recalls: "We see why in later years, despite his fervent political 'anti-Communist' stand in the 1950s, he would do left-leaning, bleeding-heart things like bring home a hobo, and he didn't seem to notice if they were Black, white, Latino, or Native American." He would invite them to stay with us for a short time, do odd jobs, and sit at our dinner table (sometimes even when money was meager, and my mom had to dream up amazingly yummy concoctions such as spam with soy sauce spaghetti and stretch a small can of Pillsbury butter-flake biscuits into a cake to feed a family of seven).

Given how he came to America as a teen, was held at Angel Island for nearly a year, then traveled back and forth between China and the United States in what would be the normal education years, it's amazing how well educated he was in Chinese history, philosophy, and culture. Victoria remembers how the curator of a major Chinese exhibit at the Asian Art Museum in San Francisco was so delighted by his exhaustive knowledge that she had Dad spend the day at Golden Gate Park singing the songs/poems for each of the paintings on exhibit, as she and other "experts" didn't know the accompanying music for these ancient works of art.

How he knew all this was something we took for granted, as if his love and knowledge of such matters were simply embedded in his DNA. But his skill at composing songs and poetry and putting them down in gorgeous calligraphy was well known among the Chinese community. He became the go-to guy for writing couplets for weddings, funerals, and other events. He also was known for his ability to create Chinese names that really nailed the personalities of friends and family, even those who weren't Chinese. I sometimes think that my career in marketing/branding came from inheriting some of those genes and watching/listening as he created just-right names with compact and apt meanings.

As Victoria notes, he was a true Chinese scholar but also a contradiction in that he loved working with his hands, which Chinese aristocrats would NEVER do. But Dad was never ashamed of his calloused and dirty-fingernailed hands or his sun-darkened skin from toiling as a farmer and, later, as an agricultural inspector for the state of California.

Our dad also played an active role in Chinese politics. At one time, he headed the national Wong Family Association and was also very involved with the Bing Kung Tong. But there is another episode in his life that reveals more about the never-ending conflict between his soulful side and his business urges. For a few years, he and our mom moved from Salinas to San Francisco to live out his dream of being a film and opera impresario when they took over the legendary Palace Theater in the Chinatown–North Beach district. Victoria remembers how Dad single-handedly renovated the Palace and its adjoining dressing rooms. Of course the concession stand went from featuring popcorn and candy to being well stocked with Chinese favorites such as watermelon seeds and stinky dried squid. Later, out of financial necessity, they shared the theater with the infamously wild Nocturnal Dream Shows featuring the Cockettes.

When that venture became too unwieldy and a victim of changing entertainment tastes, he and my mom moved back to Salinas and took jobs at a friend's supermarket. For the first time, he was employed in a steady job with a guaranteed paycheck, which relieved my mom and the rest of us. But I see now that this probably contributed to his restlessness and frustration, as he began to build a new dream about creating a dim sum empire, which was never realized.

But while he may have considered that a failure, we—his kids—look at his other achievements and what he instilled most in us: "a relentless belief in the American dream that a better life is possible, NO MATTER WHAT," as my brother Michael pointed out at Dad's funeral. Victoria adds, "He infused us with an unshakable pride in our Chinese heritage with which he fought white racism. He never felt or acted inferior to anyone due to race, nationality, or wealth, and by example, he showed us how to stand up for ourselves."

Maybe our dad was crazy. Maybe he never adapted to the realities of American life. Maybe he could've achieved more in business. Maybe he should never have left his beloved China. (He told us from his hospital bed that he wanted to go back to his ancestral village to die.) Maybe he could've been a more easygoing husband and father. But maybe, just maybe, his heart was so filled with ancient dreams and songs that he couldn't help but listen to them above all else. In combination with our salt-of-the-earth mother, he helped to make us who and what we are. And for that, as his children, we are most grateful.

Edwar Lee, Interpreter:
"A Certain Amount of Fairness"

Editor's note: Through the Chinatown grapevine, we managed to find two Chinese interpreters to interview in the 1970s. Edwar Lee was one of them. Born in San Francisco Chinatown in 1902, he was the third son in a close-knit family of nine children. His father was an herb doctor, and his mother, a well-educated woman from Shanghai. Lee was a charter member of Troop Three, the first Chinese Boy Scout troop in the United States, and the first American-born Chinese to become a Methodist minister. He earned a B.A. degree from the College of the Pacific and a master's degree in political economics from the University of California, Berkeley. But unable to find employment in any white American firm, he decided to accept the position of Chinese interpreter at the Angel Island Immigration Station. Lee worked there from 1927 until 1938, when he resigned to become the full-time pastor of the Oakland Chinese United Methodist Church.

Lee cofounded the Chinese Christian Youth Conference at Lake Tahoe and the National Conference of Chinese Churches in America and was the first Asian American minister to be appointed superintendent of the Oriental Provisional Conference. Drawing from his work experience at Angel Island, he started two Methodist agencies to assist Chinese war brides and refugees who were resettling in the Bay Area after World War II. In recognition of his achievements in overcoming prejudice within the church and his service to the Chinese community, the University of the Pacific awarded him an honorary doctorate of divinity degree in 1952. Rev. Edwar Lee retired in 1970 but remained an active member of the church and many community service groups until he died in 1996.

The following story about his experiences and insights as an immigration interpreter at Angel Island is based on two oral history interviews and his biography, *Growing Up in Chinatown*.[1]

1 Edwar Lee interviews; Moonbeam Tong Lee, *Growing Up in Chinatown.*

I had just graduated from UC Berkeley with a master's degree in political

FIG. 3.25
Immigration employees in front of
the administration building, 1937.
Edwar Lee is in the fourth row,
fourth from right. Courtesy of
California State Parks, 2014.

economics and was looking for a job. I tried several commercial firms without success. I was told either that the job had been filled or that it was against company policy to hire Orientals. Deaconess Katharine Maurer, whom I had befriended through my student pastor work at Chinese Methodist missions, asked if I would like to work for the Immigration Service, and I said yes, I'd give it a try. So she made an appointment for me to see the head inspector, Mr. P. B. Jones. I went over to Angel Island, met him for an interview, and was immediately hired. The main selection criterion at that time was one's competence in handling the different Chinese dialects. Having grown up in Chinatown and taught English to Chinese immigrants, I could converse in Sze Yup, Sam Yup, and the Chungshan dialects with ease.[2] So that's how I landed the job as interpreter, not knowing that I would stay there for the next ten years. In those days, there wasn't a ghost of a chance for a Chinese to be an inspector, even if you had a very high education. I knew there was racial discrimination in the whole system, but I still felt that I could render a service to the government and to Chinese immigrants as well.

In the heyday, there were nine Chinese interpreters, and we all commuted. I was living in Berkeley. Every morning, I would walk two blocks to catch the train to the pier, take the ferry over to San Francisco, and walk over to Pier 5 to catch the 8:30 government cutter over to Angel Island. We would begin work at 9:00 or 10:00, take a lunch break, quit at 4:30, and get back to San Francisco by 5:00. We did that five days a week. It was a pretty

2 The Sze Yup districts include Sunwui, Toishan, Hoiping, and Yanping, and the Sam Yup districts include Namhoi, Punyu, and Shuntak (see map on p. 5).

good job. The starting salary was $130 per month, compared to $30 for Chinatown grocery clerks at the time. We weren't considered part of civil service until the 1930s, so we had no pensions and could be fired summarily. But we were given thirty days of sick leave. There was quite a bit of camaraderie among the interpreters, but very little between the interpreters and the inspectors for the obvious reason that we didn't want people to think we were in cahoots with them. All the years I was with the service, I never once attended their annual picnic.

No one interpreter sat throughout the same case. Because they were afraid of collusion between the interpreters and the applicants, they assigned one case to two or three interpreters. One interpreter would translate for the father, another one for the son, and another one for the mother. That could extend a case to one day, two days, or three days. The length of time all depended on whether the case was complicated or not. They would ask for names of relatives, how many houses in the village, different aspects of village life, what the applicant had been doing in China, and so on. Sometimes there was a contradiction between the father's and son's testimonies, and then they would have to call the father back from San Francisco. It depended also on the inspector, whether he was long-winded, drawn-out, and detailed. There were some inspectors who could, if they sensed something was wrong, get right on to it. They got through a case very fast. It took longer to take care of a doubleheader—a mother and son coming as newcomers—or tripleheader—three in the family. The father may already have had some sons over here, so the sons would serve as corroborating witnesses. Or sometimes a friend or fellow villager would be a witness. So you had to take testimonies from two or three persons representing the petitioner. Then you had to interrogate the applicant—one or two times or even more. If the only witness lived out of town, like in New York or Chicago, they took the testimony out of the New York office or the Chicago office. That's why it took a lot of time adjudicating some of these cases.

The applicants were all pretty young, because by the very nature of it, claiming to be sons and daughters of natives or merchants, you couldn't apply once you turned twenty-one. If it was a wife of a merchant, she could be any age. But nobody's going to bring in an old woman. During the interrogation, some were very calm and nonchalant. You asked a question, they answered. Then there were some who were very nervous, so I generally told them to just calm down and take their time answering. Some were a little hotheaded, with a chip on the shoulder. "Why should you ask me all these questions?" and so on. In general, I think it was remarkable that the applicants, kids and women, were rather stoical. They took it matter-of-factly, knowing that they could always appeal the case and finally be landed.

One time, a Chinese woman who was a prostitute applied for admission. She came over on first class. Because there was a "knocking letter"[3] filed against her, they detained her. Usually first-class passengers were landed from the boat. But they took her over to the island and gave her a very exhaustive examination. And this woman physically attacked the inspector. She was that angry with the number of questions asked of her and all the damaging evidence in the knocking letter. This was the only time in all the years I was there that I saw a Chinese woman attack an inspector. Needless to say, she was deported.

The interrogations were so tedious, in such minute detail, that you were bound to trip. Let me give you a humorous situation. I think it was a case of a tripleheader. A mother and two kids came in at the same time, and a question by the inspector was: "Is there a dog in the house?" If you lived in the same house, you would know whether there's a dog or not, especially if the dog is your pet. So the mother said, "Yes, we have a dog." And another son, "Yes, we have a dog." And the third son, "No, no dog." So they called in the mother again, and the son, and they both said, "Yes, yes, we had a dog." And the other son was called in again. "Did you say that you have a dog in the house?" "Oh, we had a dog, but we ate that dog before we left. No dog!" Well, this was true. By the time he left home, there was no dog. Otherwise, it would be a very serious discrepancy if you lived in the same household and two said there's a dog and the other one said no.

The Board of Special Inquiry consisted of one inspector who was the chairman, a second inspector, and the stenographer who took down all the testimony and had decision-making power. The interpreter didn't count in the ruling. We just interpreted what the applicant said or what was asked. But we did render an opinion as to that person's dialect. Because if I said the son spoke in the Chungshan dialect and another interpreter said the father spoke in the Toishan dialect, immediately, the inspector would smell a rat. And then, of course, the inspector would also make a judgment as to family resemblance, and that went into the record. This was very important because the appeal was often based on the fact that there was a close resemblance.

Most of the time, the board was unanimous in their decision to land or deny admission into the country. Once in a long while, you would have a second member who disagreed with the chairman. At the end of the hearing, he would be allowed to state his reason for disagreeing. I remember one time a woman stenographer disagreed with the two inspectors, and she was in tears arguing with the chairman. She thought that the inspectors had been rather prejudiced against the applicant, so she voted to dissent. So even the stenographer had the right to question the applicant and rule in the case, but we interpreters didn't have a voice whatsoever.

3   An anonymous letter sent to immigration officials about an illegal entry.

By and large, I think the inspectors were good people. Most were very fair-minded and impartial, like one old man, George Washington Kenney. He said, "I don't care if he is a fake. If he can pass my examination, he lands and good luck to him!" Well, that's fair. After all, he answered all the questions correctly. Then there were some who were very technical, very prejudiced, who had no love for the Chinese. They would go out of their way to trip you up and deny you admission. Working there day in and day out, and asking the same questions all the time, they got very impatient and irritable, and some were not as kind as they should've been toward these new immigrants.

I remember one case. Someone came on a birth certificate and landed. Another person came and claimed the same identity and that he was born in this country, but that his birth certificate had been stolen. He was denied admission, but Washington[, D.C.,] sustained his appeal on the grounds that he might've been the true one. The first one that came may have really stolen his paper. Then a third one came claiming the same thing, that the first two were false. So it was brought up to the U.S. district court, and he was also landed. The court proceeded on the standpoint that no matter how many were fraudulent, one person was true, and it had not been proven that this third person was not true. So there was a certain amount of fairness in all this.

Surprisingly, I don't remember any breakdowns when detainees were told their case had been denied. But there was one case of suicide while I was there, over in the women's quarters. This woman was destined for Chicago. She brought in a real son and a ringer. It was clear in my mind that one of them was a ringer. So this woman, when told her case was denied, felt that the whole thing was washed up, that she might be deported back to China, a most terrible shame. So she sharpened a chopstick and stuck it in her brain through the ear. Died immediately. And even before Washington had a chance to deliberate on the case, the commissioner phoned Washington about the suicide. So promptly the word came, "Land them." So they landed the two sons.

I would say at least half of the cases were denied. Look at it this way. For each boat that arrived, you had ninety-five sons against one daughter. So you know that a lot of them were false. We might as well admit it. But 60 to 70 percent of the cases that were appealed to Washington were sustained, usually on the grounds that the questions were unfair or too prejudiced. That's before blood tests were done. It was just based on how well you did at the interrogation. If you passed, you were landed.[4]

It didn't happen often, but I do remember a case or two of someone asking me to bribe the inspector, and I said, "Oh, no, no, no. Don't waste

4   Our research shows that 9 percent of the Chinese applicants were rejected, 88 percent appealed their cases, and 55 percent of the appeals were successful. See table 2 in the appendix.

your money!" Sometimes it was very awkward when you were offered a bribe. You told them you didn't want the money, and they'd turn around and say it was because you felt it was too little, or they'd accuse you of being uncooperative and having no love for country or countryman. But we had to protect ourselves against accusations from applicants. It was generally the *bao wai*, the broker who took care of the case, who told them, "I have to give money to the inspector and the interpreter." But actually, he pocketed the money and just hoped the case would get through. If it didn't, he told them it was because the money wasn't enough.

I remember I once went to Gilroy to hear a case involving an herbalist who wanted to bring his wife in as a merchant's wife. So we had the hearing in his store. It was during wintertime and I had a big overcoat. I was in the store a long time, so I took my overcoat off and laid it on the counter. And he said, "I'll hang it up for you." So he took it to the back of the store and hung it up. When I left the store, I found this money in my pocket. Not much—$20, I remember. Well, I couldn't account for it and I couldn't tell the inspector that I had received this $20, because I would only jeopardize that case if I said so. But I never asked for the bribe. It was just tea money—they hoped you would put in a good word for them.

Our interpreting services were used in other situations, like scanning mail for coaching notes or investigating cases in the community. I remember once being asked to smooth things out after a food riot. You see, the concessionaire only received so much money from the steamship company to pay for the board of these people until they were released, sometimes for six weeks, two months, or even three months. So naturally, the company tried to pay as little as possible to the concessionaire to feed the people. This concessionaire then hired the Chinese staff and tried to think of the cheapest meal they could produce. Another problem was that the kitchen was designed for serving American food or large quantities for the army. So they had a lot of steamers instead of woks. You can imagine the difficult situation. No wok to cook Chinese food. And then they would buy the cheapest grade of rice and steam it in these big steamers. So the detainees got mad and started a riot. That's when they sent us in to calm everyone down.

There's no question in my mind that the Chinese immigrants who came through Angel Island went through quite an ordeal. It was a very harrowing experience for them to be cooped up in close quarters for long periods of time. Their cases usually didn't come up for a hearing for at least two weeks, and if they were denied, their wait on the appeal might take anywhere from three months to six months. And all that time, they were in a very sad situation. It was all because of the Chinese Exclusion Act. You'd think the government could think of a better way of handling these immigrants. But

FIG. 3.26
The Reverend Edwar Lee was
pastor of the Oakland Chinese
United Methodist Church from
1935 to 1970. Courtesy of Joyce
Horowitz.

the inspectors by and large felt, "We didn't ask them to come to this country. They themselves applied for admission to this country, so it's only right that they prove they have a right to come into the country." On the part of the Chinese, they realized that while the immigration laws and policies discriminated against them, their chances of landing on final appeal were very good, so they were willing to put up with it. Actually, the present system is best. Why bring them over to this country, give them a hearing, and then deny them entry? Why go through all that heartache, expense, and everything else? Predetermine the case in Hong Kong—that's the best solution.

Helen Hong Wong:
"No Gold to Be Picked Up"

Editor's note: I first met and interviewed Helen Hong Wong (aka Yuen Lan Heung) in 1982 for an exhibit about the history of Chinese women in America. A petite and spry woman of seventy-four years, Helen immigrated to the United States in 1928 as a newlywed with dreams of making it rich in Gold Mountain. To circumvent the Chinese exclusion laws, she had to pose as a member of the exempt classes, as a paper daughter traveling to Paris with her father and brother, who were really her husband and cousin, respectively. She had a good memory for details and was quite candid about her experiences at Angel Island and her hardworking life afterward in small midwestern towns.

When she left home for the United States, Helen had promised her mother that she would return in ten years, but she was unable to do so until 1965. By then, her mother had passed away. Although she never realized her Gold Mountain dream of a life of wealth and leisure, she nevertheless found fulfillment in her work and family. Helen made her home in Chicago, where she lived to be ninety-three. The following story is based on my interview and numerous interviews conducted by Helen's daughter Nellie Leong from 1992 to 2001.[1]

I was born in Hom Gong village in Sunwui District in 1908. My *gung* [paternal grandfather] and father owned a hemp business in the nearby town of Nam How. The Chans and the Lums were feuding, and we were caught in the middle. As a result, our house was burned down in a fire and we had to escape to *jou poh*'s [maternal grandmother's] home in Oy Hoi. We didn't have much money, just put some bedding and clothes in some large baskets and had some hired hands help us carry them to *jou poh*'s. I was only four months old and my brother was two.

When I was seven, we moved to Hong Kong, where we had a hard life. My father worked at a furniture store and only made a few dollars a day, so

1   Helen Hong Wong interviews. An earlier version of this story was published in Yung, Chang, and Lai, *Chinese American Voices*, 157–64.

FIG. 3.27
Helen Hong Wong (aka Yuen
Lan Heung) in Hong Kong, 1928.
Courtesy of Linelle Marshall.

we could only afford to rent one room for the four of us. Then carne my baby sister. I had to help my mother fetch water, wash clothes, cook meals, and carry the baby. My brother got to go to school, and he became a carpenter's apprentice at sixteen. They were just starting to educate girls, but my mother would not let me go to school. There was no time and no money. After dinner, I had to help make rattan chairs. Since my mother had bound feet and couldn't go out, I had to do all the shopping as well. So there was no time to play, hardly any time to sleep.

I lived in Hong Kong until I got married at twenty and left for America. A friend of my old man [husband Harry Wong] who played mahjong with my father introduced us. He was a *Gam Saan haak* and had a restaurant business in Fort Wayne, Indiana. He said he made $200 a day in America. My father asked me if I wanted to marry him. I thought about how poor we were, sleeping on wooden planks and with hardly enough food to eat. Where we lived, I could see the harbor where many of the big ships docked. Every time I heard the tooting of a ship, I would watch all the *Gam Saan poh* [Gold Mountain wives] get off the ship, wearing all their jewelry and followed by their *mui nui* [slave girls]. I thought Gold Mountain must be a nice place. So I didn't answer my father. If he told me to go, I would go.

My husband was fifty years old when he returned home to retire. But after two years of living in Gong Moon, he was called back to Fort Wayne [Indiana] by his uncle to help with the restaurant business. By then, his immigration papers had expired and he had to go to Hong Kong to fix the problem. This he did by acquiring the identity and papers of Lee Wai Mun, a forty-five-year-old merchant who was supposedly traveling to Europe with his sixteen-year-old daughter, Lee Heung, and eleven-year-old son, Lee Sam. After our wedding, I was to go to America with him, posing as the daughter, and my cousin Lum Sam, as the son.

We came together on the *Tenyo Maru*. It took twenty-one days, during which time I wasn't seasick at all. There were many Chinese, but most of them traveled in steerage. We had second-class tickets, so we had a private cabin for three and were allowed to go on deck and eat in the first-class dining room. We never missed a meal—breakfast in our room at 6:00, a second breakfast in the dining room at 8:00, lunch at 12:00, tea at 3:00, dinner at 6:00, and evening snack at 9:00. My husband pretended that he was a new immigrant who did not understand any English. But he didn't fool any of the waiters, who all remarked that he dressed, acted, and used his knife and fork like an American.

When we got to San Francisco, we thought we were going to be inspected on the ship. But it was a Saturday, so we had to go to Angel Island instead. My husband and Sam stayed in the men's barracks, while I stayed in the women's barracks. We all answered wrong at the immigration hearing. They were very strict then, and we had not prepared for the interrogation. They asked all kinds of questions, about the type of stove we used in the village, the tiles on the floor, even how many steps in the stairs. I had lived in Hong Kong all those years and didn't remember anything about the village. They asked where things were in the kitchen and your lineage going back three generations. How could anyone remember all that?

Because we failed the interrogation, they would not let us land. So we had to appeal the case. I was stuck there from the end of November to the beginning of January the next year. I still remember the Jesus woman [Deaconess Katharine Maurer] bringing us each a parcel at Christmas that contained some cloth, a toothbrush, towel, and some candy. There was a woman from Heungshan who had to stay there for three years with her son and daughter. Her husband made the mistake of mentioning his first wife's name. When she saw the Christmas tree again, she said she had seen it three times. Three times, can you imagine that?

Editor's note: According to Lee Wah Mun's immigration file, the father was a bona fide merchant with $2,000 in gold and a traveler's certificate. He and his son and daughter were visitors in transit to Paris. Six days after they arrived at Angel Island, they were called before a Board of Special Inquiry, and each was interrogated twice about their family background, living arrangements in Canton, and the children's schooling. The father and daughter were ill prepared. He contradicted the information on his traveler's certificate, and there were a number of discrepancies in their testimonies regarding their living quarters, the death dates of the wife and mother, and the birthdate of the son. The daughter answered "I don't know" to many of the questions. They were summarily excluded on the grounds that the father had failed to establish his status as a bona fide visitor and the children had failed to establish their statuses as the son and daughter of a temporary visitor. The father opted to appeal the decision to the secretary of labor in Washington, D.C., during which time the family was detained on Angel Island for more than a month.[2]

The women's barracks where I stayed was one big room with three tiers of beds. We only used the bottom two tiers. Young children generally stayed with the mothers and slept in the bottom beds. Everyone got along. There were people from Sunwui, Heungshan, and Toishan. There were very few women then, but every ship always had a few that failed the interrogation. We weren't allowed visitors, couldn't talk to anyone or receive any mail or packages directly. They were afraid of coaching notes being sneaked in. The matron called out, "Chow, chow!" when it was time to eat. Every time we went downstairs to the big dining hall, a *fan gwai* would stand by the door to watch us, afraid that the kitchen staff might sneak us coaching notes. They were known to hide coaching notes under the plates of food. You would take the note upstairs and read it in the bathroom. Then you would light a match, burn it, and flush it away.

There was a long table with two dishes of food at each end of the table. Do you know what it was? Usually steamed pork with *gam jum* [golden needles] or *gai choy* [mustard greens] and pork. People helped themselves to as much food as they wanted. An extra dish like fried ham and eggs cost 25 cents. Or if you were lucky, friends might send some canned fish or deli food from San Francisco.

We stayed mostly in the breezeway while watching the younger ones play ball outside. There were musical instruments, bird-watching, sewing, and lots of things to do. The Jesus woman was willing to go shopping for us. I had her buy me some material so I could do some sewing by hand. Time passed quickly. We had three meals every day. Then we would wait to hear when we would be landed. There were always people arriving and leaving. Those who answered right could go to the city; those who answered wrong couldn't. Some stayed years, like the woman who said she had seen the Christmas tree three times. During the time we were there, there was a woman who got deported. That was considered very sad because so much money had been spent.

Editor's note: On December 31, 1928, the family was admitted into the country for six months under a departure bond costing $500 per person. According to a letter in their immigration file dated January 9, 1930, "the aliens had disappeared leaving no trace." They were not found until 1952,

2   File 27442/2–4 (Lee Wai Mun), Immigration Arrival Investigation Case Files, RG 85, NARA-SF.

when they were threatened with deportation. According to Helen, after they were released from Angel Island, the couple took a train to Chicago, stayed there for a week, and then went to live in Fort Wayne. Her husband took back his real name—Harry Wong—soon after they were landed. Her American name—Helen—was given to her by her daughters when she applied for naturalization in 1956.

There were very few Chinese in Fort Wayne then, just two restaurants and two laundries run by bachelors. I was the only Chinese woman. There was no one for me to socialize with, and I felt lonely as a result. We lived upstairs above the Cozy Inn Restaurant, which served both Chinese and American cuisine. Almost as soon as I arrived, I put on an apron and went down to help peel potatoes, cut vegetables, wash rice, do the dishes, everything. I was young then and didn't feel it was hard work. When I had free time, I took my daughter Lillian, who was a year old, with me and went browsing in the dime store. No one bothered me. Fort Wayne had an open marketplace on Tuesdays, Thursdays, and Saturdays. So at night, I would go there and walk around. After I had the second daughter, Nellie, I didn't go out as much.

FIG. 3.28
Helen Hong Wong working in Fort Wayne, Indiana, 1930. Courtesy of Linelle Marshall.

When we first arrived, the restaurant business wasn't bad. We made $200 during the lunch hour alone. But then came the Depression and things got difficult. People had no jobs and no money to spend. We made only $2 during lunchtime. A year later, we closed the restaurant because we couldn't pay the rent. We moved to Chicago for a year. The federal government was giving out corned beef, cabbage, potatoes, and bread to needy families, but my old man was afraid to go stand in line. Instead, he went to Chinatown and borrowed money from the gamblers. A one-hundred-pound bag of rice only cost 80 cents, but we couldn't even afford that.

We rented a flat with six rooms for $19, but there was no electricity. Even when my son William was born, we couldn't afford it. We could only afford one bushel of coal for the week. During the winter, the windows were all frosty and we closed all the doors and stayed in one room by the open

After her husband died in 1943, Helen Hong Wong (seated) moved to Chicago with her four children. Left to right: Betsy, Lillian, Nellie, and William. Courtesy of Linelle Marshall.

furnace. We wore multiple layers of clothes, and I wrapped the two girls in blankets. It got to be 40 degrees in the house. A year later, a friend opened a laundry, and we moved to Anderson, Indiana, to work for him. That's how we got into the laundry business.

We lived above his laundry in two rooms. Our fourth child, Betsy, was born in Anderson. I helped out with the washing, pressing, and ironing. It was hard work, long hours. We did everything ourselves. We worked Monday through Saturday, even Sunday if we didn't finish on time, or I would clean house on Sunday. We did this for four years. Then his nephew carne from Hong Kong and caused trouble, so we left and went to Kokomo, Indiana, to open our own laundry.

Kokomo was a small town about one hundred miles away. We lived on the premises again. Business was so-so. We started making $20 a week, and that grew to $100 a week. It was still hard work from morning to night, washing and ironing one hundred shirts a day. If we got behind, no Sunday off, no time to sleep. I helped at the front when someone came to pick up laundry. Even though I couldn't read, I knew how to find the package by the number. There was no time for anything else, only time to go get my hair cut. Again, we did this for four years. Then their father [Harry] died. It was wartime, and there was no one around to hire. I couldn't do it alone, so we moved to Chicago to live and work for his [Harry's] granduncle.

I worked at his store, the Dong Kee Bakery. I only made $20 a month working more than ten hours a day. After work, I had to do all the cooking and housework, but the kids helped out. I stayed there for about eight years, from 1944 to 1952. It wasn't a better or worse job, just a matter of having enough to eat and a place to live. There wasn't anything to put in the bank. But whenever I could, I would send money home to my family in Hong Kong.

I left the bakery to go work for Nabisco cookies, folding boxes and packing cookies. An Italian neighbor introduced me to the job. I was the second Chinese woman to be hired. Everyone was good to me, called me "Mama, Mama." They asked me why I never complained to the union. There really was no reason to. I took the bus to the west side at 5:10 a.m. in the winter, 5:30 a.m. in the summer. I had to take three buses. I worked until 3:15 p.m. It was only 75 cents an hour when I started, but the white employers always give you better working conditions—raises, insurance, vacation benefits. By the time I got home and had dinner, I was tired and went straight to bed. I did this for twenty-nine years. When I retired in 1977, they threw me a big party.

Life has been better for me in America, but I must admit that my Gold Mountain dream was never fulfilled. Instead of becoming a rich *Gam Saan poh*, I ended up working like a slave. When I came in 1928, things were cheap. String beans were 2 cents a pound; pork chops were 25 cents for three pounds. But no one had any money to spend, and there was no food in the house. We didn't know any better at the time, only that we saw these *Gam Saan poh* with their jewelry, fine clothes, and *mui nui*. So we assumed life was easy in Gold Mountain. But there was no gold to be picked up. Instead, all we found was hard work.

Jann Mon Fong:
A Gold Mountain Man's Monologue

TRANSLATED BY MARLON K. HOM

Editor's note: Jann Mon Fong (aka Smiley Jann) was born on July 9, 1913, in Pong Tou village, Longdu, Heungshan District. He was the only son in a family of four children. Jann completed eight years of schooling before he found a way to fulfill his dream of reaching Gold Mountain. He bought papers to immigrate as Sue Sow Fong, the son of a U.S. native, Sue Chong On. In 1931, Jann boarded the *President McKinley*, bound for San Francisco. Upon arrival, he came to a rude awakening when his hopes for a better life were dashed by the "cruel treatment" he received at Angel Island. His three-week confinement there so angered him that he decided to write home about it. "I wanted my classmates to know that America is not as great as everyone thinks, that we actually suffered a great deal of humiliation," he said many years later.[1] His essay, "A Gold Mountain Man's Monologue," sat on his desk for four years before he decided to send it, not realizing that his friends in Shanghai would submit it to the journal *Renjian Shi* (People's world).[2] It is a rare and emotional firsthand account of how one Chinese immigrant responded to his imprisonment at Angel Island. It is also one of the earliest publications of the Angel Island poems, as Jann thought to include five of the poems in his essay.

We were lucky to have been able to interview Smiley Jann in 1976, because he not only called our attention to this essay but also shared his notebook of ninety-nine poems that he had carefully copied from the barracks walls when he was detained there. "The poems were written all over the walls at Angel Island, wherever the hand could reach, even in the lavatories," he told us. Jann remembered feeling overwhelmed with grief and bitterness as he copied them. "They are not great poems," he said, "but they express real feelings."

Whenever there was an air-horn-blasting, foreign steamship arriving at port, there would be our countrymen among the passengers returning

1   Smiley Jann interview.
2   Jann Mon Fong's essay was published in *Renjian Shi*, March 5, 1935, 15–16.

home after striking it rich in foreign soil. Their suitcases were filled with foreign dollars that would enable them to purchase all the comforts they needed for their triumphant homecoming. They would also speak of the sights and sounds of Gold Mountain and show off their riches. This was indeed the envy of everyone. I, too, could not resist that envy and temptation of wealth and for some time had so wished for the opportunity to go overseas.

Time passed, and without realizing it, I had become a young adult. Money also became a desperately needed commodity in those years of worldwide depression. My mind was preoccupied with the thought of leaving home to seek a living. Three years ago, at the time of the summer solstice when apricots were ripening, I spent a huge sum of money in silver dollars to buy a slot to come to America. By next summer when the lychees were in season, I left home, bidding farewell to my beloved parents.

It took only a few hours to get to Hong Kong from Chungshan. But the U.S. consulate in Hong Kong dictated that all U.S.-bound Chinese people must report at least half a month in advance for pre-departure immunizations and the physical examination. It was done, as they said, so that we would go to the wonderfully sanitized United States with a clean and healthy body, after clearing all the dirty and harmful substances inside our bodies. For the sake of economic advancement in America, and like all my fellow countrymen, I subjected myself to this ridiculous process. Still, I didn't comprehend the implications behind it.

After braving the winds and waves for twenty days, the ship finally docked. The returning Gold Mountain old-timers left the pier soon after their immigration inspection. We, the newcomers, were transferred by a small boat to an island located inside the Golden Gate, which was, as told by old-timers, the immigration detention center for all incoming Chinese immigrants.

The moment we were put on the small boat, we lost all our freedom. The Americans treated us like cattle. Those green-eyed people must have thought Chinese were the offspring of pigs and goats. Carrying a cloth bundle on my back and a suitcase in my hand, I was herded into the detention center under their wolflike authority. Tears flowed down my face. Fight back? Not a chance. How could I, since I had yet to learn their language upon arrival in their land?

First, we were put inside a small room surrounded with barbed wire. Their intention was obvious, but they claimed it had to be done as they re-

FIG. 3.30
Smiley Jann (aka Jann Mon Fong), 1932. Courtesy of Arliss Jann.

FIG. 3.31
Smiley Jann and his family
in front of their house in San
Francisco, 1955. Left to right:
Smiley Jann with his wife,
Mildred; daughter, Dale; and
sons, Citron, Arliss, and Michael.
Courtesy of Arliss Jann.

3   As a rule, guards did not
    carry weapons at the im-
    migration station except
    during a period in the 1930s
    when federal prisoners were
    temporarily housed there.

ported our arrival to their superior officers. At that moment, I was saddened by the realization that my country and my people were powerless, and that I, myself, was facing an unknown and uncertain future. Now we went from being treated like a herd of cattle to being treated like hapless birds confined to a cage, ready for slaughter.

On that first day, we had breakfast before daybreak, and it wasn't until evening that we heard the call for supper. I didn't feel hungry all day, probably because I was full from being fed up with the cruel treatment there. Soon we were led into a huge prison. The moment we were all inside, they locked the door tightly. I found my bunk. Several fellow countrymen who had been detained there for some time asked me to join the Self-governing Association that had been established by the Chinese detainees. About two hundred of us detainees attended the meeting, during which the association officers told us the rules and regulations.

We were subject to yet another physical examination the next day, and the procedure, targeting our entire race, was particularly humiliating. The physician ordered us to disrobe and bear the chilly sea breeze for hours. He felt our chest and spine and ordered us to jump around like monkeys. I was not sure if this was a physical examination or, rather, an act of insult. Well, it was said that my treatment was actually light and easy. In the past, they would draw blood from our flesh to test for hookworm disease.

In the Self-governing Association office were a phonograph, some record albums, and fiction books. There was also a small playground outside the detention barracks. Like the dormitory, it was also surrounded by barbed wire. The Caucasian guards kept the key to the playground's gate. In fact, there were armed guards on patrol both inside and outside the detention barracks.[3] Don't ever think of trying to escape; they would send you off to another world. For the Chinese held up there, there was little if any freedom accorded them!

All over the walls of the dormitory were numerous scribbling of poems, rhymes, ditties, and parallel couplets written by Chinese detainees. Being idle there, I copied them down verbatim in a notebook without any editorial changes. Here are a few examples [see poems 128, 94, 16, 83, and 111].

These writings are the testimonies of hardship on their journey to America. Among these writings are references to suicides due to frustration and humiliation. As I was copying them from the walls, I was overwhelmed with grief and sorrow. I wrote the following in response to what I saw on the walls [poem 18]:

When I left, my parents regretted it was so hurried.
The reason I tearfully swallow my resentment is because of poverty.
Wishing to escape permanent poverty, I fled overseas.
Who caused my destiny to be so perverse that I would become
    imprisoned?
Victims of aggression, the people of our nation mourn the desperate
    times.
I feel sorely guilty for having not yet repaid my parents' kindness.
The chirping insects moan in the cold night.
Not only do I sob silently, but my throat tastes bitter.

Altogether, I spent twenty days in detention at the wooden barracks, two of which were for interrogation and deposition.[4] On the afternoon of the twentieth day, I was ferried out, and I finally landed in this place erroneously called since my childhood years the heavenly "Gold Mountain."

Perhaps we should think this over: We are dealt all this difficulty and adversity when going to another's country. Yet, when they come to our country, why do they behave so superior on our home soil?

Editor's note: After he was landed, Jann Mon Fong adopted the name Smiley Jann and forged ahead with his life in America. He started out in Santa Barbara, California, where he worked in a relative's dry goods store and, later, as a houseboy for a wealthy family while he attended high school. In 1938, Jann returned to San Francisco, where he found a job as a waiter and married Mildred Lee. They had four children. For a brief period, he tried farming in Loomis, California. Then he settled on the grocery business, operating the West Side Market in San Francisco for more than thirty years. Jann broke the racial barrier when he became the first Chinese member of the San Francisco Wholesale Grocers Association. He was an officer of the Tung Sen Benevolent Association and helped establish a scholarship program for its members. "My feeling is that if I can't achieve my goal of success, the second generation will," he told us.[5]

Smiley Jann took pride in seeing all four of his children graduate from college and become successful dentists, a teacher, and a computer programmer. But he never once mentioned Angel Island to them, not even after he

4   According to Jann's alien file, his alleged father, alleged sister, and he were thoroughly investigated. They were interrogated for days and asked a total of 455 questions about their family background and the layouts of their house and village. Jann was able to answer all their questions with confidence, even as to how many children his mother's younger brother had, what the floors in their house were made of, when his sister started bobbing her hair, and whether his mother had any gold in her teeth. The summary report indicated that their testimonies were in "good agreement" and each of them had shown "excellent demeanor" throughout the examination. Alien File A11814436 (Sue Sow Fong), obtained via Freedom of Information Act request to the U.S. Citizenship and Immigration Services.

5   Smiley Jann interview.

voluntarily participated in the Confession Program and cleared his name in 1959 so that he could become a U.S. citizen in 1963.[6] According to his son Arliss, "We did not even know that he had gone through the Confession Program until he said we are changing our last names from Sue to Jann."[7] Nothing more was said, but the children did notice that following this incident, their father was able to return to China periodically for visits. Smiley Jann passed away in 1997 at the age of eighty-four, leaving behind his notebook of Angel Island poems, which he titled "A Collection of Autumn Grass: Voices from the Hearts of the Weak."

6   According to the FBI investigation on June 2, 1959, Jann admitted to his fraudulent entry in 1931 and named members of his paper family and his real family. After a brief interview and a criminal background check, he was granted permanent residency as Smiley Mon Fong Jann. See Alien File A11814436.

7   Arliss Jann, e-mail correspondence with Judy Yung, July 18, 2009.

Xie Chuang:
Imprisonment at Angel Island

TRANSLATED BY CHARLES EGAN

Editor's note: Xie Chuang (aka Xavier Dea) was born in Yijing village, Tangkou, Kaiping District, in 1905, the oldest of five children. His father immigrated to the United States when Xie was six years old. He received an elementary school education and began to participate in revolutionary activities at a young age. In 1922, he married Kwan Sau Kau, who gave birth to a daughter before he was summoned by his father to join him in America. Leaving behind his family and the revolutionary cause in which he fervently believed, Xie said, he crossed the Pacific Ocean in tears, only to land at Angel Island. In an interview with a newspaper reporter in 1981, he recalled his stay on Angel Island. "I was detained there for over forty days, during which time I thought of how China had been carved up by foreign aggressors, and how we Chinese immigrants were just as oppressed. I thought if China were to become strong one day, our status would change. Life at Angel Island reaffirmed my patriotism."[1]

Upon his release from Angel Island, Xie settled in San Francisco Chinatown, where he attended St. Mary's School during the day and worked at his father's fruit and candy store at night. Thinking that his life lacked political meaning, he decided to leave home and strike out on his own. He moved across the bay to San Rafael, where he started high school and found a job as a live-in houseboy. But a year later, Xie had to give up his education when he became unemployed. He spent the next five years as a rabble-rouser supporting the Chinese revolution and organizing Chinatown workers through his involvement with the San Francisco Chinese Students Association, Kung Yu Club, Chinese Unemployed Alliance, and the U.S. Communist Party.[2]

In 1930, Xie was arrested for his subversive activities and thrown in jail. He was released two weeks later after the International Labor Defense, a legal organization associated with the U.S. Communist Party, posted bail of $2,000 on his behalf. He immediately went back to his political work, helping Chinese laundry workers win their first strike and spearheading

1. Transcript of an interview with Xie Chuang for *Unity* newspaper, San Francisco, 1981, in possession of Gordon H. Chang.

2. In 1927, Xie Chuang co-founded the San Francisco Chinese Students Association to support the Chinese revolution through street rallies and mass meetings. In 1928, he became the leader of the Kung Yu Club, which focused on organizing Chinatown workers. After the Great Depression hit, he established the Chinese Unemployed Alliance to organize mass demonstrations in Chinatown and participate in citywide hunger marches. See Fowler, *Japanese and Chinese Immigrant Activists.*

FIG. 3.33
Xie Chuang (Xavier Dea),
certificate of identity, 1922.
Courtesy of National Archives,
San Francisco.

the first mass protest in Chinatown for unemployment relief. In May 1931, he was again arrested for his political activities and incarcerated on Angel Island for one year while the International Labor Defense appealed his case. In the end, the courts dismissed his appeal and granted him voluntary departure to the Soviet Union via Germany.

Xie stayed in the Soviet Union for three years, touring factories and studying at the Lenin Academy. He returned to China in 1935, taught school in Kaiping, remarried and fathered six children, and led the resistance against Japanese aggression in central Guangdong. Xie was appointed to a number of important government posts after the Communists took control of China. However, in 1958, he was purged by leftists for being too soft on landlords and was purged again during the Cultural Revolution. He was rehabilitated in 1979, returned to visit the United States in 1981, and retired three years later with benefits equal to that of a provincial deputy governor. During his retirement, Xie wrote his memoirs, helped overseas Chinese reconnect with their families in China, and used his pension to help educate poor children and provide welfare to the elderly. He died of cancer in Guangzhou in 1995, at the age of ninety.[3]

The following story of his second imprisonment at Angel Island is excerpted from his autobiography, which was written in Chinese and published in 1993.[4] A rare account told from the perspective of a Chinese Communist and deportee, it is full of rich details and new information about the food riots, suicide poems, political divisions among the inmates, and interactions with the Chinese consulate and immigration officials. Written sixty-two years after the events, errors and misinterpretations understandably occur in his retelling. I have noted these errors in the footnotes whenever verifiable.

Angel Island—what a beautiful name! Yet in the period before the 1930s, in the minds of overseas Chinese in America, it was a terrifying place. This island is situated in San Francisco Bay, about five nautical miles from San Francisco, and covers an area of ten square kilometers.[5] There are no residents on the island, only navy camps.[6] Transportation to and from the island is concentrated mostly on a single pier. The U.S. immigration station was established on a hillside there. All new immigrants who arrive on the West Coast—especially those from the Far East—must come to the station for interrogation and medical examination. Only when the authorities are convinced that travel documents have not been forged will immigrants be

3   Him Mark Lai, *Chinese American Transnational Politics*, 182; "Xie Chuang," *Guangzhou Local History*; Mary Fong and Peter Ja, e-mail correspondence with Judy Yung, February 22, 25, and March 4, 2013.

4   Chuang, *Chongyang nan zu baoguo xin*, 20–25.

5   Angel Island is three miles away from San Francisco, and its area is 1.2 square miles (3.1 square kilometers).

6   The U.S. Army, not the Navy, occupied Angel Island from 1863 to 1946.

allowed to enter the country. As for those foreign nationals awaiting deportation, they are also detained here.

This immigration processing station is in fact a detention center—there's not much difference between it and a jail. While at the station, Asians (Japanese, Filipinos) and Chinese are kept in separate dormitories. In those years, because China was weak and its people poor, the treatment Chinese received at the station was worse than that of the Japanese and Filipino immigrants. As for the time required for processing, Japanese immigrants could leave the station and enter the country within twenty-four hours of their arrival; for Filipinos, it could take from two weeks to a little more than a month. For Chinese, the quickest was more than a month, and there were those who still did not receive permission to land after periods as long as two years. This is obviously due to China's weak status as a nation, which has resulted in discrimination against its people. The Chinese were also given worse food and lodging space than the Japanese and Filipinos.

The Chinese live separately in a two-story brick and wood building.[7] Each floor has an area of about 150 square meters [1,600 square feet], where three-tiered bunk beds are placed in four rows. All of the windows in the building are sealed with wire mesh. Even the empty yard on the south side, where Chinese immigrants can get air twice a day, is completely surrounded by a wire-mesh fence four meters high. When the immigrants go to the dining hall for meals, guards tail them to keep watch on their activities. For daily meals, the freshly cooked rice is usually mixed with yesterday's, and horse is the chief meat.[8] Since the prisoners have no proper recreation, and their activities are limited, gambling became popular. *Pai gow*, *fan tan*, and mahjong are all available. A few old criminals who had been detained the longest formed a clique and established a little pawn business. They loaned money at usurious rates, thereby exploiting their fellow sufferers.

Before the Xinhai Revolution,[9] many Chinese who came to America to make a living did so because they felt their lives were at an impasse. Bankrupt farmers, small craftsmen, and even a few sons of scholarly families in decline were compelled to debase themselves and cross the sea. Believing that America was Gold Mountain, they did not hesitate to sell their land and property, even mortgage their own bodies, in order to secure the necessary travel funds to cross the vast ocean. Yet how could they have foreseen they would be stopped by the harsh regulations that America enforced upon Chinese immigrants? Not only were they barred entry to the country; they

广东党史资料丛刊

重洋
难阻报国心

谢 创 著

FIG. 3.34
Cover of Xie Chuang's autobiography *Seas and Oceans Cannot Block an Intention to Serve the Nation.*

7   The detention building was made entirely of wood, and the room that housed the Chinese measured 2,700 square feet.
8   Pork and beef, not horse, were the chief kinds of meat served.
9   Also known as the Chinese Revolution of 1911, the Xinhai Revolution overthrew the Qing dynasty and established the Republic of China under the control of the Nationalist Party in 1912.

were deported to China. More than a few believed there was no outlet for their suffering and felt compelled to hang themselves at the station. Before they died, some left behind poetry. Their fellow prisoners carved these on the walls, and they accumulated over time until there were more than a hundred. Among them is one poem by a student from Toishan whose testimony was inconsistent. He was denied entry to America and so hanged himself. I still clearly remember his suicide poem.[10]

走投無路別家鄉，
乘風破浪渡重洋，
一言之差河橋斷，
困囚木屋兩年長.
英雄難過美人關，
進退兩難夜靜嘆:
謝絕浮生僅一途，
冤魂飄蕩莫奈何。

My life at an impasse, I left house and home;
I braved the winds and broke through waves to cross the seas.
Yet with one wrong word, my bridge across the sky was broken;
Now I've been imprisoned for two years in a wooden building.
It's hard for heroes to cross the barrier to America;
Both going forward and back are hard, and in the quiet night I sigh.
I leave behind this floating life—there's only one road for me now;
My wronged soul is doomed to wander—what else can I do?

From the Qing dynasty [1644–1911] to the Nationalist period [1912–49], all the officials at Chinese embassies in America fawned on foreign powers for their own self-advancement. They were never concerned with the sufferings of overseas Chinese people. For their part, the U.S. Immigration Service tried to assuage the anger of the prisoners by frequently inviting pastors from Chinese churches to the island for consolation visits. These pastors promoted the "humanitarianism" of capitalism, "freedom," "democracy," and "material civilization." All of this was just intended to make the prisoners submit completely to tyranny.

In May of 1931, after I was arrested by the American government, I was sent to Angel Island. Life for the Chinese prisoners had not changed much, except for the addition of the Self-governing Association and less gambling. Because the masses there had been subjected to Nationalist anti-Communist propaganda and had a good impression of Chiang Kai-shek, they instituted a practice of "remembrance meetings" on Mondays to commemorate

10 For other poems that memorialize Chinese who died while in detention, see poems 111 and 112.

Sun Yat-sen.[11] They were frightened of the Communist movement. By the time of my arrival at the immigration station, they had already learned from the Chinese newspapers that I was a Communist Party member, and so they didn't dare approach me. I remained solitary and isolated for several months. Yet I thought to myself, even if I were locked up and isolated, I still should strive to be an effective and useful member of the Communist Party.

I sought out a few young people among the mass of prisoners and got close to them by teaching them English and translating for them. Once we became friends, I used the September 18th Incident in China to teach them that if they loved the motherland, they must follow the road of "Resist Japan for National Salvation"—exactly what the Chinese Communist Party had consistently advocated.[12] After awhile we reached a mutual understanding, and their attitude toward me changed. I took this opportunity to organize seminars and explain to them the essence of the Japanese bandits' aggression against China and the trends of the developing war. These young people felt they had benefited substantially. With that, I just let them spread the news to everybody else. Overseas Chinese are always patriotic. They were very concerned by what they had heard. One after another, they entreated me to give a lecture to everyone. Naturally, the Nationalist clique was adamantly opposed, as they believed that allowing me to talk about these topics was no different than promoting Communism. In contrast, the masses held that even if it's the Communist Party speaking, as long as it promotes "Resist Japan for National Salvation," it's a good thing. The Self-governing Association called a meeting to discuss the issue and unanimously agreed that I should give a lecture to the assembly during the weekly "remembrance meeting."

Seeing that the Nationalist Party had begun to lose favor among the prisoners, I used the platform of the weekly meeting to publicize the Japanese bandits' ambition to invade China. I pointed out how the Nationalists had adopted a policy of nonaggression and had prevented the heroes of the Nineteenth Route Army from resisting the enemy.[13] I then elucidated the policies my party had consistently advocated of uniting and resisting Japan. The masses were extremely happy to hear this and applauded to show their support. Not long afterward, the Self-governing Association held an election. The previous chairman (a member of the Nationalist clique) was defeated, and I was elected. Once I took over the reins of leadership, I focused on the urgent desire of the masses to improve their living conditions and treatment on the island. The members and I gradually concluded that we had to take some form of action before the authorities would negotiate. We decided to rise in revolt on the day when the food was worst. After we entered the dining hall, at a prearranged signal, everyone began to throw plates, knives, and forks at the guards. The guards were completely unpre-

11 The Nationalist Party (Kuomintang) was founded by Sun Yat-sen shortly after the 1911 Revolution. It worked closely with the Soviet Union and Chinese Communist Party (CCP) in the 1920s, but after Sun died in 1925, his successor, Chiang Kai-shek, mounted a vicious attack on the Communists, nearly wiping them out at their base in Jiangxi. In 1949, the Communists defeated the Nationalists and assumed full control of mainland China while Chiang and the Nationalists retreated to and governed the island of Taiwan.

12 The September 18th Incident is also known as the Mukden Incident. On September 18, 1931, the Japanese army chose to sabotage a few feet of track on the South Manchurian Railway line as a pretext for attacking Mukden and subsequently occupying northeastern China. Chiang Kai-shek, intent on fighting the Communists, chose not to resist, while the CCP and overseas Chinese communities advocated a united front to resist Japanese aggression.

13 Following the Mukden Incident, Japanese troops attacked Shanghai on January 18, 1932, bombing, burning, and killing soldiers and civilians alike. Against Chiang's orders, General Cai Tingkai's Nineteenth Route Army resisted, fighting valiantly against superior forces for thirty-four days before retreating.

pared and were so scared that they rushed for the exits to escape. There was rubble all over the dining hall, with knives and forks scattered in disorder. We sounded the retreat and withdrew our forces.

Immediately upon returning to the dormitory, we called an emergency meeting. We reckoned there were two possible responses forthcoming: first, the ringleaders would be immediately arrested; and second, the immigration authorities would be forced to negotiate with us. Under these circumstances, we resolved that if the authorities wanted to arrest someone, then the organizers of this action should take the initiative to assume responsibility. Two core members and I immediately indicated that if anyone was to sit in jail, it should be us, and that we would definitely not implicate the masses. If the authorities wanted to negotiate, then we would raise the following conditions: (1) no more rotten rice or horsemeat; increase the supply of vegetables; eating implements must be sanitary; promote hygiene; (2) the exercise yard should be opened to prisoners three times per day, each time for three hours.

The next day, the superintendent of the immigration station invited us to send representatives to negotiate. Everyone elected me to represent them. I was only too glad to attend in my role as chairman of the Self-governing Association. The negotiations had only just begun when the superintendent offered me a bribe. He professed that he first wanted to improve the quality of my treatment, and so every day I was to be provided with three Western meals, two apples and two oranges, and one pack of cigarettes. I immediately declared that I had not come to solve my own problems but was representing all the Chinese prisoners. I said that I could only represent everyone's wishes, and that if he would not accept that, then we would struggle to the end. The superintendent saw that my attitude was resolute, and he could only agree to the conditions we had proposed. The negotiations a success, the masses were overjoyed.

In February 1932, the Chinese consulate in San Francisco informed us by letter that Consul General Ye Keliang would personally come to visit the station to console the compatriots. The Self-governing Association discussed the matter and unanimously agreed that on all previous occasions the consulate representatives had made superficial promises to alleviate our difficulties and suffering but in fact had never honored their commitments. Ye coming this time would most likely be equally insincere. We wanted to think of a way to expose his false benevolence and false righteousness and to put him in an awkward position.

As expected, Ye arrived punctually, in the company of a clergyman. He repeated his hackneyed platitudes about how the Nationalist Party was concerned about overseas Chinese. All of us angrily interrogated him: why was it that one year after the consulate had promised to intervene with the Immigration Service to improve our living conditions and treatment, still nothing had happened? Ye explained that this kind of issue had to go through diplomatic channels to be resolved.

Everyone snorted in contempt at Consul Ye's hypocritical and bureaucratic answer and retorted, "How could we dare to trouble the Honorable Consul? Recently, after we undertook a forceful act of resistance, we got the immigration authorities to concretely improve our living conditions. So why do we need to go through any so-called diplomatic channels? Obviously you are just making excuses to put us off."

Ye immediately replied, "In a word, you are now in the U.S. sphere of influence and in future must under no circumstances act provocatively." This reply laid bare Ye's true purpose in coming here—all he wanted was to placate us and keep us from again causing any trouble with the immigration authorities. So everyone rebuked him and demanded that in the future Ye never again use blandishments and affected manners to dupe the masses. This made Old Master Ye ashamed and speechless.

At that point, the masses again questioned him, "Disaster is imminent, so why doesn't the Nationalist government support the resistance of [General] Ma Zhanshan in the northeast and [General] Cai Tingkai in Shanghai?"[14]

Ye replied, "These are great matters of state, and must not be discussed recklessly." Everyone indignantly criticized the Nationalist Party for only looking out for itself, without any concern for the life and death of the common people. They also said that the nonaggression policy toward the Japanese would only result in calamity for the nation and its people.

This shamed Ye Keliang into anger, but faced with the righteous anger of the masses, he did not dare show it. We just saw his face turn red and then white. It was really laughable. The clergyman who accompanied Ye never said a word; no words could have released the Honorable Consul from his embarrassment. Eventually the two men dejectedly beat it back to San Francisco.

Ever since I was arrested again and detained at the immigration station, the U.S. Communist Party never stopped working for my release. It arranged for lawyers from the International Labor Defense to appear on my behalf. In order to avoid the danger that I would be executed by the Chiang Kai-shek regime if returned to China, an appeal was lodged in district court opposing my deportation and insisting that I had the right to reside in America. Of course the district court did not agree to their demands. They then brought the suit to the U.S. Supreme Court. Yet how could the Supreme Court allow the number one most prominent Chinese political offender to be released? As before, the suit failed. The lawyers for International Labor

14 Dissenting from Chiang's policy of nonresistance against the Japanese, General Ma Zhanshan and his troops fought back heroically at Mukden, and General Cai Tingkai did the same in Shanghai.

FIG. 3.35
Comrade Xie Chuang.
Courtesy of Peter Ja.

Defense, realizing that there was no possibility anymore of my being granted permanent residence, came up with a plan to apply to the Supreme Court for voluntary departure. At the same time, the Central Committee of the U.S. Communist Party sent out an appeal to the working masses to launch demonstrations in every major city protesting my deportation to China by the authorities. Finally, the U.S. Supreme Court, influenced by the mass protests, was forced to rule that I be given voluntary departure. The U.S. Communist Party obtained permission from the Communist International for me to go to the Soviet Union. At that time, the Soviet Union and Germany had diplomatic relations, and so after going through diplomatic channels, I was able to travel to the Soviet Union via Germany.

In May 1932, I finally left capitalist America for a working-class country—the Soviet Union. The day I was to leave the country, I was transferred under escort from Angel Island to a police station in San Francisco. The commander of the station declared to me, "Henceforth you must never return to America. If you do, you will not only be fined $5,000 but also be sentenced to five years in jail."

Laughing, I said, "Wait until I am the honored guest of the American Soviet. Then I will certainly visit this country again."

This angered him, and he said scornfully, "Now that you are off to the Soviet Union to seek refuge with Stalin, do you think you can muster 100,000 Red Army troops to attack us?"

I said, "The Red Army of the Soviet Union will never invade other countries; it is a people's army that will only defend socialism and the sacred national territory."

Faced with such a thoroughly obstinate person as me, who dared to go toe to toe with him, the police station commander seemed completely at a loss. So he promptly ordered policemen to escort me to the German passenger liner.

Once I was on board the ship, I saw countless masses of workers there on the pier to see me off, holding up placards with slogans and red flags that billowed in the wind. I felt a surge of emotion, and my eyes filled with hot tears. Again and again I waved my hands to acknowledge them. As the ship cast off to begin its journey, the masses of workers on the shore continuously called out martial slogans. I stood respectfully on the deck and raised my hand in salute to my dear class brothers. When all traces of them disappeared from my eyes, in my mind I silently called out, "Good-bye, comrades! Good-bye, America!"

Tet Yee: "All Because China Was a Weak Country"

Editor's note: Tet Yee (aka Yee Tet Ming) was born in 1911 in Ha Jick village, Longdu, Heungshan District. He was the oldest of four children. His mother died when he was four, and his father was often away on business, running a fabric store in Hong Kong and, after 1922, the Canton Fish Market in San Francisco Chinatown. Yee attended school in the village while living with his grandmother, stepmother, and siblings in a large house with servants. At eighteen, he married Low Wing Hin from a nearby village in an arranged marriage. They had a daughter before Yee was summoned by his father to join him in America as a merchant's son. He would not see them again for fourteen years.

We got to know Tet Yee from his political activities in the Chinese American community. Back in the 1930s, he was involved with the Chinese Workers Mutual Aid Association and local labor unions, organizing Chinese workers and supporting the war effort in China. At the time that we interviewed him in 1976, he was active with the Chinese Progressive Association and its efforts to promote better relations between China and the United States. Aware of the importance of our research project, Yee was more than willing to talk to us about his six-month detention on Angel Island, during which time he served two terms as chairman of the Self-governing Association and took the time to copy down ninety-six poems from the walls into a notebook, which he generously shared with us. "The younger generation must know how difficult and painful it was for the earlier generations to come to America, and the hardships and discrimination they suffered on Angel Island," he told us. The following story is taken from two interviews that we conducted with him in 1976 and 1984.[1]

I came in 1932. At the time, Japan had invaded China and I was involved in the anti-Japanese movement. I did not want to come to America, but my father insisted on it. He wanted me to attend school and help out at his

1   Tet Yee interviews. Tet Yee is prominently featured in Felicia Lowe's film *Carved in Silence.*

poultry and fish market on Grant Avenue. So I came as a merchant's son. My papers were real. I never had to lie.

I arrived on Angel Island in September of that year. Because I failed the interrogation and had to appeal my case, I was detained there for six months.[2] Time passed very slowly in the wooden barracks. A day seemed like a year. It was like being in jail. We were locked in, with nowhere to go except the fenced-in recreation yard. Every day we had three meals in the dining hall—breakfast, lunch, and dinner. After we were marched back to our dormitory, we were locked up again. Then we could do whatever we wanted. Some played cards or Chinese chess. Others listened to the gramophone or read the newspapers.

We were all in trouble so the Chinese were very united. The Self-governing Association welcomed newcomers and oriented them to life and the rules in the dormitory and on the island. People were encouraged to make donations, and the money was used to buy books, school supplies, gramophone records, and recreational equipment. Because I was detained there for such a long time, they elected me chairman twice. One of the first things I did was to negotiate with immigration officials for toilet paper and soap. Other detainees—Germans, Italians, Japanese—all had toilet paper and soap, but not the Chinese. They had to get their supply from San Francisco. I felt this was inconvenient and unfair. In the end, we were victorious. The immigration officials gave in.

Many Chinese immigrants passed the time gambling. I didn't like that because a lot of people who lost money got into deep trouble. The association decided to forbid gambling. No more *fan tan* or *pai gow*, but mahjong within certain limits was alright. There were quite a few children with nowhere to go and not much to do. We decided to organize a Chinese school for them in an adjacent room. Those of us with some education took turns teaching them reading, writing, and math. The officers also helped detainees solve their interrogation problems. We usually got to sit at the front table in the dining hall and were served special dishes. If the Chinese kitchen staff came by and said, "The chicken is especially good today," most likely there would be a note wrapped in wax paper and taped to the bottom of the dish. We would take the note back upstairs and give it to the right detainee. We all knew that if any of the guards ever caught us, we would start a ruse to make sure the note was not confiscated. That never happened on my watch.

We all worried a lot. I worried about my future and about what would happen to me. "Will I ever be landed?" That was the way we all felt. "Will we ever be able to leave Angel Island and go to San Francisco?" Many of the Chinese who had gone into debt to come to America and were now stuck

2   Although Tet Yee was the real son of a real merchant, and he had carefully studied the coaching book before leaving for America, he was a poor interviewee. The summary report in his immigration file indicates that he was evasive and slow in responding to the questions raised and that he often changed his testimony or resorted to pleading inability to remember matters that he should have known well if his claims were true. The Board of Special Inquiry also found major discrepancies in his answers regarding his brother's illness, trips to Hong Kong, and schooling in the village.

on Angel Island became very depressed. There were people who had borrowed as much as $4,000 or $5,000 to pay for their papers and passage to America. Many had to sell their homes and personal belongings to come to America. It was very hard for them to face the possibility of deportation. How could they go back to China and face their families? Where could they ever get that much money to repay their loans?

Some of the detainees released their sorrow and frustrations by writing poems on the walls. Many of the poems were full of anger, self-pity, resentment, and even bitterness. They talked about being separated from their wives and families, about the money they owed people back home in China. Some wrote that once China was strong again, it must send soldiers to the United States for revenge. Others were more tempered, writing about how to better themselves and their future. No one signed their names to the poems. They just carved it deep into the wooden walls with a knife. I had plenty of free time and there was nothing else for me to do, so I would copy down a few poems every day. I felt very sad for them.

For me, the hardest thing to forget was the prejudice and discrimination that Chinese suffered on Angel Island. It was most unjust and unfair. There were white guards stationed there to watch us. They treated the Chinese like animals, always yelling at us, especially at mealtimes. During the interrogation, if you talked too slow or didn't speak clearly, they would use a threatening tone and try to rush you. Some of the immigration officers even pounded the table, and many of their questions were unreasonable and insulting. It was all because China was a weak country, so America took advantage of this and discriminated against the Chinese people.

The injustices that I witnessed on Angel Island motivated me to later become a political activist and labor organizer. I have never placed a high value on money. Instead I have always fought for the equal rights of overseas Chinese. That has always been top priority for me. That was why I became involved in the Chinese Workers Mutual Aid Association, helping new immigrants find work, a place to live, and making sure that the Chinese were fairly treated.

I remember in 1940, when I first joined the machinist union on Market Street near Sixth Street. The dispatcher at the window would yell at the Chinese when they came to the window to apply for work. They would say, "Get out, we don't want any Chinese here." They would not give us any work. Whenever a black or Chinese worker was sent to a construction site

FIG. 3.36
Tet Yee (center) walking the streets of San Francisco with two friends, 1940s. Courtesy of Irene Yee.

FIG. 3.37
Private Tet Yee at the time of his honorable discharge from the U.S. Army, December 1944. Courtesy of Irene Yee.

for work, inevitably the big boss would send them back to the union hall. We made a list of these employers, and to get back at them, we had the union purposefully send Chinese or black workers to them, because even if they refused to hire them, they still had to pay them one full day of wages. Finally, rather than lose money, they began accepting minorities to work for them. That was the only way we could end some of the discrimination.

Despite all the injustices, I still volunteered to fight in World War II, because I felt we had to defeat fascism. I found discrimination in the army as well. I remember there was this officer by the name of Doyle, who was always yelling at the Chinese and saying bad things about us. He complained that we always sent our money back to China and that we all acted dumb because we wanted an early discharge. Every morning at reveille time, he would stand next to me. It was very irritating to hear him insulting the Chinese. I told Doyle that when he insulted the Chinese, he was insulting me. I wasn't going to physically fight him since he was much bigger than me. Finally I told him, "Doyle, your name is on this shell. When we cross the enemy line, I will kill you before I kill the enemy." I said that to him every day for a week. He not only stopped insulting us, but he was so scared that he went AWOL.

When I returned to Angel Island for a visit in 1976, I noticed the place had changed. Instead of a prison, Angel Island was now like a paradise. There was nothing left except for this one wooden barracks. When I entered the building, I saw that many of the poems were faded or marked over. I decided to write a poem to reflect how I felt about returning to Angel Island after forty-four years.

On Revisiting Angel Island

I cannot forget my imprisonment in the wooden building.
The writing on the wall terrifies me.
Returning here after forty-four years,
I seek out poems now incomplete.
But still I remember the past hardships of overseas Chinese,
All because China was a weak country.
Today amidst prosperity in our Motherland,
We can stand tall as Chinese Americans.[3]

3   Tet Yee originally wrote this poem in Chinese upon his return visit to Angel Island in 1976. I translated the poem into English for Felicia Lowe's film *Carved in Silence* in 1984 but have not been able to find the original Chinese poem.

FIG. 3.38
The Tet Yee family at home in Oakland, 1988. Left to right: Ed, Barbara, Low Wing Hin, Tet Yee, and Irene. Courtesy of Irene Yee.

Editor's note: The Chinese exclusion laws kept Tet Yee separated from his wife and daughter in China for fourteen long years. Only after the laws were repealed and he was honorably discharged from military service and granted U.S. citizenship was Tet Yee finally able to sponsor them to come to America under the War Brides Act. He and his wife had three more children and settled in Oakland, where they bought a home and ran a grocery store for many years. Tet Yee remained active in progressive causes and made many trips back to China before he died in 1996 at the age of eighty-five.

Koon T. Lau: "Why?"

Editor's note: I found Koon T. Lau through the visitors' logbook at Angel Island. He had immigrated to the United States in 1934 at the age of fifteen and was detained on Angel Island for ten days. He signed the logbook during a return visit on June 28, 1987, and agreed to let me interview him.

A small-framed, energetic, and spry man, Lau came prepared to the interview. He had carefully written down his biography in Chinese and what he remembered of life at Angel Island on eight sheets of paper. Throughout the interview, he referred to these notes and answered with deliberate care. Although fifty-six years had passed since his ordeal at Angel Island, his memory was intact, and he re-created the experience as if it had just happened yesterday. I was particularly struck by his honesty, exactness, and willingness to reveal his true feelings about Angel Island.[1]

At seventy, Lau was still working as chief steward on passenger liners when I interviewed him in 1990. "When I'm home, I'm beside myself with boredom," he said. "It's when I'm at work at sea that I'm truly on vacation." Koon Lau formally retired in 1999 and lived to be eighty-eight.

I was born in Cheung Ping village, Toishan District, on April 4, 1919, the oldest son in a family of four boys and three girls. My father had a small store in Chung Lau Heui and also a *Gam Saan jong* in Hong Kong. It was a service station for relatives and friends on their way to or from the United States, Europe, or South America. People would live and board there while waiting for their ship to arrive. Father would also make necessary arrangements for them and deliver remittances sent home from abroad. The income from these services was enough to support our family in the village.

After I finished elementary school in the village, I had one year of schooling in Hong Kong. It was a private school, upstairs from my father's *Gam Saan jong*. We learned the classics—Lao-tzu, Confucius, Mencius—and how to write couplets and poems. Then my father decided to send me

1   Koon T. Lau interview. An earlier version of this story was published in *Chinese America: History and Perspectives*, 1991, 157–68.

to Canton, where I studied three years at a secondary school. After that, he told me to go to journalism school. It was while I was a student there that my father and uncle planned my trip to America. I didn't even know about it. At that time I was only fifteen and my parents decided everything for me. My uncle was already in America, and my father thought going to any country would be better than staying in China. So he wrote my uncle, who made the necessary arrangements for me.

When others returned from America, they always had pretty clothes and money to spend, and they had cookies for the whole village. I always envied them and thought going to America would be a good thing. So when I heard my father say I was to go to America, I was happy. But he explained to me that I had to go as a paper son, otherwise I would have no right to go. Along with the papers was a coaching book this thick [about one-half inch]. The paper father also had to study the same coaching information. For example, I had to know how many people lived in our house, how many brothers and sisters, what were the ages of my father and mother, where did I sleep, how many steps up the stairs, and so on. My father said I had to be extremely careful. If I didn't learn it well and answered wrong, I'd get deported. So I was happy about going to America, but also scared.

After the Mid-autumn Festival passed, I returned to my village in Toishan for two weeks. After paying respects to my ancestors, I was accompanied to Hong Kong by my grandmother and father. The day my ship was to leave, my father instructed me not to pick up bad habits, and Grandmother told me over and over again to be careful. She said, "I hope you will return in two or three years to see me. But if I'm not here when you do return, bring a box of American cookies to my gravesite." Tears were streaming down her face as she said this. I stood there with tears in my eyes as I watched this seventy-five-year-old woman turn back to look at me with each step that she took.

I boarded a huge ship called *President Hoover.* I went in steerage. The area where I stayed was very big, as wide as the width of the ship. There were canvas beds arranged in two tiers. The area could hold about two hundred people. All the Chinese stayed together. There were Filipinos, but they didn't stay or eat with us. The women and children were in another section. Sometimes we ate with them and saw them walking on deck.

First we went to Shanghai, where we stopped for one day to pick up passengers. Then we went on to Yokohama. Do you know how the Japanese treated us Chinese there? They told all of us to go up to the front of the ship and stand there like soldiers. They said the Japanese doctors had to examine us. We waited for over half an hour and no one came. Then a couple of Japanese with mustaches in white uniforms, along with the

FIG. 3.39
Koon Lau with Fifth Uncle in
San Francisco, 1934. Courtesy of
Cynthia Ip.

ship's officers, walked back and forth in front of us. Finally, they asked us to hold our hands out. They touched our foreheads and looked into our eyes and mouths, tapped our chests, and things like that. This procedure took almost two hours. The Japanese had taken Manchuria by then. They hated us and we hated them. Standing there like that so long, we hated them even more. But we couldn't do anything about it.

After Yokohama, we went on to Hawaii and stopped there for one day. Before the ship reached Hawaii, this clansman whom my father had instructed to take care of me asked me if I had learned all the coaching notes. I said yes. He told me in another two days I would have to throw it overboard. Otherwise, if caught with it, I might get into big trouble. His bed was next to mine, and he proceeded to test me. He reminded me not to forget. He then helped me tear it up, put it in a bag, and throw it overboard.

The entire trip took eighteen or nineteen days. The ships weren't that fast then. It was crowded and noisy, and there was absolutely nothing to do except study my coaching book and eat three meals, maybe go upstairs for some fresh air. There were no recreational activities, no entertainment at all. Some of the passengers and workers gambled, but not for high stakes. The bed was not that comfortable, but it was better than our hard boards at home. We ate in the dining room. The food wasn't too bad. We usually had *jook* or noodles for breakfast and Cantonese-style meals at lunch and dinner. After the meal, we could take an apple or orange back with us. Every night at around ten o'clock, the Chinese crewmen would make a big pot of chicken *jook* or pork *jook* to sell to us. This way they made some extra cash on the side.

As soon as the boat docked in San Francisco, the old-timers took their luggage and cleared customs. They were all smiles, whereas the fourteen or fifteen of us newcomers wore the opposite expression. The immigration officials confined us to a fenced-in area at the pier. Nobody was allowed to talk to us. Even the real sons and daughters couldn't see their relatives. We were kept at such a distance that relatives couldn't even make out our faces. We must have stood there in the cold for two hours or so. Fortunately, we had listened to the people on board the ship who had advised us to wear wool garments beneath our Western suits. We were finally herded like ducks down this fenced-in route to the boat at the pier. No one said a word during this time. We were frightened as well as depressed. We knew we had to get through this criminal process before we could enter America.

When we got to "En-gin Island," as the Chinese mispronounced it, I thought, "What a beautiful place!" It had green grass and trees, flowers, birds. I wondered why the old-timers had said it was a bad place. Later I realized that they weren't saying the place was no good, but that the imprisonment was bad. All the buildings were made of wood. We had to climb up a long stretch of stairs before we got to the dormitory. When we arrived, all the Chinese inmates stared at us blankly. Inmates who spoke some English translated for us. We were told where to sleep. I still remember that my bed was the bottom bunk to the left of the entrance. Two or three hours later, our luggage arrived in the barracks. An inmate told us to take out some clothes and our toothbrushes and put them by our beds. That's when I realized that our luggage had been searched, because my grandmother had neatly packed my things and they were now topsy-turvy.

The exercise yard was right outside the back door of our dormitory. The yard was as wide as the room. That was all the space we had. The door to the building's main entrance was always closed. Only during mealtimes would the Westerners open the door and yell, "Sik fan la!" [Time to eat!]. Then everyone would follow them down the stairs into the dining room. The food was all arranged on these long tables before we arrived. I soon learned that, regardless of whether they were real fathers and sons or not, many received crib notes through the kitchen staff. They would hide the note at the bottom of a thermos filled with herbal soup from a relative in San Francisco, or they would hide it in the food. The guards in the dining hall probably never suspected because they never searched the food before delivering it to the designated person. So that was how crib notes were sneaked in.

The food was worse than what we had on the ship. For breakfast, we had oatmeal, bread, and coffee. For lunch and dinner, we had Chinese food—soup, vegetables, and meat, usually pork. The food was all boiled—pork, beef, or whatever. One day in the dormitory, I heard the old-timers talking. They were probably illegal entrants who had been caught by immigration officers in the city. Some of them spoke English pretty well. I heard them discussing how bad the food was and what changes we should demand. Later, in the dining room after everyone was seated, one of the old-timers who knew English told us, "Don't eat until I've talked to them." So we sat and he negotiated with the Westerner who was in charge of the dining hall. He told him we Chinese didn't like the food, that it was very, very bad. We wanted such and such done. After ten minutes of conversation, he told us that the immigration official had promised to improve the food.

The question that crossed my mind was, what was the Immigration Service's budget for food? Because if the government didn't allocate enough money for food, it was the government's fault. If the government gave enough to the cook and the cook kept some of the money, then it was Chinese cheating Chinese. But no matter whether the government gave enough money to the cook or not, or whether it was the government or cook who bought the food, they should not have boiled the food every day. After that confrontation, the food was cooked better. They sometimes stir-fried the food or steamed the pork. So we decided that the cook was the one to blame.

After meals, most people would sit around the phonograph to listen to Chinese opera records. Sometimes we young ones would go outside and play ball. But most of the time, we would listen to records. There were no arguments during the time I was there. We were all in the same sad situation, so everyone was pretty friendly. I remember there were one or two who kept to themselves. They refused to talk to anyone. They just walked back and forth with their heads bowed, or they lay in bed deep in thought. I didn't know how long they had been there, but I figured they were having a hard time. All of us who came through Angel Island had a hard time. Those who had been interrogated repeatedly and still were not allowed to land were the most tragic of all.

When I saw the poems on the wall, I felt very sad. I knew how those poets must have felt, although I had not gone through the same experience. Nevertheless, I sympathized with them. I heard some had been imprisoned for over a year. I didn't know what the immigration authorities thought they were doing. If someone was illegal, why didn't they just send them back to China? Why keep the people here so long? Some were very meticulous about carving their poems into the wall. They had time and were well educated. Anyone who finished high school in China could write good classical poetry.

Of the fourteen newcomers who came with me on the ship, they summoned the youngest boy for interrogation first. Then after he was interrogated, the next morning the same tall Westerner opened the door again. Every time he opened the door, we knew it had to be something. Everyone would look toward the door automatically, because if there was nothing happening, the door would remain closed. So he called this kid's name and then said in Chinese, "Seung ngon!" [Landed!], followed by "Gung hei nay!" [Congratulations!]. So everyone rushed around to help him pack. As we watched that kid go out that door, we all had mixed feelings. We envied him and wondered when our turn would come.

On the ninth day, I was lying in bed after a meal and after playing ball outside. I was thinking, "It's the ninth day. I wonder how many more days?

Another month or two is no matter; the worst would be if I were deported to China. What would I do then? How would I face my disappointed family?" Many thoughts crossed my mind. I thought about my school days in Canton, of the time my grandmother saw me off. All of a sudden, a voice called my name on that ninth day. The second time he called my name, I got up quickly and walked between the beds. "What's your name?" he asked. Then, "Come, come, come." I didn't think of putting more clothes on. I just went down the stairs, past the dining hall, farther down the stairs and into a room on the left.

When I went inside the room, there was a pleasant-looking Westerner sitting behind a large desk. There was also a Chinese man—a fat man who interpreted. He sat at the end of the table. I was told to sit across from the inspector. Then the Westerner told the Chinese interpreter to tell me not to be afraid. He smiled and said through the interpreter, "You don't have to be afraid. There are no tigers in this room. I won't eat you. I prefer steaks myself." We all laughed. After he joked like that, half of my anxiety and fear vanished. If he had been mean, perhaps I wouldn't have been able to utter a word. I guess he was used to seeing Chinese get scared. He asked me if I liked candy, American oranges. Then he began to ask me, "What is your father's name? How old is your mother?" He asked a few more questions and then joked some more. So the only time I was scared was right when I entered. He asked me when I planned to get married and how many kids I would have. He asked me what I wanted to do when I grew up. "Would you want to be a football player?" I thought he meant soccer, so I said no. Then serious questions would follow: "How many brothers and sisters? Their ages? Where was the dining room table? Where was the stove? Where did you sleep?" They asked everything. They even asked how many steps there were in the stairs. You know how our stairs in China are really ladders. It was so unreasonable! Who would remember all that? If you said eight steps and your father said ten, you're wrong. These were stupid questions. Stupid! But what could we do?

After over an hour of interrogation, another Caucasian took me back to the dormitory. As soon as I got back, many of the inmates crowded around me and asked me how it went. I said, "You don't have to be afraid. The inspector is very nice." I didn't know then that there were many inspectors and not all of them were kind.

The next morning, they called me again. It was the same inspector, the same interpreter, and the same room. The second time was called the reexamination, an inmate told me. Perhaps you said your home had four chickens the first day and your witness said seven. On the reexamination, the same question would be asked, and if your answers still did not agree, then you were in trouble. I stuck to my original answers. After the reexamination, I returned to the dormitory. Many said they would decide whether to admit you or deport you after that. So I think the time after the reexamination was the worst. I knew I had answered carefully, just like in the coaching book, but maybe the paper father had not. I didn't know. So that time was the hardest for me.

As I lay in bed, this older man—one of those who knew how to speak English—said to me, "I've been here for eight, nine months." As a young man, I didn't dare ask why. I didn't know whether he had been arrested in the city and detained for eight, nine months or newly arrived and detained for eight, nine months. Then he gave me a letter and said, "They will either let you land or not. If you are landed, please help me deliver this important letter to this address. But you must hide this and not let anyone see it." So I hid it among the clothes in my suitcase. I was still young and didn't think about the consequences. He gave it to me, and I sympathized with how long he had been there. I just thought I should help him.

Then we went to lunch, but I didn't have the heart to eat. I was so worried about my fate. I was feeling very anxious. After the meal, we all went back upstairs. I lay in bed again, eyeing the bottom of the bed above me. Many thoughts ran through my mind. "What's going to happen? What's going to happen?" That's all I could do. They told me I would know in a day or two. I didn't know how many more times I would be interrogated. If I had answered wrong, how much longer would I have to stay? The worst was, what if I was deported? Suddenly I heard my name called again. I was more frightened at that moment than the time when I was first called for the hearing. It was as if I had lost consciousness. The second time they called me, I got up. Chew, who had come with me on the same ship, said, "They're calling you! They're calling you! You're landed!" But the Westerner hadn't said so yet. The third time he called my name, he said, "Seung ngon!" My heart was jumping up and down. Chew and the man who had given me the letter hurriedly helped me pack.

As I was putting my things together, one of the guards said, "Fai di, fai di!" [Hurry, hurry!]. I stood there transfixed, and it was only through the help of Chew and the man who gave me the letter that my things were put in order. I quickly put on my shoes, and Chew picked up my suitcase and walked me to the door. The man who gave me the letter dragged my other bag. I could not stop the tears and clutched both of their hands in farewell. Then two Westerners each took one of my bags and escorted me down the stairs.

We went into the interrogation room. The inspector and interpreter were not there, but my paper father and brother were. Because we had seen each other's pictures, I recognized him. As soon as I entered the room, I said, "Go Bak" [Uncle Go]. He right away said, "Shhh!" Fortunately, the inspector and interpreter were not there, because I had slipped. Scared, Uncle Go quickly said, "Call me Baba [Father]." Later I saw the inspector and Chinese interpreter on the same boat. They were probably going off duty. So we all went to San Francisco together. My paper father smiled and nodded at them. My paper brother, I recall, said, "Thank you, thank you," to them. I couldn't understand what the inspector said to me in English, but he patted me on the head and said a few words. The inspector then went into a small room. After the boat docked, we had a car take us straight to Washington Street to the Chan, Woo, and Yuen Association. My paper father, who was a Chan, lived there in one of those bachelor rooms. His room had no electricity. He used an oil lamp, lighted it with a match. We shared a communal kitchen with other men. The next day, I moved in with Fifth Uncle, a carpenter who lived at 730 Commercial Street.

FIG. 3.40
Koon Lau traveled around the world several times while working in the U.S. Merchant Marine. Here, he stands next to the ship's commanding officer on board the *R. J. Pfeiffer* in 1997. Courtesy of Cynthia Ip.

Editor's note: Koon T. Lau attended English classes in various Chinatown churches and public school for two years. He later worked for a lumber company with another uncle in Santa Cruz, California. He said he was exempted from the draft during World War II because he couldn't speak English. Lau studied welding and worked at the Moore Dry Dock shipyard in Oakland for the duration of the war. There he met his wife, Jenny Leung, a sheet-metal worker, and they were married in 1943. They had three sons. Wanting to return to China to see his family, Lau joined the merchant marine as a cook. He was promoted to chief steward in 1965. Unfortunately, his grandmother had died during the war and he was not able to reunite with her as planned. In 1987, at the urging of his niece, he returned to Angel Island for a visit. The following are his thoughts upon seeing Angel Island again.

As soon as I arrived, I could see things had changed. Except for our dormitory, everything, including the dining hall, had been destroyed. Even the stairway, which was pretty long, had been destroyed. The offices on both sides of the stairway had also been destroyed. As I entered the dormitory, I

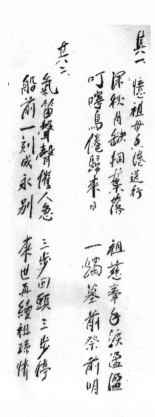

其一
憶祖母香港送行

保秋月缺桐葉落
叮嚀鳥倦歸來日

祖慈牽手淚盈眶
一獨墓前祭前明

其二

氣笛聲聲催人急
船前一別成永別

三步回頭三步停
來世再續祖孫情

FIG. 3.41
Koon Lau did not leave a poem on the walls of Angel Island, but his niece Cynthia Ip found this poem, "Remembering Grandma's Farewell in Hong Kong," in his room after he died and read it at his funeral: "The autumn moon was pale, the leaves were falling, / Gentle grandmother held my hand, she was weeping. / Reminding me to come home when I was tired, / Burn incense at her gravesite, if she was no longer there. / The horn was blaring, the ship was sailing, / Walking forward, but my head kept turning. / The ship departed, good-bye forever, / In my next life, again be my grandmother." Translated by Cynthia Ip

could see the door leading into the exercise yard, and I said, "Same thing." And I thought, "How many Chinese had languished in this dormitory and then been deported?" My heart told me that the older ones who had finally been landed were probably no longer alive. I looked at the poems and carefully read them in silence. My mind tried to understand the meaning of those poems. As I thought about it, I was overcome with grief. I thought about the ones who were deported and how heavy their hearts must have been. I also thought about the ones who were landed. How many became rich? How many returned to China to die? Myself, I am not rich, nor so poor that I cannot afford rice. But I have managed to support my family with my two hands. Most important, I am still healthy and alive. So I consider myself a lucky man.

Angel Island did not adversely affect my livelihood, but it did affect me psychologically. I felt I was not equal. We were judged guilty although we had committed no crime. The main points I want to make are, one, the food was bad. Second, the space we were confined to was too small. Why wouldn't they give us more freedom since we couldn't escape from the island anyway? Besides, even if we could swim, we couldn't swim that far or know where to go. Why wouldn't they let us go beyond the exercise yard? Third and worst of all, they would not allow our relatives to come see us. I heard others say on the ship and in the barracks that criminals in America have visiting rights. If they allowed criminals that right, why not us, who had not committed any crime, like robbing or killing anyone? Maybe we were considered criminals for coming as paper sons, but what about those who were real sons? Why not let their relatives see them? Since landing here until now, I still wonder about this. I am seventy now and still do not understand why they treated us like that.

Lee Show Nam: "We Were Real, So There Was Nothing to Fear"

Editor's note: On February 5, 1935, thirteen-year-old Lum Ngow (aka Lee Show Nam) and his mother, Ow Soak Yong, arrived in San Francisco from China on the *President Taft*. They had come to join his father, Lum Piu, a merchant who ran Lun Kee, a roast meat deli in Oakland Chinatown. Family members of the merchant class were exempt from the Chinese Exclusion Act, and they should have been admitted into the country. Instead, mother and son were detained on Angel Island for eighteen months, fighting a legal battle to prove that they were in fact the wife and son of Lum Piu. At issue was a major discrepancy in their testimonies and those of other witnesses regarding the wedding date of Lum Ngow's parents. Seventy-five years later, Lee Show Nam offered the following explanation:

Before my aunt [Mo Shee] came to America with my uncle [Lum Yun] in 1921, they knew she would have to answer questions from the immigration bureau, like when did your brother-in-law [Lum Piu] get married? And if he had married, there would be more questions, like where is the wife from? What is her surname? How many were at the wedding? Who introduced them? Did she ride in a sedan chair? And so on. To avoid all these kinds of questions, she was told to say, "My brother-in-law is not married." But they did not tell my father that was what she said at the interrogation. So when we arrived in 1935, they saw from her immigration file that she had said my father was not married when she left China for America. Yet my father had said he got married in 1920 and was sponsoring his wife and son to come to America. So it was all wrong![1]

Editor's note: I met Lee Show Nam at the annual Angel Island Immigration Station Foundation gala in 2009 and knew right away that I should interview him. He looked much younger than his age of eighty-seven, and he obviously had a great memory for details about his long stay at Angel

[1] Lee Show Nam interview. An earlier version of this article was published in *Chinese America: History and Perspectives* (2012): 19–26. Lee Show Nam was prominently featured in the Hong Kong television series *Roots Old and New* directed by Chen Zhuoling.

FIG. 3.42
Lum Ngow with his parents
in China, 1925. Courtesy of
Lee Show Nam.

Island. He attributed his robust health and jet-black hair to his *hei gung*
and *luk tung kuen* exercises as well as his stoic attitude toward life: "I don't
let things get to me." Lee told me things that I had not heard before about
the Self-governing Association, the smuggling of coaching notes, the "dark
room" (or isolation cell), and the role of missionary women like Donaldina
Cameron in helping immigrants get landed.[2] I was also intrigued by his im-
migration case file, which, when combined with his oral history interview,
clearly showed how thorough and suspicious the immigration officials were
in their investigations of Chinese applicants and how a real son of a real
merchant could still fail the test and be deported.[3]

Due to no fault of his own, Lum Ngow was caught in the pact of lies
that Chinese immigrants often devised in their attempts to circumvent the
Chinese Exclusion Act and pass the rigorous cross-examination at Angel
Island. Many did not realize that the Immigration Service had detailed
records of all past Chinese immigration cases at its disposal and that, as
happened to Lum Ngow's family, once a lie or inconsistency in the tes-
timonies had been uncovered, it could not be easily retracted. As far as
the immigrant inspectors were concerned, it was a question of "how do
we know they are telling the truth now when they have lied before?" Par-
ticularly with Chinese cases like Lum Ngow's, the assumption was almost
always that the applicants were not telling the truth, in this case, even
after Donaldina Cameron wrote three letters of support vouching for the
family's credibility.

2   Donaldina Cameron served
     as superintendent of the
     Chinese Presbyterian Mis-
     sion Home in San Francisco
     from 1900 until 1934. She
     dedicated her life to rescuing,
     educating, and Christianizing
     Chinese prostitutes and other
     abused women.
3   File 34831/2–2 (Lum Ngow),
     Immigration Arrival Inves-
     tigation Case Files, RG 85,
     NARA-SF.

The following story is based on my interview and reading of his immigration file.

I was born in 1923, the second month and fourth day, in Fu Chung village, Heungshan District. I had an older brother who died soon after I was born and a younger sister. The custom then was that when a child died, the next child would be named after an animal. So I was given the nickname Ngow [Cow]. Later, my teacher in Shekki changed my name to Show Nam [Longevity] so that it would sound better.

Life wasn't bad in China. My father was a merchant in America, and he periodically sent money home to support us. I helped with the farming and attended school in the town of Shekki. Still, I wanted to go to America for a better life. People returning from America were able to buy land, build new houses, and get married. So everyone wanted to come to America. No one wanted to remain in the village, especially after the world depression set in and money began to lose its value.

In 1935, my father was finally able to sponsor my mother and me to come to America. We had to go to Hong Kong for inoculations and the

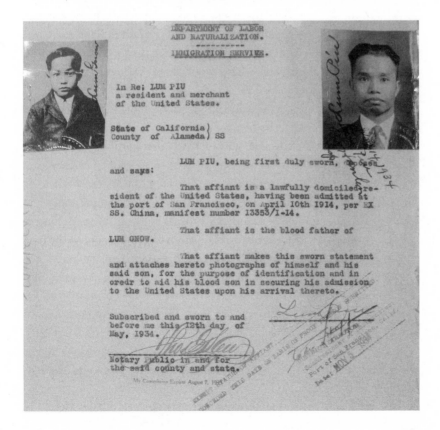

FIG. 3.43
Affidavit of Lum Piu, U.S. resident and merchant, stating that he is the blood father of Lum Ngow. Note the strong resemblance between father and son. Courtesy of National Archives, San Francisco.

physical exam. Then we had to book passage to America. After we took care of everything, we returned to the village until it was time to sail. Father sent us a coaching book to study, even though we were a real family and did not have to lie. It included answers to questions that would likely be asked in the immigration interrogation and a map of the village.

We traveled special third class on the *President Taft*, a 20,000-ton ship. We had a small room to ourselves with two bunk beds and a small table. It was December and quite stormy. We were seasick and stayed in bed. When we felt better, we went to the dining room for our meals. The food—Chinese food—was pretty good. The voyage took more than twenty days, with stops in Shanghai, Japan, and Honolulu. We got off the ship in Shanghai to go shopping at the large store owned by our Chungshan people. We refused to step foot in Japan. After all, they had attacked and invaded China! But when we got to Honolulu, we got off the ship to walk around. We met up with an uncle there.

Our ship docked at Pier 5 in San Francisco. A large station wagon drove us to Pier 35 to catch the ferry to Angel Island. They just took the two of us, since the rest of the people were going elsewhere—to Panama, Peru, New York, and so on. After we arrived at the island, some *lo fan* [barbarians] took us to the dormitories. There was a men's dormitory and a women's dormitory. The Chinese had their own dormitory, and Indians, Japanese, and Mexicans lived in another dormitory. Since it was past dinnertime, they took us to the dining hall, where we ate alone. The food—corned beef, cabbage, and rice—tasted awful!

From then on, this was the daily routine. In the morning, a loudspeaker blasting the radio woke us up at 5:00. Then at 6:00, they opened the door, and we went down the covered stairway to the dining room for breakfast. Those too lazy to go have breakfast could keep sleeping. Lunch was at 10:00—usually bread and jam, coffee and tea. Dinner was at 3:00. At 12:00 noon, a white guard by the name of Pete would open the door and yell in Chinese, "Jing sung lo ho!"—in other words, bring your dishes of food to the dining room for the Chinese cooks to warm up. That would be the food that relatives sent from the city, like salted fish, bean cakes, and barbequed chicken that could be added to the meal. Otherwise, it was one main dish and one small dish, like beef and *cha gwa* [cucumbers], *lam gok* [pickled olives] and bean curd, and things like that. The food was of poor quality, and we were seldom served chicken. If you had money, you could buy milk, cookies, or a piece of pie for 5 cents from Henry, the Italian guy who ran the concession. He also sold us stationery paper and envelopes, pencils, toothpaste, and notebooks.

We had a Self-governing Association run by sixteen officers elected to

these positions: a chairman, vice-chairman, secretary, treasurer, two nego-
tiators who spoke English, a public safety officer, general affairs officer, four
investigators, and four law enforcers. They usually asked kids like me to be
law enforcers. Whenever we saw anyone throwing cigarette butts or spitting
on the floor, we were to tell the officers, and the offender would be confined
to the "dark room" for half an hour. It was a closet where they stored old
newspapers and brooms. I was confined there once for not shutting off the
water faucet in the bathroom. One kid caught stealing 50 cents was confined
there for a whole week.

There were basketball and volleyball games, ping-pong, dominoes, and
mahjong, also Chinese chess, newspapers, and musical instruments like
the *yeung kam* [butterfly harp] and *yi wu* [two-stringed fiddle]. There were
also two radios and a phonograph. The Self-governing Association put out
the money to buy these things with the onetime membership dues they col-
lected from the new arrivals. The officers read outgoing letters to be sure
there was no coaching information in it, and they were also responsible for
receiving coaching notes from the Chinese kitchen help. How did they do
this? The cooks would pick up coaching notes in the city on their days off
and wrap them in foil paper that came in a pack of cigarettes. (This was be-
fore the days of plastic wrap.) All the big shots [officers] sat at the first table
near the kitchen and were served special dishes like green beans, chicken,
steamed eggs, and so on. The cook would indicate there was a coaching
note hidden in the food by putting a drop of soy sauce on top of the dish of
steamed eggs, two drops for two notes. All the time I was there, I never saw
anyone get caught passing coaching notes.

There were many kids my age. We played ping-pong, read newspapers,
listened to records, and played dominoes. We were never bored. Someone
taught me how to play the *yi wu* and another guy who was a pilot taught
me the English alphabet and simple words like "good morning," "how are
you," "table," and "chair." One time when we were outside in the recreation
yard, Lau Wai You shot a bird with a slingshot. Then he threw the ball over
the fence and shouted to the guard, "Outside ball!" So the guard opened the
door to let him go outside to retrieve the ball. Wai You got the bird, plucked
it, and had the cook make us *sang gai jook* [chicken congee]. That was the
only time I ever saw a bird like that. It looked like a fat pigeon, but it was a
gray color and could not fly.

Once a week, I would be allowed to go visit my mother in the adminis-
tration building, where the women were kept. Sometimes I would run into
Miss Maurer [Deaconess Katharine Maurer] on the way. She had a room
full of school supplies and playthings, and she would give me things like a
ruler, pencil, eraser, or puzzle. She really liked Chinese people and would

help us write letters and purchase things from the city. She was very nice to me and did not want me to leave. I remember she hugged me and kissed my cheek. She was a very nice woman. There was also a Miss Cameron at the Presbyterian church who was very helpful to the Chinese. My father got her to write a letter on our behalf. Her letters usually helped people get landed, but not us.

Sometimes I was asked to serve as a messenger on these visits. I remember this case of a brother and sister who were living in different dormitories. After they were interrogated, he asked me to take a letter to my mother and tell her to give it to his sister. Then another time, the sister gave my mother a coaching note to give me to take to her brother. The guards never searched me, and I was able to help them out in that way.

I waited ten days before they called me for the interrogation. It took place in an office on the second floor of the administration building with two immigrant inspectors and interpreter Hall Lan present. I was well prepared. We were real, so there was no need to be afraid. I remember the interpreter asking me, "Is your grandmother *joy sang* [still alive]?" I didn't understand what she meant by *joy sang*. Then she asked, "Do you still have a grandmother?" I said no. Then she asked when my father got married, and I said I didn't know. Who would know that my aunt had said my father was unmarried? So that was the mistake!

In those days, things were very crooked. Someone told my father he could give a $350 bribe to get us admitted. My father said, "Three hundred fifty dollars is a lot of money. I could buy a new Ford automobile for that amount." So he didn't want to pay that much money. He thought there was nothing to fear since our papers were real. So he took it to court instead. The appeal process took eighteen months, during which time I lived there on Angel Island. In the end, the appeal failed, and my mother and I were deported to China in 1936.

Editor's note: According to Lum Ngow's immigration file, he passed the medical exam and was called to appear before a Board of Special Inquiry fifteen days after he arrived at the immigration station. He and his parents were interrogated for four days and asked a total of 808 questions regarding their family background and village life. Their answers were compared to testimonies given by six relatives who had immigrated to the United States earlier. The board was thorough in its summary report, which was eight pages long. It denied Lum Ngow and his mother, Ow Soak Yong, admission on the grounds that their relationships to the alleged father and husband Lum Piu had not been "satisfactorily established." Aside from finding no resemblance between father and son, Chairman Moore noted many discrepancies in their testimonies regarding marriage and death dates, sleeping arrangements in the house, their neighbors, details of their wedding and the birth of their first child, the number of trips Lum Piu made to Hong Kong, and whether the sister-in-law had bound feet or not.

In response, Lum Piu went to great expense and trouble to appeal the decision. He retained attorney Thomas Lew to file an appeal to the secretary of labor in Washington, D.C., and when that failed, he retained attorney Chauncey Tramutolo to petition for a writ of habeas corpus in the U.S. district court. Three months later, mother and son were informed that the petition had been denied. Tramutolo then asked that the case be reopened to hear the testimony of two new witnesses—Aunt Mo Shee and business partner Low Pung—in order to address the discrepancy in the date of Lum Piu's marriage to Ow Soak Yong. Mo Shee claimed that she had attended Lum Piu's wedding before she left for America but that her husband had instructed her not to say so at her interrogation because of a family quarrel over money matters.

Q. In view of the fact that you have on one occasion deliberately given false testimony under oath before this Service, can you state any reason why this Board should regard your present testimony as that of a person entitled to be believed?

A. After all, I am sorry for what I said when I first came in. She is my sister-in-law, and I thought I should tell the truth or she would never be admitted.

Low Pung likewise testified that he was present at the wedding but was confronted with the answer he gave at his own interrogation, that he did not attend any weddings during his visit to China in 1921.

A. (*After a long hesitation*) I did not think it was important, so I just said no.

Q. Then your judgment as to whether or not a matter is of importance determines whether or not you will tell the truth about that matter?

A. I have told you how I felt. I have nothing more to say in that respect.

Lum Piu, Ow Soak Yong, and Lum Ngow were again cross-examined separately and asked a total of 171 questions. The following exchange involved Ow Soak Yong:

Q. Was your previous statement that you had never seen your sister-in-law, MO SHEE, the result of a mistake on your part or a deliberate mis-statement of the facts?

A. It was my mistake. I was too hasty in making the answer.

Q. The record shows that you were not at all hasty and that you were repeatedly questioned on this point, eliminating any possibility of an honest mistake. . . . Do you wish to make any additional explanation or comment?

A. I really have no explanation than what I have already given. I know I made a mistake, such a mistake that I don't blame you a bit for denying my admission. However, I was not deliberately telling you an untruth.

Q. It seems very strange to this Board that at the previous hearing you were unable to identify a good clear photograph of this MO SHEE taken about the time you were supposed to have last seen her and that you can now promptly identify a photograph of this woman taken at the present time which is some 14 years after you last saw her. How do you explain that?

A. Her picture was shown to me at my first hearing. I really was able to recognize her, but when I said I had not met her, I could not say I knew that picture.

Q. According to that, your previous testimony concerning MO SHEE was not an honest mistake on your part then but a deliberate mis-statement of the facts. How about that?

A: I know I made a mistake, but I didn't know I could correct my mistake at the time, and I realize now that I did wrong.

In his four-page summary, Chairman Moore concluded that the evidence presented at the hearing "in no way cures any of the adverse features" of the case. "On the contrary, I believe there is further proof that the testimony given as evidence to support the applications is false and perjured." He moved to deny both applicants admission into the United States on the same grounds as before, and board members Cole and Silver concurred.

Lum Piu did not give up. His attorney Chauncey Tramutolo made another appeal to the secretary of labor in Washington, D.C., which was turned down, and followed with another petition to the U.S. district court, which was also denied. Mother and son were to be deported on the next available ship. By now, they had been detained on Angel Island for more than a year. Tramutolo then contacted Donaldina Cameron for help. According to her first letter, dated April 2, 1936, to District Director Edward Haff, she had conducted her own investigation and was "convinced beyond any doubt that they are in fact husband, wife, and son." She requested that deportation be delayed so that attorney Tramutolo could present further evidence. As she explained in the letter, "Please remember that my underlying motive for interceding on behalf of this family is the deep desire I hold to further decent family life and right home influences among the Chinese people, who because of Immigration Regulations have missed so much of the blessing that other nationalities have enjoyed."[4] Her request was granted.

Tramutolo next took new photographs of the father and son and had a physiognomist attest to their similar features, but to no avail. In a second letter to District Director Haff dated April 10, 1936, Cameron proposed that the wife and son be landed on parole for six months, during which time Lum Piu and Ow Soak Yong would marry according to the laws of California and Cameron would stay in close contact with the family. Although parole was often granted to European immigrants, and Japanese picture brides were admitted on the condition that they remarry in an American civil ceremony, these same privileges were seldom accorded Chinese applicants.

Cameron stayed involved and wrote a third letter on April 21, 1936, requesting that the Board of Special Inquiry interview a new witness, Chun Wai Hin, who remembered meeting Lum Piu's wife in China on two separate occasions. Unfortunately, Cameron warned, Chun, like many other Chinese immigrants, had told immigrant inspectors at his own interrogation upon return from China that he did not know the family for fear of becoming involved in "other people's business." Sure enough, the board questioned Chun's credibility as a witness on that score.

Q. When you returned to this country in 1922, you stated before this Service that during that trip to China you had not visited any resident of this country who happened to be at his home during your trip and that you had not met the wife of any resident of this country during that trip. How do you reconcile those statements with your present testimony?

A. The reason that I replied "No" to some of the questions asked was that I did not want to appear as witnesses for anyone coming to this country. During my trip to China at that time, I did visit the home of LUM BEW, and the home of WONG JONG, and the home of WONG YOUNG and WONG SUNG, and the home of WONG YUK LUN; the home of QUAN SING

Q. Then you admit that whether or not you answer these questions truthfully is determined by your own wishes and convenience at any particular time. Is that right?

4   Ibid.

A. Yes.

Q. Under those conditions, how is the Board going to know or not whether you are telling the truth at this time?

A. I am telling you the truth now—every word of it.

But the board evidently did not believe him. Even though Lum Piu and Ow Soak Young gave similar details about their encounters with Chun Wai Hin, the board dismissed the new evidence on the grounds that "the parties have had ample opportunity to prepare themselves for examination on this matter, the principals having been permitted to visit frequently and for considerable periods."[5] Moreover, they doubted Cameron's judgment on the case. "We feel that Miss Cameron probably is not in so good a position from which to judge the truth or falsity of the statements in question as is this Board." Mother and son were sent back to China on June 19, 1936.

Asked how he felt when he heard the bad news, Lee Show Nam said sadly, "When you fail at something, it's always depressing. I was at school age—what a waste of time and expense! What a waste of eighteen months of my life!" Upon reflection, he added, "The way I look at it, if I had been admitted, I probably would have been drafted in World War II and been killed. If I had been admitted, I wouldn't have had a Chinese education and my Chinese wouldn't have been as good. So there's good and bad in being landed or not."

Lee Show Nam attended school for about a year before Japan invaded China. "Japan bombed everywhere—the bridges, the electricity plants, the bus stations," he said. "Our teacher died and our school closed." He fled to Hong Kong and found a job fixing radios in a machine shop. In 1941, Japan occupied Hong Kong, forcing him to return to farming in his native village. He got married and had three children. Then after the Communists took over the country in 1949, his family lost all their land. Lee was accused of listening to the Voice of America on the radio and was about to be arrested when he fled with his family to Hong Kong. There he opened a drugstore. His mother was able to immigrate to the United States in 1958, but he had to wait until 1963, after his father "confessed" to the Immigration Service that he had used a false identity to enter the country, before immigrating to the United States with his family. Compared to his first trip in 1935, Lee said, "it was very quick. We got the papers signed in Hong Kong and came by airplane. There was no detention or interrogations when we got here." By then, he was forty-two years old. "So much time and opportunity wasted! So much of my youth lost!"

5 Chinese applicants were allowed visitors after the Board of Special Inquiry had rendered decisions on their cases.

FIG. 3.44
On a recent visit to Angel Island, Lee Show Nam pointed out the mark he had made recording his height on the barracks walls when he was detained there in 1935. Photo by Roy Chan.

The family settled in Oakland. Lee Show Nam worked at his father's deli in Chinatown until he retired in 1980. He bought an eight-unit apartment building, which he continues to manage, doing all the repairs himself. He is an accomplished photographer and has traveled all over the world. As Lee proudly showed me pictures of his three grown children, he said that Eric worked in Hollywood as a martial arts actor and instructor; Elaine married a Chinese chef and lived in the suburbs; and Anna became a floral designer and an acclaimed Cantonese opera singer.

When asked about his feelings about Angel Island after all that he had been through, Lee did not hesitate to say, "The Chinese exclusion laws discriminated against the Chinese and made it hard on them by imprisoning them in the wooden building. Now it's much better. Who would have guessed that so many Chinese would be allowed to come to America, become educated, and even run for political office? We now have a Chinese mayor in Oakland [Jean Quan], and we had a Chinese governor in Washington [Gary Locke]. If this keeps up, we may even have a Chinese president someday!"

Emery Sims, Immigrant Inspector: "A Square Deal"

Editor's note: When we began our research in 1975, we had a difficult time finding former employees to interview about the operations of the immigration station. With the help of the Immigration and Naturalization Service, we found Emery Sims, who had worked as a clerk and immigrant inspector on the island from 1929 to 1940. He led us to another immigrant inspector, whom we were able to interview as well. A slim and soft-spoken man, Sims proved to be the better informant of the two. He patiently answered all of our questions about how he came to work at Angel Island, how immigration laws were enforced at the immigration station, and how he felt about his job as an inspector. Sims told us that he had not intended to stay long with the Immigration Service, but the work was so interesting, the hours short, and the pay good that he ended up putting in thirty years of civil service before he retired in 1957. He was eighty-five years old at the time of our interview and lived to be eighty-nine.[1]

Emery Sims was born in 1892 and grew up in North Dakota. His parents were immigrants from Canada. Sometime after he graduated from high school, Sims moved to Tacoma, Washington, where he worked first as a salesman in a lumber company and later for the Veterans Bureau. In 1929, he decided to move to San Francisco with his wife of three years to look for work. After passing the civil service exam as a stenographer, Sims was assigned to work as a clerk at the Angel Island Immigration Station. Six years later, he was promoted to immigrant inspector after he passed the civil service exam with flying colors. He had no previous legal training except for a correspondence course in immigration laws and procedures. A diligent worker, he earned the reputation of being a "fair" inspector, one who believed in giving every applicant "a square deal."

I moved to San Francisco when the big depression was coming on, and I just took any job that I could find. I started as a stenographer and was assigned

1   Emery Sims interview.

to the record vault at Angel Island. There were masses of records of people from foreign countries, especially from China. My first job was to retrieve records from the vault.[2] You see, when Chinese or Japanese people came from the Orient and were detained, a file was started on that person with a file number made up of his ship's number and the page and line of the ship's manifest. Now suppose the ship had come to New York and there was a Chinese newcomer among the passengers. The New York office—then Ellis Island—would send out here for any records we might have on that person's relatives. My job would be to go through the San Francisco records and pick out the file of the person's father or any brothers or sisters, bundle them up, and send them to New York. It was the same way with Boston, Philadelphia, Seattle, and Los Angeles. Large numbers of Chinese immigrants were arriving in New York and Boston at that time.

About 90 percent of our files were on the Chinese because we handled persons of Oriental descent—Chinese, Japanese, Indians or Hindus, and Filipinos. Some of the files were quite thick, since the Chinese were usually questioned at length when they first arrived. The Japanese were processed more quickly because they were mostly children who had been born here and had been taken to Japan for their education. It wasn't too hard to definitely identify them. Filipinos were rarely detained or interrogated because the Philippines was a part of the United States, so their status was different from other immigrants'.

At that time, a new arrival was held for a hearing before a Board of Special Inquiry, as we called it. That consisted of two inspectors, a stenographer,

2   The large fireproof vault was kept in the administration building. In 1914, it held close to 750,000 Chinese records. See Architectural Resources Group and Daniel Quan Design, "Final Interpretive Plan," C-4.

and an interpreter. The interpreter was not really on the board, but the other inspector and the stenographer had the privilege of asking questions if they desired. The inspector to whom the case was assigned was handed the file with any related files of that person's family. And then it was up to him to review these old files and start questioning the applicant about his birth, family, home, and in the course of the testimony, it would develop that the applicant was either very much in accord with the old files or there were rather serious discrepancies between him and the others. It was the only means we had, although it wasn't a very good method, because in a way, the Immigration Service built a way for them to be coached, to learn their testimony and get by. We just worked on the theory that this was the law and we had to carry it out. Some of the inspectors held prejudicial views against the Chinese and gave them a harder time during the hearing. I felt each one was entitled to a square deal, and I tried to give it to him as much as I could. In a way, the Chinese exclusion laws did touch me, and when they were repealed, I thought that was a good thing.

I remember that the interrogation rooms were bright, airy rooms. There would be the stenographer's desk and another desk or two. When the applicant was brought in, he would be given a seat where he could be at ease and talk as he wished and where the interpreter could communicate with him. Around 15 percent of the cases I handled were women. I don't remember any prostitutes, except one instance after World War II. There were many, many boys coming through—twelve, fourteen, fifteen years old, a lot of them smart kids. They were very sure of themselves. I've known of families of four or five coming together. They would question one briefly, just to a certain point, and the other one briefly just to a certain point. Then they would call back the first one and go a little further. That way, the family couldn't get together and talk about what had been said.

The testimony was taken directly on the typewriter in shorthand. Usually you would start with the immigrant himself and check his testimony against his relatives'. The applicant would be questioned about his birthday, about his parents, about his brothers and sisters, and about the village he lived in. That might be quite brief, or it might drag out with some inspectors to forty or fifty pages of typed testimony. All together, it could take from one to three or four days for him and the witnesses. If the testimonies matched, we had to give them the benefit of the doubt. A minor discrepancy would not carry much weight. If it was something serious . . . I remember a case of a boy whose father was bringing him in. He said his mother was so-and-so, but his father said the mother was so-and-so. Still the boy insisted she was so-and-so. Well, he didn't stay.

After the board heard the testimony, they would be pretty much in accord as to what was right and what was not. Any disagreement would mean a denial for the person. If two voted to land him and one voted to deny him, the dissenting member could appeal the case. But if he didn't wish to appeal, the person was landed. Then the file would be sent to the detention quarters with an order to land. If denied, the person was not notified until the testimony was all summed up, but he would be given that notice eventually. If the applicant wished to appeal, a copy of the testimony would be sent to the central office in Washington, D.C., and the attorney handling the case would be given a copy from which he made his appeal. Washington would probably make its decision based on the transcript alone.

More than 75 percent passed the interrogation at Angel Island and were released within two months of their arrival. There could have been indications of fraud in some of them, but nothing that would stand up in court to debar them. Of those who were denied entry, there was always an appeal to Washington, and probably only 5 percent of those who were denied were actually deported. Some who were deported came back and tried again, and made it. They knew you knew they were here before. If we found they were using another name, they could be excluded. All those deported had their photographs taken before they left. They were kept here and could be checked if the person returned.

The interpreters we had were pretty good on most of the dialects. We would use one interpreter with the applicant. Then when we had the witness, we would change interpreters. The inspector in charge had to rotate the interpreters, so the first interpreter might not be available for the recall. One time I asked one of our interpreters what percentage of cases were fraudulent. I asked if 90 percent were, and he said probably. I was aware of it from the beginning. I remember one case I was very sorry about. A father had brought a boy in when it was a daughter that he really had. She later came, and I forget how he brought it up that she was really his daughter, and she really was, but the boys that he had gotten paid for bringing in had spoiled things for her. She was deported, but she married a G.I. and later came back

I know bribes did happen, but the cases were very rare. I don't think I ever had anything offered to me, but in a few cases, some of the others had. It was something that was hard to prove. I was aware that coaching notes were being sneaked in. The administration tried to prevent it by checking the mail. I heard of a capsule being put in a bowl of soup with a little note inside. They got the capsule but nothing developed from it. I know the kitchen help used to give them a lot of help, but there was nothing we could do about it. Overall, I found the law work interesting, and I enjoyed matching wits with the applicants. A lot of them had sharp minds.

Mock Ging Sing:
"Just Keep a Hopeful Attitude"

Editor's note: At the ripe old age of ninety-five, Mock Ging Sing (aka William Mock) still looks at life with a hopeful attitude. He was born in Cheuk Suey Hong village in the Wong Leung Do area of Heungshan District in 1919. That same year, his father Mock Yee Keung left for America to join his own father in the floral nursery business in San Carlos, California. Mock Ging Sing followed in 1937. However, his attempt to enter the United States as the paper son of a U.S. citizen failed, and he was detained on Angel Island for ten months while waiting for a decision on his appeal case. "Those prison days on Angel Island are forever etched into my heart," he told Felicia Lowe when she interviewed him for her film *Carved in Silence*. With great clarity and sincerity, he told her why.[1]

I came to America when I was eighteen years old. I was going to school in China and had heard from other people that you could earn a lot of money in one month in America. So I wrote my father and asked him to find a way to bring me over to America. He then bought me false papers to immigrate to the United States, costing $1,600. We had to sell some of our land in China to pay one-third of the fee as a deposit. The agreement was that once I was landed, my father, with his own money and some borrowed from relatives and friends, would pay off the rest of the debt. That was a lot of money in those days.

At that time, "nine out of ten" Chinese immigrants were coming to America on false papers. Even if an immigrant did not have to buy false papers to come, his father who came earlier probably did, or his grandfather did. I did not feel that I was doing anything illegal. My only thoughts were of coming to America. I had big dreams about my future, about making a lot of money in America.

When I left home, my maternal grandmother accompanied me out of the village. She said, "I am over seventy years old. I don't know if I will be

1   Mock Ging Sing interview, April 9, 1984. Mock Ging Sing is featured prominently in Felicia Lowe's film *Carved in Silence*.

FIG. 3.46
Left to right: Mock Ging Sing with his mother, older brother, and grandmother, 1926. Courtesy of John Mock.

around when you return." When I heard that, my heart felt very sad. The tears started to flow, and I wanted to throw down my luggage and run back home, not come to America. However, I thought further and decided that I must think ahead to my future. And so, I made up my mind to come to America.

Before I came to America, I thought finance was going to be my only problem—how much money it was going to cost. Little did I know then that I was going to be imprisoned in the immigration station for over ten months. It was like being in jail. The doors were locked and we were all confined in this very small space—about 100 by 200 feet. The beds were made of steel and stacked in three tiers. There was a recreation yard outside where we could play basketball, but the entire area was enclosed by a wire fence. There was no way you could get out. The suffering I endured there on Angel Island made me feel very depressed, and time passed very slowly.

Every morning, we would get up around 6:00 or 7:00. We had breakfast at 8:00—usually bread, butter, jam, and saltine crackers. At lunch, we had rice, beef, and vegetables all boiled together, sometimes salted fish, pickled vegetables. The food was quite bad, but because there was nothing else to eat, we had to eat it. At 3:00 in the afternoon, we had coffee, bread, crackers with butter and jam. Around 5:00 or 6:00, we had dinner. The recreation yard was opened at 8:00 or 9:00 in the morning and closed at around 6:00 at night. There were Chinese phonorecords and musical instruments for us to play. There were also mahjong sets and books to read. Most of us didn't have any money, so we played mahjong for fun or for small stakes. The Chinese newspapers were sent over to the island by the publishers in San Francisco. The detainees all had their own interests. Some played musical instruments quite well. Some liked to sing and some liked to read or write. Many of the teenagers had completed middle school and could write well. There were very few fights or arguments among us; we all got along. Every night at 10:00, they would turn out the lights except for the bathroom lights. That was our daily routine.

The guards would stand watch outside. I guess they were afraid that we might escape from the island. They were indifferent toward us and just went by the rules and regulations, opening and locking the doors as required. But there was a janitor who was very nice, especially to the children. He even shared his lunch with them. He had no power whatsoever, but he was sympathetic toward us Chinese. He often said that the immigration people did not treat us fairly, that they should not lock us up.

The Self-governing Association was formed to help the new immigrants adjust to life on Angel Island. There were always new arrivals who did not know anything. So those who had been detained there the longest, sometimes for more than a year, would brief the new arrivals on what to do and what not to do. For example, most of the detainees were paper sons. If they brought their coaching books with them to the island, they were told to destroy them. To avoid any trouble, they were also warned never to say anything about their real names.

The organization also helped immigrants who became sick by calling for medical help. It also complained to the immigration authorities about the poor food. When any of the immigrants did not behave properly—stealing or fighting—the Self-governing Association reprimanded him and even punished him by locking him in the *haak fong* [dark room]. It was called *haak fong* because that was what it was—a dark room with no light. There was only a chair inside to sit on. We would close the door and leave him there for two or three hours. Although the Self-governing Association had no real power, we still had to unite. There is always strength through unity.

Locked up on Angel Island, everyone felt depressed and worried. First of all, we all worried about whether or not we would be admitted into the United States. Second, the place was so small and confining, it made us moody and even more depressed. Some committed suicide because they had sold everything they had in China or borrowed heavily to buy the papers to come to America. Here he was, up to his neck in debt. If he were deported back to China, there would be no way for him to ever repay his debts. So to relieve himself of these kinds of problems, he committed suicide. Again, I have only heard people talk about suicides. I did not see it for myself.

Other people released their anger and frustrations by writing poems on the walls. There were poems inside and outside the building. Some were written and some were carved with a knife into the wall—all expressing pain, sorrow, and bitterness. Many of the poets had been detained on the island for a long time. They had plenty of time to worry and feel frustrated. Many of them hurt inside so deeply that they needed to vent their feelings by word of mouth. But since they could not talk about it, they wrote about it so that they would not be forgotten. There was no other way for them to rebel against the immigration officials. There was no other way for them to express their sorrow or unhappiness. There was no other way for them to ever forget this painful experience. That is why they had to use the written word to express their inner feelings and deep thoughts. If not for the poems, they perhaps would have committed suicide because the frustration and depression would build up day by day. And when depression sets in too deeply, something is bound to happen.

The person who came to America with me—my paper father—told me that I would be interrogated. "They will ask you many questions. What questions they will ask you, I do not know. But they will definitely ask you lots of questions. You must study your coaching book and know it well. If you give the wrong answers, it will be disastrous!" I began to worry and became frightened. I made up my mind that, no matter what, I would study and memorize everything that was in the coaching book. I didn't care how big the book was, I was determined to know it all.

It was about three or four months before it was my turn to be interrogated. My biggest worry was that I might answer a question wrong and not be allowed into the country. They asked me about our house and our neighbors, the size of the village, and how far away was the marketplace. They even asked me how many rooms there were in our house and what type of furniture we had. It may have been because of my youth, but I was very bold and fearless. I answered their questions so thoroughly that they couldn't open their mouths to ask me any more. I later heard from a number of people that certain Chinese interpreters were very mean and disrespectful to them. They told me, "The interpreter pounded the table deliberately to scare me. If I should be landed and someday see that interpreter on the streets of San Francisco, I am going to beat him up!"

That did not happen to me, but in those days, the Immigration Service was very unreasonable. If they said that you did not pass, you did not pass. And if you did not pass, you had to hire a lawyer to appeal the case. That was why I was there for more than ten months. The immigration officials said that my papers were fraudulent. They said I didn't speak the Heungshan dialect, but the Sunwui dialect. That was because my village was close to Sunwui. I told them that there was no big difference between the two dialects, but they said, "It is not the right dialect." I replied, "If that's what you say, that's your business, not mine." That was how I answered him!

Editor's note: According to the alleged father's immigration case file, Mock Ging Sing came to America, claiming to be Chang Hall Hoy, the son of Chang Lin Hoy, a U.S. citizen.[2] Father and son arrived on the *President Coolidge* on May 5, 1937, and were taken to Angel Island. The father was briefly interrogated on May 7, at which time the case was deferred, pending the receipt of files from Honolulu, Los Angeles, and San Diego. "Knocking letters" from Chang's relatives in China had been mailed to the immigration offices in these cities as well as in San Francisco, asserting that father and son were using false papers to enter the United States. There were also Chinese letters that had been confiscated in another immigration investigation in Coronado, California, which indicated that Chang Lin Hoy's brother, Chang Lin Siu, was really the son of Wong You Dong.

When the alleged father Chang Lin Hoy was interrogated a second time on July 21 and 22, he was asked a total of 234 questions about his family, the village, the schoolteacher, and his brother Chang Lin Siu. He was also confronted with certain discrepancies between testimonies he had given in 1920 and at the time of the hearing.

Q. Do you know the name of the schoolteacher you had?
A. MAH WAI DOO.
Q. How did your father engage him to teach in your village?
A. He went to LIK KEE VILLAGE to get him; the teacher belongs to that village.
Q. When was it your father went to the LIK KEE VILLAGE to engage this teacher?
A. My father wrote to my mother and had my mother employ that teacher.
Q. Are you contradicting your statement that your father went to the LIK KEE VILLAGE to engage the teacher?
A. I didn't mean to say that; I meant to say my father got my mother to employ that teacher. . . .
Q. But although your father was in the U.S., other people in the village left it up to him to engage a teacher for the village school, is that right?
A. Yes.
Q. Then how do you account for the fact that your father was unable to

2   File 37176/12–17 (Chang Lin Hoy), Immigration Arrival Investigation Case Files, RG 85, NARA-SF.

name the teacher you had in the village when he was testifying at the time you were an applicant for admission?

A. I don't know.

Q. According to that, your father and mother go to the LIK KEE VIL-LAGE and select a man there, without knowing who that man was. Is that what we are to understand?

A. Possibly my father, at that time, did not name any particular teacher—just left that matter to the judgment of my mother to select a good teacher.

On October 18, 1937, Chang Lin Hoy was interviewed again. At one point, the questions focused on letters that his brother Chang Lin Siu had written to his father, Wong You Dong.

Q. (*Showing Chinese letters that are marked SD 4, SD 6, and SD 8*) These three letters are in the same handwriting as that on the letter, which you have identified as having been written to you by your alleged brother CHANG LIN SIU. Each one of these letters is dated several years subsequent to the date you give for the death of your father, but each letter is addressed to the father [Wong You Dong] of the writer, and each one is signed in the name of YAT CHEUNG, same characters as given for the marriage name of your alleged brother, CHANG LIN SIU. How do you account for the fact that this alleged brother wrote several letters to his father long after your father died?

A. I deny that these letters are in CHANG LIN SIU'S handwriting, and as to the name, YAT CHEUNG, it may be just a coincidence.

The Board of Special Inquiry concluded that while the incriminating letters from China "are of no probative value," the investigation into the applicant's status showed disagreements between the present testimony and evidence on which the applicant was admitted in 1920. Chang Lin Hoy was denied admission on the ground that his original admission to the United States as the son of a U.S. citizen was fraudulent. By implication, his son Chang Hall Hoy [Mock Ging Sing] was also denied admission.

Father and son decided to appeal the exclusion decisions by retaining attorney William Jack Chow. Three months later, on December 15, 1937, a telegram from the INS in Washington, D.C., ordered Chang Lin Hoy to be landed immediately. His son Chang Hall Hoy had to wait another three months before he was finally admitted to the United States on March 1, 1938. By then, he had been detained on Angel Island for ten long months.

FIG. 3.47
Mock Ging Sing enlisted in the
U.S. Army in 1944. Courtesy of
John Mock.

FIG. 3.48
Mock Ging Sing's chrysanthemum
nursery in Palo Alto, California,
1968. Left to right, front row:
John and Larry; second row: May
and Henry; third row: wife Chew
Young Kay and Stewart; back row:
Ann. Courtesy of John Mock.

Today, Mock still believes that their appeal succeeded because his paper father's brother-in-law worked as a cook at Stanford University and was able to get his employer to put in a good word with the INS.

After his release from Angel Island, Mock attended San Mateo High School while working part-time in his father's chrysanthemum nursery. "It was fifteen hours a day for $50 a month and no days off," he recalled. He joined the Army in 1944 and served one year in Europe. In 1947, he returned to China and married Chew Young Kay. The couple had seven children. They were able to build a profitable business growing chrysanthemums in Palo Alto, California, despite the racial discrimination they faced.

We were treated unfairly not only by INS but also in our daily lives. We could not buy houses in certain areas. We could not join the unions or compete for the better jobs. Restaurants and barbershops would not serve us, and gas stations would not allow us to use their restrooms because we were Chinese. At that time, we had no choice but to walk away. There was no way to handle these types of situations. I could only hope that things would somehow get better in the future. Just keep a hopeful attitude; that was all we could do.

FIG. 3.49
Mock Ging Sing and family
visiting China, 2007. Courtesy of
John Mock.

Later on, Chinese became better educated and more Chinese went into business and politics. The world became more open-minded, and opportunities opened up as a result. All my children were able to get a college education and establish successful careers. From 1938 to 1981, I invested a great deal of sweat and energy into the flower business. Although I never made it rich, I have had a comfortable life. In 1956, we Dowmoon (previously part of Chungshan District) people formed the San Francisco Bay Area Chrysanthemum Growers Association in order to strengthen our bargaining power in negotiations with suppliers, shippers, and florists. I served as the first secretary and remained actively involved with the association for many years. After I retired, I sold my business and land holdings and invested in commercial real estate. In 1987, I founded the Mock Ging Sing Foundation to do charitable work in my ancestral village, helping to fund schools, libraries, hospitals, and senior centers. Although the foundation is small, I am very proud of our work. It makes me happy and keeps me healthy.[3]

Editor's note: In 1964, during the Confession Program, when the U.S. government offered to clear the status of any Chinese immigrant who had entered the country fraudulently if they "confessed," Mock Ging Sing became one of 30,000 Chinese aliens to confess and become a naturalized U.S. citizen. Initially, he had been reluctant to do so. "It wasn't because I was afraid of being deported," he told me in a phone conversation. "I just did not want to cause any trouble for my paper mother, who did not want to participate in the Confession Program." But when one of Mock's paper brothers decided

3   Him Mark Lai, "Potato King and Film Producer"; Mock Ging Sing interview, November 13, 1995; Wu Rijun, "Tianshidao shou nan zhe."

to confess because he needed to be a U.S. citizen in order to work for the federal government, Mock changed his mind. His attorney was right—there was nothing to fear. He vaguely remembers a brief interview at the INS office, during which time he joked with the officers about the floral industry. Two months later, he passed the citizenship exam and changed his surname and that of his children to Mock.[4]

My children did not seem to mind what their surnames were, but I felt bad about changing my name when I left China. My surname is Mock and I wanted to remain a Mock. I felt very good about the confession. Before that, I was always worried about some immigration officer coming to my house to arrest me. It was a big load off my mind.

About those prison days on Angel Island . . . although my sufferings there did affect my mental outlook, I did not let it affect my future. It made me think ahead, "How can we overcome this type of injustice?" It did not discourage or dishearten me. Rather, it made me work harder to better my future.[5]

4   Mock Ging Sing, phone conversation with Judy Yung, August 14, 2009.
5   Mock Ging Sing interview, April 9, 1984.

Ja Kew Yuen:
"Treated as Second-Class Citizens"

Editor's note: We all fondly called him Ja Bak (Uncle Ja)—the father of my Chinese-school classmate Ja Wing Chi, the owner of the M & J Children's Shop on Grant Avenue, and the political activist known for his pro-China stands. Ja Kew Yuen was born in Tam Kai village, Hoiping District, in 1913, the second son of four children. When he was still a young boy, his father left for America, where he learned the restaurant business in San Francisco before opening the Bon Ton Restaurant in Prescott, Arizona. His remittances home supported the family and Ja Bak's schooling through college in Canton. By then, the Japanese had invaded China, and Ja Bak knew it was time to leave for America. A well-educated man knowledgeable about Chinese immigration history, Ja Bak contributed to our book by providing the Chinese calligraphy for the book cover and title pages and by allowing us to interview him about his one-month stay on Angel Island.[1]

I had just graduated from Chungshan University in 1938 when the Japanese bombed Canton and the country went to pieces. We were afraid that our communication lines to America would be severed, which would have meant no more remittances from my father. We would have starved to death! So I wrote Father to make arrangements for me to come to America. He had intended to send for me after I finished elementary school, but he never got around to taking care of the paperwork.

At the time, there weren't too many native-born citizens, since the Chinese Exclusion Act had effectively stopped the immigration of Chinese women and the formation of families in America. But after the 1906 earthquake and fire destroyed all the birth records in city hall, the Immigration Service was forced to accept claims of birthright citizenship from anyone. So my father reported he was born here, and that gave me the opportunity and right to come to America as the son of a native.

1   Ja Kew Yuen interview.

But first, my family had to escape to Macao by sampan since the Sze Yup area was under Japanese attack. We stayed in Macao for three or four months, while I took care of all the paperwork in Hong Kong. In those days, you didn't have to go through the U.S. consulate. Fathers here filed an affidavit and sent it to Hong Kong, and you used that affidavit to purchase your ship ticket. I had the *Gam Saan jong* help me get my ticket. I was to come alone, while the rest of my family stayed in Macao.

Before a son or daughter immigrates, the father must send a coaching book. To be careful, he would usually have someone hand-deliver it. But if he were in a rush, he would have to mail it. What did the coaching book say? It talked about family relationships, the village and the living quarters in China. If you memorized all the answers, you should've been able to pass the interrogation. But it was very tricky, especially if they didn't ask the essential questions but something else like, "Where was the clock in the house?" or "Who were in the photos?" So if the immigration people wanted to trip you up, it was quite easy. There was no way to prepare for it all. After the Immigration Service caught on that most of the Chinese applicants were frauds, they asked more difficult questions. So the Chinese here in America developed specialists who wrote down detailed answers to questions that were likely to be asked of applicants and their witnesses. Once you received the coaching book, you calculated how long it would take you to memorize it and worked your departure date around that. In my case, the coaching book had more than ten pages of questions and answers, so I needed about a week. Many people took the coaching book with them to study, but before they reached Hawaii, they knew to throw it overboard or flush it down the toilet.

I remember I came on the *Coolidge* in 1939. There were more than one hundred newcomers aboard the ship. I had $10 in my pocket when we arrived in Hawaii. It was money that my father had sent to my mother from America—she had kept it for years. When I heard about the fresh fruit in Hawaii, I gave $1 to someone to help me buy some bananas. After our ship arrived in San Francisco, new immigrants were not allowed to go ashore or speak to any relatives. Instead, we were transferred to a small ferry and taken over to Angel Island for inspection.

After we were registered, they took a group of us to a large dormitory and assigned us bunk beds. There must have been two or three hundred people—all Chinese. Then we were given a cursory medical exam. I later went to see the doctor because I was suffering from insomnia and felt tired. I saw that the hospital was nicer and quieter than the dormitory, so I asked this Korean man who was in charge [Paul Whang] if I could stay there for a few days. It was very comfortable, and I was able to get some rest.

Lee Bak Yeung, an old-timer who had been deported for narcotics and who was now seeking admission under another name, was there to greet the new arrivals. Everyone went to him whenever there was a problem. He told me that in the past, there were all kinds of bad habits—gambling and fights among the inmates. So the Self-governing Association was formed to maintain order. It forbade gambling—only mahjong, poker, and small stakes were allowed. I was elected president right away. When enough people complained, the organization requested longer hours for the exercise yard and better food. It also helped people buy food and things in San Francisco by sending an order list to Sing Chong or some other store. Officers of the Self-governing Association started the practice of chipping in money for *siu yeh* [midnight snack]. We would send for a pig's head to throw into a pot of *jook*.

FIG. 3.50
Ja Kew Yuen at work in the M & J Children's Shop, 1950s. Courtesy of Alvin Ja.

There was no set time for getting up. If you got up late, you missed breakfast—usually plain *jook* with fermented bean curd. After breakfast, some exercised or played ball outside. The fenced-in yard was opened after breakfast and closed before dinnertime at five or six o'clock. After lunch, people slept, played chess or mahjong, read newspapers, or chatted. Sometimes I wrote in my diary or read books I had brought with me. Lights went out around 9:00 or so.

I remember the interrogation took no more than two days—an hour or two each day. After they asked me questions, they had to ask my father the same questions. Then they came back to me again. It was not very difficult. I still remember the inspector. His name was Sims. He was small in stature—calm, not mean or hostile. The Chinese interpreter was polite too and didn't rush me. They asked me questions about the village, how many houses in each row, the layout of our house, who lived in front and behind us, the birthdates of my parents, how many trips did my father make to America, how many brothers and sisters, where I went to school, and so on. I think they did not give me a hard time because I resembled my father. I was landed a few days later.[2] Then after another week, I went to pick up my certificate of identity, what we called *fo lim beng* because it resembled a Chinese cookie by that name.

2   According to Ja Kew Yuen's Alien File A11408999, obtained from the United States Citizenship and Immigration Service through the Freedom of Information Act, he was detained on Angel Island for seventeen days. The Board of Special Inquiry noted only two minor discrepancies in the cross-examination, and Ja's attitude during the hearing and his strong resemblance to his father convinced the board to admit him as the son of native Ja Siu.

事通 周家京　席主邑三 周　棠　席主州岡 李賢華　席主慶肇 周廬韶　十二月撮　民國卅年　席主陽寧 黃起煬　席主和合 謝僑遠　席主和陽 周錦朝　席主和人 陳東初

FIG. 3.51
Ja Kew Yuen (third from right)
representing the Hop Wo District
Association on the board of
directors of the Chinese Six
Companies, 1941. Courtesy of
Alvin Ja.

I didn't see anyone commit suicide or go crazy at Angel Island while I was there. In general, people were all anxious to get the interrogation over with and to leave the island. No one was happy living there. At the time, we didn't understand the laws. Although the conditions were bad and the treatment unfair, we learned to bear it. For those who passed the interrogation and were landed, Angel Island did not play a big part in their lives. But you can't blame those who were detained for a long time while on appeal, after spending a lot of money to come in the first place, for feeling anguished. They were the ones who suffered the most and who wrote the angry and bitter poems on the walls. But after you have been in the United States for a while, you will come to see that America treats Chinese as second-class citizens.

Editor's note: After he was admitted into the country, Ja Kew Yuen settled down in San Francisco Chinatown. He married Mabel Mar of Victoria, B.C., in 1945, and the couple had one daughter and one son. They, along with a son from a former marriage, lived in and ran the M & J Children's Shop

FIG. 3.52
Ja Kew Yuen speaking at a
community event to promote
U.S.-China relations, 1950s.
Courtesy of Alvin Ja.

(with the two hobby horses in front of the store) at 952 Grant Avenue for more than thirty years. A respected community leader, Ja Bak was a board member of the Hop Wo District Association, Chew Lun Family Association, and Chinese Six Companies. He also taught Chinese school, wrote for two Chinese newspapers, and founded the Chinese American Association of Commerce in 1978, which he served as president for many years.

A Chinese patriot at heart, Ja Bak was persecuted by the FBI in the 1950s for his pro–Communist China views and actions, including a clandestine visit to China in 1957. He was stripped of his immigration status and U.S. passport as a result. Rather than return to China, he chose to remain in the United States, where he worked on improving U.S. relations with China through the establishment of Kuo Feng Travel and Tours and organizing such cultural exchange programs as a Ping-Pong diplomacy tour. After he recovered his legal status in the early 1980s, Ja Bak was finally able to make four visits to his beloved homeland. He became a naturalized U.S. citizen in 1990. He had planned to attend the ceremony marking the return of Hong Kong to China on July 1, 1997, but passed away seventeen days before the event, at the age of eighty-four.

Lee Puey You:
"A Bowlful of Tears"

Editor's note: In 1975, we were fortunate to find Lee Puey You through a mutual friend of her daughter Daisy Gin. I had heard that she was detained on Angel Island for close to two years, probably the longest stay of any Chinese detainee, and she was willing to be interviewed! So one Saturday afternoon, Him Mark Lai and I paid Lee a visit in her North Beach flat in San Francisco. She had a remarkable memory and thoughtfully answered our questions one by one, until we ran out of questions to ask after an hour or so.

That afternoon, we learned that Lee Puey You was born in Chung Tow village, Heungshan District, in 1916. She was twenty-three years old when she immigrated to the United States in 1939 as Ngim Ah Oy, the paper daughter of a U.S. citizen. Once admitted, she was to marry a *Gam Saan haak* thirty years her senior in order to prepare the way for the rest of her family to come. Lee had expected to be detained at Angel Island for a few weeks, until she successfully passed the physical examination and interrogation; however, because of discrepancies in her interview and that of her alleged father, she was denied entry.

Slated for deportation, Lee was told by her relatives that they would hire an attorney to appeal her case to higher authorities in Washington, D.C., and that she needed to be patient. The appeal went from the U.S. district court to the U.S. circuit court of appeals, and finally to the U.S. Supreme Court, without success. By this time, the war with Japan had escalated in China, and the United States was about to enter World War II on the same side as China. The hope was that Lee would be allowed to land, because it would be too dangerous to send her back to China. Instead, after twenty months of confinement at Angel Island, she was deported to Hong Kong. Here, her story took another unique turn. In 1947, she returned to the United States, posing as a war bride, to marry the same man. The immigration station at Angel Island had since closed and been moved to San Francisco, and the

Chinese Exclusion Act had been repealed. This time, she was allowed to enter immediately. But the twenty months of prisonlike detainment at Angel Island had been forever etched into her mind and heart.

Mindful of the psychological scars of Angel Island that she still bore, Him Mark and I trod carefully, perhaps too cautiously, in asking our prepared list of questions. As a result, we saw only a partial picture of the circumstances of her immigration to the United States. Nine years later, when I reinterviewed Lee with Felicia Lowe for her film *Carved in Silence* and pursued a different line of questioning, I got a fuller picture of her life before and after Angel Island and learned how she was able to endure twenty months of confinement at Angel Island. The following story is drawn from the two interviews.[1]

I didn't want to come to America, but I was forced by circumstances to come. When I was very young, my father was a wealthy farmer. A flood destroyed all his land, and he lost all his money. It was then that our family's fortunes changed. My father died and my brother had to go to work to support my mother and me. I saw how hard he worked, just one job. It was barely enough. So my mother arranged a marriage for me. I had a passport to come when I was sixteen, but I didn't come until I was twenty-three, after the Japanese attacked China. They bombed Shekki and everywhere, and there was nowhere to hide so I had to come to America. But my fate was not good. I had never seen my fiancé before, but I knew he was a lot older than me. He said he would give me the choice of marrying him or not after I arrived. My mother wanted me to come to America so that I could help bring my brother and the rest of the family over later. Because of that, I was afraid to oppose the arranged marriage. I had to be a filial daughter. The situation forced me to sacrifice everything to come to America.

In 1939, I arrived at Angel Island. They told us to store our luggage in the shed, and then they directed us to the wooden building. We were allowed to bring only a small suitcase of clothes. The next day, we had to take a physical examination. When the doctor came, I had to take off all my clothes. It was so embarrassing and shameful. I didn't really want to let him examine me, but I had no choice. Back in China, I never had to take off everything, but it was different here in America. I found it very disturbing.

There must have been more than one hundred people detained on Angel Island. The men had their dormitories and the women had theirs. They assigned us to beds, and there were *gwai poh* [female foreign devils] to take care of us. Every day we got up at about 7:00. They yelled, "Chow, chow!" They would wake us up and take us to the dining room for breakfast—usually a plate of vegetables and a plate of meat catering to the Chinese pal-

1 Lee Puey You interviews. An earlier version of this story was published in Hune and Nomura, *Asian/Pacific Islander American Women*, 123–37, and *Frontiers*, 25, no. 1 (2004): 1–22. Lee Puey You was prominently featured in Felicia Lowe's film *Carved in Silence*.

2 Most of the women were
from the Sze Yup districts
(Sunwui, Toishan, Hoiping,
and Yanping), while Lee Puey
You was from Heungshan
District, where the Longdu
dialect is spoken. (See map
on page 5.)

ate. Sometimes scrambled eggs, sometimes veg-
etables mixed with meat. Their food was pretty
bad, not very tasty. But then most people didn't
eat their food. Many had relatives in the city who
sent them Chinese dishes—barbecued duck and
sausages, packages of food every day. After we ate,
they took us back and locked the doors. That's all.
Just like in jail. Followed us out and followed us
back, then locked the doors. They treated us like
criminals! They were always afraid that we would
go over to the men's side and talk to them or that
we might escape or commit suicide. Where would
we escape to? I never saw anyone attempt suicide,
but people did cry to die because they were suf-
fering so.

There was really nowhere to go. Just a little
breezeway that was fenced in for us to sun, exer-
cise, or play ball. There was a long table for us to
use for writing or sewing. From the windows we
could see the boats arrive daily at about 9:30 or
10:00 in the morning. At the end of the day, we
would watch the inspectors and newly released
immigrants leave the island on the same boat.
That's all. We couldn't have any visitors, but there
was a Miss [Katharine] Maurer, a churchwoman who came once or twice
a week. She was very nice to me, bringing me yarn or fabric. Sometimes I
read or knitted, made some clothes, or slept. When you got up, it was time
to eat again. Day in and day out, eat and sleep. It was hard, and time went
by so slowly.

We had a bed to sleep in and the bathrooms were adequate, but it was
noisy with so many people—fifty or sixty women at one time and a few
young children besides. Sometimes the people next to you talked or people
would cry in the middle of the night, so you couldn't sleep. Sometimes
people didn't get along and argued, but because we were in the same fix,
we were generally good friends. We shared food and helped each other out
even though I couldn't understand the Sze Yup dialect.[2] Often, those who
had been there awhile cried when they saw others leave. So much mental
anguish; we all suffered emotionally. No one had any energy. You know,
sitting at Angel Island, I must have cried a bowlful of tears. It was so pitiful.

When I was in China, I didn't know it would be so hard in America. Ev-
erybody said that coming to America was like going to heaven, but at Angel

Island they treated the Chinese as if we were all thieves and robbers. The bathroom was filled with poems expressing sadness and bitterness. They were about how hard the stay at Angel Island was, how sad and depressed the women were, not knowing when they would be allowed to leave the island. Sometimes I wrote poems to console myself. That helped to release some of the tension. I would write and cry at the same time. During one of my more painful moments, I wrote this poem:

遠涉重洋到美洲，
離別家鄉與親朋—
誰知困在木樓中，
不知何日得出頭？

Crossing the faraway ocean to arrive in America,
Leaving behind my hometown, family, and friends—
Who would have expected to be stranded in a wooden building,
Not knowing when I can hold my head up with pride?

Translated by Marlon K. Hom

In my darkest moment of sadness, I could only turn to God for help. I just prayed every day. That was the only way I could bear those hardships. I had no choice but to be strong. I had to take care of myself so that I might survive. I had to fulfill my duty as a filial daughter. That was all!

Two or three weeks after my arrival, I was called in for the interrogation. I knew I would be interrogated, but I was still nervous when the time came. There was a typist, an inspector, and an interpreter—three in all. Just looking at them made me scared. It went on for three days. We started at 9:30 or 10:00 in the morning. At 11:30 or 12:00 there was a lunch break. Then we went back at 1:00 until 4:00. They asked me about my grandparents, which direction the house faced, which house I lived in, how far from one place to another. It took a long time because after they asked me questions, they would ask my father, then my uncle, and then the two witnesses. That's why it took so long. Sometimes the interpreters were cranky. When I said I wasn't sure or I didn't know, they would tell me to say yes or no. They just treated us like criminals!

After the interrogation, if you failed, they didn't tell you. But when you were allowed to see your father or witnesses, you knew they were going to deport you. You see, if I had passed, I wouldn't have had to see the witnesses. I would have been immediately called to land, to gather my things and leave. That's how it usually was. Relatives later told me that they would appeal my case to the higher authorities in Washington, D.C. They told me to be patient. My appeal failed the first time and then a second time. They were hoping that when the United States finally entered the war, I would be released. But instead, I was stuck on Angel Island for twenty months. I was there the longest. Most people stayed three weeks or so. Those on appeal left after a few months. But my case was more "crooked" because my paper father had reported that I was a twin and I didn't know that.[3] So I wasn't landed.

That was the system then, and there was nothing you could do about it. But this is how I look at it now. If things checked out at the American consulate in Hong Kong, they should let us come. If not, they shouldn't let us come. That would have spared us suffering twenty days aboard ship, seasickness and all, and then imprisonment at Angel Island. In my case, I had to endure twenty months of prisonlike confinement. And then to be deported to Hong Kong, how sad!

During my trip back to China on the boat, my heart felt very heavy. I had "no face" to see my family. My spirit was broken. I finally had to put some rice, some hot rice, against my chest to ease the pain inside. The anguish that I had suffered is more than anyone can bear. I can't begin to describe it. Then all of a sudden, I had a dream. My appeal was successful! It was like a message from God. Then my heart was at peace. So that's my story from start to finish. It took me fourteen years to come back to America, fourteen long, long years.[4]

As for my life in America . . . As long as you are willing to work hard, you can make a better living in America than in China. We had a grocery store, and since there were enough people working in the store, I was not needed. Later on, after my father-in-law passed away, that left only my husband and me to run the store. I would work every day from 7:00 a.m. to 9:00 p.m., fourteen hours a day, seven days a week. But I only did that for five or six years. Now my life is quite settled. I saved enough money to buy a building so that I can live in one apartment and rent the rest of the units out. I should be able to support myself for the rest of my life.

My mother had wanted me to come to America, hoping that later on I would somehow bring the rest of the family over. Twenty years later, my mother, my brother, his wife and their four children, my sister and her husband and children all came to America on a ship. It cost me thousands of dollars, but my mother's hopes have finally been fulfilled! Now all of them are doing well. They all have good jobs and their own homes. All the children have finished college and are making good money. Everyone is happy and my responsibility to them is finally over.

3 The final report in Lee Puey You's immigration file shows that the Board of Special Inquiry did a thorough cross-examination of Lee and the four witnesses, citing contradictions in the alleged father's former testimonies and present claim of relationship and discrepancies in Lee's testimonies about her birth date and status as the older twin. The credibility of one of the witnesses was also called into question. The board concluded, "The character of these discrepancies afford clear proof that the alleged father's claim of American citizenship is based upon fraud, and that he falsely claims the applicant to be his legitimate blood child." See file 39071/12−9 (Ngim Ah Oy), Immigration Arrival Investigation Case Files, RG 85, NARA-SF.

4 It took Lee Puey You fourteen years to come to America, counting from 1932, when she was betrothed and first issued a visa, to 1947, when she was finally admitted into the United States as a war bride under the War Brides Act of 1945.

Editor's note: Sixteen years after the second interview for the film, I came to a different understanding of Lee Puey You's immigration history and her life in America. It had not been as "easy" as she had said. By then, Lee had passed away after a heroic battle against cancer in 1996, and I turned to her daughters, Daisy and Debbie Gin, for help in clarifying some discrepancies in her interview. Based on the immigration and court files that they found at the National Archives and through a Freedom of Information Act request, we learned that in 1955, someone blew the whistle and reported her illegal entry to the INS.[5] A warrant for her arrest was issued on the grounds that the immigration visa she had used to enter the country in 1947 had been procured by fraud. She was ordered to appear before the INS in San Francisco to show cause as to why she should not be deported. The stakes were just as high as they had been for her at Angel Island in 1939, but this time she had the benefit of an attorney, Jackie Sing, to represent her as well as the support of her second husband, Fred Gin, whom she had married in 1953. She was also apparently prepared to tell the whole story. According to the transcript, partway through the interrogation and at the prompting of her attorney, she said through the interpreter, "I wish to volunteer the whole facts in the case." Then she proceeded to tell the truth about her difficult journey to America and what really happened to her after she was admitted into the country.

FIG. 3.54
Lee Puey You and daughter Eva Chan, 1950. Courtesy of Debbie Gin.

I was born in Cr 5–5–3 [June 3, 1916]. My name was Lee Puey You at birth. When I was about 13 years old my father died, and he did not leave us anything and my family was very poor. It was during the war and my family was having a hard time to make a living. One day a cousin of Woo Tong talked to my mother and told her that he has a cousin in the United States whose wife died recently and that he would like to remarry again and asked my mother whether she was willing to consent to having her daughter marry his cousin in the United States. Later Woo Tong's cousin tell my mother to have a photograph of me to send it to Woo Tong to see whether he liked me or not. Some time later Woo Tong's cousin came and told me that I was to go to the United States under the name of Ngin Ah Oy as a daughter of a son of a native—I was known as Yim Tai Muey at that time—and that after I came to the United States I was to marry Woo Tong as his wife, and I came to the United States in 1939. When I arrived here in San Francisco, I was

5   "In the Matter of Ngim Ah Oy on Habeas Corpus," folder 23099R, Admiralty Files, U.S. District Court for the Northern District of California, RG 21, NARA-SF; and copy of Alien File A6824153, obtained via Freedom of Information Act request to the Immigration and Naturalization Service.

detained at Angel Island for almost two years. During all of that time I had a very hard time and I was very sad, and every time that someone was released from there I felt sick all over again. I did not know what was happening to my case. I even attempted suicide. Then later I was deported back to Hong Kong. On my way back to Hong Kong I wanted to commit suicide again, but I was thinking about my mother, of the hard times we had together. When I arrived back in Hong Kong, I sold rice on the street in Hong Kong. I was having a very hard time because it was during the war at that time. My mother told me that we have used some of Woo Tong's money and no matter how hard a time I am having I must not get married. She already promised my marriage to Woo Tong. She said that I should wait until after the war, when she could correspond with Woo Tong again and that he will make arrangements for me to go to the United States again. After the war, in about 1947, Woo Tong came to Hong Kong and he came to our house and talked to my mother. Later then, we invited some friends for dinner; then my mother told me it was considered as my marriage ceremony with Woo Tong. Then Woo Tong told me of his plan to bring me to the United States. He said I was to get a marriage certificate with Sai Chan and said I was to come to the United States as Sai Chan's wife and said he would accompany me to the United States.[6] After Sai Chan and I obtained our marriage certificate from the American consular office in Hong Kong, he told me that I must go to a husband-and-wife relationship with him before he could bring me to the United States. I objected to that, but he forced me into that, so I lived with him as man and wife in Hong Kong. Sai Chan and I came to the United States together in 1947. After we arrived in the United States, he took me to Woo Tong's place at 1141 Stockton Street and he left me there. When I get there I learned Woo Tong's wife was still living and that I was not actually to be Woo Tong's wife, but his concubine. I objected to it, but there was nothing I could do because I was now here in the United States. I did not know of anyone to go to for aid, so I stayed with him. During all those times I was living there I was treated very badly by his wife. She treated me as a slave girl. I had to do all kinds of work in the house, take care of her, and I also had to take care of one of Woo Tong's buildings. On January 8, 1949, I gave birth to a daughter fathered by Woo Tong. While I was in the Stanford Hospital during my maternity period, Woo Tong made all the arrangements for me. He filled out the birth certificate for my daughter and he filled out the father's name as Sai Chan. Woo Tong died August 18, 1950, in San Francisco. After he died, his wife forced me to continue to work for her. When Woo Tong died, he did not leave money or anything for my daughter and myself. I met Fred Gin in about 1953 and learned his wife had passed away several years before. I found he was a person of good character.

6   Sai Chan (pseudonym) was a U.S. citizen and World War II veteran.

I went with him about six months before we got married. I went to Reno and obtained a divorce decree from Sai Chan to clear the record on January 16, 1953. Fred Gin had two sons by his first wife in the United States, and after we were married, I bore him a daughter on February 4, 1955.

Editor's note: Lee Puey You admitted to no wrongdoing and insisted that she was following her mother's orders, that she had agreed to marry Woo Tong believing he was a widower, and that Sai Chan had forced her to have sex with him after their bogus marriage. In the cross-examination by her attorney, Lee emphasized her newfound happiness in her marriage to Fred Gin and her desire to remain with her family in the United States.

Q. What would happen if you were separated from Fred and the rest of your family?

A. I would have a hard time, because I have no one else to go to if I should be separated from my family.

Q. Would Fred go with you in the event you should be deported?

A. I will not allow him to go with me even if willing, because I don't want him to sacrifice his life for me.

Q. Would you take your blood daughters, Eva and Daisy, if you were separated?

A. No. I will leave them in the United States. Even if they have to beg or starve in the United States, I would leave them because the living conditions here in the United States are better.

When asked by the INS officer if she had anything further to add before the hearing came to a close, she responded:

I just wish to say that you give me a chance so that I can remain in the United States to be with my family. I found happiness after I married Fred Gin. Prior to that time the wrongdoing was not due to my fault. I was just obeying my mother, which she make all the arrangements with Woo Tong that I apply for a marriage certificate as the wife of Sai Chan to come to the United States.

Editor's note: The INS officer H. H. Engelskirchen was evidently not convinced or moved by her testimony and ordered her deported on grounds that her immigration visa had been procured by fraud and that "she lived in an adulterous relationship with Woo Tong" while still married to Sai Chan. Lee Puey You did not give up. She had associate counsel Lambert O'Donnell appeal the decision before the Board of Immigration Appeals in Washing-

FIG. 3.55
Lee Puey You and Fred Gin with
their children, 1955. Left to right:
Eva, Daisy, Calvin, and Melvin.
Courtesy of Debbie Gin.

ton, D.C. The attorney first argued that she was "not innately a bad person
of criminal tendencies . . . but a mere pawn—indeed a slave—of men who
deserve severe condemnation." Next, he pointed out that because her mar-
riage to Sai Chan, a citizen veteran, was consummated and deemed valid,
she had immigrated legitimately as a war bride. This time, the Board of Im-
migration Appeals sustained Lee's appeal and terminated the deportation
proceedings on March 25, 1956. Lee Puey You became a naturalized U.S.
citizen in 1959, which paved the way for her to send for her family in China.

Detention Time for Chinese Applicants at Angel Island, 1910–1940, and Chinese Exclusions and Appeals at Angel Island, 1910–1940

The following tables are based on *Lists of Chinese Applying for Admission to the United States through the Port of San Francisco, California, 1903–1947*. It is the most complete source available on the numbers of Chinese applicants, their length of detention on Angel Island, and the disposition of their cases. The handwritten lists provide the following information on 95,687 applicants: ship manifest number (same as immigration file number), name, class (native, merchant, laborer, student, government official, etc.), residence, BSI hearing date, and dates admitted, denied, appealed, and "departed to China." All twenty-seven rolls of microfilm have been scanned by Ancestry.com and made accessible through its website.

To compile table 1, we spent more than one thousand hours poring over fifteen thousand ledger pages to tally the number of days it took for each person to be admitted or deported. "One day" indicates that they were admitted the same day, most likely from the ship, and not from Angel Island. These included returning residents and members of the exempt classes (teachers, students, government officials, merchants, and travelers). "Two days" indicates that they were admitted the day after their ship arrived, probably after spending one night on Angel Island, and so on. In the cases of people who were paroled or released from Angel Island after posting bond and who were admitted or departed months or a few years later, we used the date they were released from Angel Island as their ending detention date. We left out fifty-six people who reportedly died of some illness, four babies who were born on Angel Island, and pages of Japanese names that were entered in error in the ledgers.

Significant findings include the following: (1) 49 percent of the Chinese applicants were admitted on the same day of arrival in San Francisco and did not even set foot on Angel Island; (2) 95 percent of the Chinese applicants were admitted, and 5 percent were deported; (3) The median days (typical number of detention days spent on Angel Island) ranged from a low of 7 days in 1918 and a high of 42 days in 1940, with the median stay being 16 days for the entire period of 1910-40; and (4) Close to two hundred people were detained for more than one year, and three people were held for more than two years while waiting for decisions on their appeals. The longest detention times were 756 days for Kong Din Quong, grandson of a native who arrived in San Francisco on November 9, 1938, and 750 days for Wong Dung and Wong Bing, merchant sons who arrived in San Francisco on April 5, 1928.

To compile Table 2, we tallied how many applicants were denied entry, how many appealed their cases, and the outcomes of their appeals. We found that immigrant inspectors rejected 9 percent of the Chinese applicants. Of these, 88 percent retained attorneys to appeal the decision, and 55 percent of the appeals were successful.

YEAR	1 Day	2 Days	3 Days	4–7 Days	8–14 Days	15–30 Days	31–90 Days	91–199 Days	>200 Days	Total	Admitted	Deported	Median Days
1910	942	376	197	486	537	406	782	152	1	3,879	3,186	693	12
1911	1,372	367	175	288	233	286	406	83	1	3,211	3,013	198	10
1912	1,405	179	164	213	205	451	598	82	13	3,310	3,116	194	18
1913	1,453	182	132	339	432	534	479	94	29	3,674	3,465	209	15
1914	1,149	140	145	850	544	612	344	73	5	3,862	3,688	174	9
1915	1,214	307	408	407	401	647	539	264	39	4,226	3,964	262	14
1916	803	199	423	591	495	522	289	73	16	3,411	3,241	170	8
1917	848	189	272	328	284	353	422	221	60	2,977	2,685	292	14
1918	766	119	162	204	155	149	117	66	12	1,750	1,691	59	7
1919	1,429	220	123	147	215	246	267	73	19	2,739	2,660	79	12
1920	1,474	166	192	232	266	513	664	129	16	3,652	3,606	46	18
1921	1,795	117	149	395	524	714	565	184	81	4,524	4,357	167	16
1922	2,695	148	222	323	416	670	935	225	54	5,688	5,429	259	20
1923	2,487	287	115	205	241	495	1002	295	106	5,233	4,944	289	31
1924	1,755	441	179	370	241	371	396	248	41	4,042	3,836	206	11
1925	1,344	302	52	57	78	139	149	152	21	2,294	2,132	162	11
1926	1,992	157	28	58	83	184	272	255	73	3,102	2,915	187	35
1927	1,805	68	34	65	145	270	186	140	25	2,738	2,602	136	23
1928	2,234	48	36	93	89	304	440	214	62	3,520	3,355	165	35
1929	1,568	94	41	70	280	282	256	169	22	2,782	2,677	105	19
1930	2,253	86	37	69	97	250	274	169	89	3,324	3,217	107	29
1931	1,885	52	45	61	71	309	330	208	47	3,008	2,893	115	31
1932	1,179	93	55	61	94	131	208	73	20	1,914	1,866	48	20
1933	1,404	74	31	54	68	66	119	39	11	1,866	1,818	48	14
1934	1,507	59	57	75	52	86	99	65	49	2,049	2,012	37	16
1935	1,412	60	78	73	45	100	80	73	24	1,945	1,917	28	14
1936	1,282	52	62	57	45	82	112	145	41	1,878	1,831	47	28
1937	1,257	96	50	91	42	69	137	114	12	1,868	1,841	27	15
1938	1,488	73	61	91	85	168	259	132	27	2,384	2,333	51	25
1939	1,584	76	48	127	101	210	408	230	63	2,847	2,774	73	35
1940	1,057	34	32	75	86	147	266	252	41	1,990	1,953	37	42
TOTAL	46,838	4,861	3,805	6,555	6,650	9,766	11,400	4,692	1120	95,687	91,017	4,670	16
PCTG.	48.95%	5.08%	3.98%	6.85%	6.95%	10.21%	11.91%	4.90%	1.17%		95.12%	4.88%	

Source: U.S. Department of Immigration and Naturalization Service, *Lists of Chinese Applying for Admission to the United States through the Port of San Francisco, California, 1903–1947*, microfilm 1476, RG 85, National Archives, Washington, D.C.

TABLE 2.　Chinese Exclusions and Appeals at Angel Island, 1910–1940

YEAR	APPLICANTS	DENIED		APPEALED		SUSTAINED	
1910	3,879	791	(20.4%)	599	(75.7%)	94	(15.7%)
1911	3,211	278	(8.7%)	21	(78.4%)	77	(35.3%)
1912	3,310	268	(8.1%)	180	(67.2%)	75	(41.7%)
1913	3,674	220	(6.0%)	136	(61.8%)	44	(32.4%)
1914	3,862	226	(5.9%)	156	(69.0%)	54	(34.6%)
1915	4,226	444	(10.5%)	337	(75.9%)	201	(59.6%)
1916	3,411	228	(6.7%)	176	(77.2%)	75	(42.6%)
1917	2,977	445	(14.9%)	336	(75.5%)	147	(43.8%)
1918	1,750	91	(5.2%)	72	(79.1%)	50	(69.4%)
1919	2,739	115	(4.2%)	110	(95.7%)	86	(78.2%)
1920	3,652	233	(6.4%)	226	(97.0%)	198	(87.6%)
1921	4,524	282	(6.2%)	282	(100.0%)	159	(56.4%)
1922	5,688	235	(4.1%)	233	(99.1%)	87	(37.3%)
1923	5,233	401	(7.7%)	388	(96.8%)	187	(48.2%)
1924	4,042	433	(10.7%)	397	(91.7%)	218	(54.9%)
1925	2,294	369	(16.1%)	344	(93.2%)	165	(48.0%)
1926	3,102	423	(13.6%)	393	(92.9%)	188	(47.8%)
1927	2,738	306	(11.2%)	258	(84.3%)	140	(54.3%)
1928	3,520	364	(10.3%)	344	(94.5%)	191	(55.5%)
1929	2,782	311	(11.2%)	306	(98.4%)	219	(71.6%)
1930	3,324	312	(9.4%)	301	(96.5%)	206	(68.4%)
1931	3,008	373	(12.4%)	360	(96.5%)	245	(68.1%)
1932	1,914	216	(11.3%)	207	(95.8%)	167	(80.7%)
1933	1,866	155	(8.3%)	122	(78.7%)	91	(74.6%)
1934	2,049	123	(6.0%)	119	(96.7%)	89	(74.8%)
1935	1,945	115	(5.9%)	110	(95.7%)	78	(70.9%)
1936	1,878	173	(9.2%)	170	(98.3%)	123	(72.4%)
1937	1,868	153	(8.2%)	151	(98.7%)	127	(84.1%)
1938	2,384	165	(6.9%)	162	(98.2%)	114	(70.4%)
1939	2,847	251	(8.8%)	247	(98.4%)	171	(69.2%)
1940	1,990	173	(8.7%)	171	(98.8%)	128	(74.9%)
TOTAL	95,687	8,672	(9.1%)	7,611	(87.8%)	4,194	(55.1%)

Source: U.S. Department of Immigration and Naturalization Service, *Lists of Chinese Applying for Admission to the United States through the Port of San Francisco, California, 1903–1947*, microfilm 1476, RG 85, National Archives, Washington, D.C.

CHINESE GLOSSARY

Ah Yum 阿任 personal name

Ai Jiangnan 哀江南 "Bewailing Jiangnan" (poem)

An Lushan Rebellion 安祿山叛變

baba 爸爸 papa

Bak Heong 碧香 personal name

bao wai 包位 immigration broker

Baohuanghui 保皇會 Protect the Emperor Society

Bing Kung Tong 秉公堂 fraternity, secret society

bok choy 白菜 leafy vegetable

Cai 蔡 former state in present-day Henan

Cai Tingkai 蔡廷鍇 general in the Nationalist Army

cha gwa 茶瓜 cucumbers

Chan, Woo, and Yuen Association 陳胡袁公所 family association

Chang'e 嫦娥 moon goddess

Chang Hall Hoy 鄭桃海 personal name

Chang Lin Hoy 鄭蓮開 personal name

Chaozhou 潮州 city in Guangdong

Che Pai 斜牌 village in present-day Dowmoon District

Chen 陳 former state in present-day Henan

Chen Jiongming 陳炯明 warlord

Chen She 陳涉 led peasant rebellion against Qin government

Cheuk Suey Hong 赤水坑 village in present-day Dowmoon District

Cheung Ping 昌平 village in Toishan District

Chew Kai 潮溪 village in Toishan District

Chew Lun Association 昭倫公所 family association

Chiang Kai-shek 蔣介石 generalissimo and president of Republic of China

Chin Lung 陳龍 personal name

choi! 啋! exclamation of disgust or displeasure

Chu 楚 former state in present-day Hubei

chu jai uk 豬仔屋 pigpen for coolies

Chun Wai Hin 陳渭賢 personal name

Chung Lau Heui 冲蔞墟 marketplace in Toishan District

Chung Tow 冲頭 village in present-day Chungshan District

Chungshan District 中山縣 formerly Heungshan District in Guangdong

Cixi, Empress Dowager 慈禧太后 regent of the Qing dynasty

Congxia 冲霞 hamlet in Nanhai District

Da Lüsong 大呂宋 Mexico

Dai Chek Hom 大赤坎 village in present-day Dowmoon District

Dai Fow 大埠 First City, refers to San Francisco

dai kam 大妗 bride escort

Dasha 大沙 village in Nanhai District

Denglou fu 登樓賦 "Ascending the Tower" (poem)

dim sum 點心 pastries

Dong Hing Mui 鄧興妹 personal name

Dong Wah 鄧華 personal name

Dowmoon District 斗門縣 formerly part of Heungshan (Chungshan) District

Du Shee 杜氏 personal name

fai di! 快啲! hurry!

fan gwai 番鬼 foreign devil

Fan Li 范蠡 (Taozhugong 陶朱公) wealthy merchant and minister in the state of Yue

fan tan 番攤 Chinese roulette

Fayuan 花縣 district in Guangdong

Feng Tang 馮唐 Han dynasty official

fo lim beng 火鎌餅 cookie, refers to certificate of identity

fu 賦 poetic form

Fu Chung 庫充 village in present-day Chungshan District

Fucha, King 夫差王 ruled state of Wu

fun gor 粉粿 dumpling

Fuzhou 福州 capital of Fujian

gai choy 芥菜 mustard greens

gam jum 金針 golden needles, vegetable

Gam Saan 金山 Gold Mountain

Gam Saan haak 金山客 guest of Gold Mountain; sojourner

Gam Saan jong 金山莊 Gold Mountain firm

Gam Saan poh 金山婆 Gold Mountain wife

George Brothers 多利 sewing factory in San Francisco Chinatown

Go Bak 高伯 Uncle Go

Gong Moon 江門 city in Guangdong

Goujian, King 勾踐王 ruled the state of Yue

Guangdong 廣東 province in China

Guangxi 廣西 province in China

Guangxu 光緒 ruler during the Qing dynasty

Guangzhou 廣州 Canton

gung 公 paternal grandfather

gung hei nay! 恭喜你! congratulations!

gwai poh 鬼婆 female foreign devil

Ha Jick 下澤 village in present-day Chungshan District

haak fong 黑房 dark room, isolation room

Hainan 海南 province in China

Hakka 客家 "guests" from central China who settled in Guangdong

Han dynasty 漢朝

Han Xin 韓信 Han dynasty general and marquis

Han Yu 韓愈 (Han Changli 韓昌黎) Tang dynasty scholar-official

Hee Tai Wo 怡泰和 meat market in San Francisco Chinatown

hei gung 氣功 qigong exercise

Henan 河南 province in China

Heungshan District 香山縣 in Guangdong, renamed Chungshan District in 1925

Hing Oi 興愛 personal name

Hip Sen Tong 協善堂 fraternity for Wong Leung Do people

ho sai gai 好世界 good luck, good times

Hoiping District 開平縣 in Guangdong

Hom Gong 潭岡 village in Sunwui District

Hop Wo Association 合和會館 district association for Sze Yup people

Huai, King 楚懷王 ruled the state of Chu

Hubei 湖北 province in China

Ja Bak 謝伯 Uncle Ja

Ja Kew Yuen 謝僑遠 personal name

Ja Wing Chi 謝詠慈 personal name

Jang (Jung) 鄭 clan name

Jann Mon Fong (Smiley Jann) 鄭文舫 personal name

Jeung Jee 長志 personal name

Jew Law Ying 趙羅英 personal name

Jiang Taigong 姜太公 (Lü Shang 呂尚) Zhou dynasty minister and marquis

Jiangsu 江蘇 province in China

Jiangxi 江西 province in China

jiaren 佳人 beautiful woman

Jin 金 state in ancient China

Jin dynasty 晉朝

jing sung lo ho! 蒸餸囉呵! bring food for steaming!

Jingzhou 荊州 city in present-day Hubei

jook 粥 congee, rice gruel

jou poh 祖婆 maternal grandmother

joy sang 在生 still alive

Jung, Laura 張玉英 personal name

Kai Gok 谿角 village in present-day Chungshan District

Kaiping District 開平縣 in Guangdong

kaishu 楷書 calligraphy style

kelü 刻律 tyrannical laws

Kung Yu Club 工餘俱樂部

Kuo Feng Travel and Tours 國風旅行社

Kuomintang 國民黨 Nationalist Party

Kwong Shee 鄺氏 personal name

Kwong Sui (Guangxu) 光緒 Qing dynasty emperor

Lai Bing 黎炳 personal name

Lai Git 麗潔 personal name

Lai Ha 麗霞 personal name

Lai, Him Mark 麥禮謙 personal name

Lai Hoong 禮雄 personal name

Lai Kwong Poon 黎廣泮 personal name

Lai Lim 禮廉 personal name

Lai Wo 禮和 personal name

lam gok 欖角 pickled olives

Lan Guan 藍關 mountain pass in Shanxi

Lau, Koon T. 劉袞祥 personal name

Lau Wai You 劉維銳 personal name

Law Shee Low 羅氏劉 personal name

Law Yuk Tao 羅玉桃 personal name

Lee Bak Yeung 李白楊 personal name

Lee Heung 李香 personal name

Lee Puey You 李佩瑤 personal name

Lee Sam 李森 personal name

Lee Show Nam 李壽南 personal name

Lee Wai Mun 李衛民 personal name

lei see 利是 lucky money

Leung, Tye 梁亞娣 personal name

Lew Sau Kam 劉秀琴 personal name

li 里 one-third of a mile

Li Guang 李廣 Han general who fought the Xiongnu

Li Ling 李陵 Han general who was defeated by the Xiongnu

Li Shimin 李世民 general and second emperor of the Tang dynasty

Liang dynasty 梁朝

Lim, Genny 林小琴 personal name

Lim Kam On 林錦安 personal name

Lim Lee 林利 personal name

Lim Tai Go 林齊高 personal name

Liu Bang 劉邦 first emperor of the Han dynasty

Liu Yuxi 劉禹錫 poet who wrote "Loushi Ming"

lo fan 老番 barbarian

Longdu 隆都 region in present-day Chungshan District

Loulan 樓蘭 former state in present-day Xinjiang

Loushi Ming 陋室銘 "Inscription about a Humble House" (poem)

Low Gun 劉根 personal name

Low Pung 劉鵬 personal name

Low Wing Hin 劉穎軒 personal name

Lü Shang 呂尚 (Jiang Taigong 姜太公) Zhou dynasty minister and marquis

luk tung kuen 六通拳 Chinese boxing

luk yi 綠衣 green clothes man, police officer

Lum Ngow 林牛 personal name

Lum Piu 林標 personal name

Lum Sam 林森 personal name

Lum Yun 林迎 personal name

Lun Kee 麟記 deli in Oakland Chinatown

Luoyang 洛陽 capital of Eastern Han dynasty in present-day Henan

lüshi 律詩 regulated verse

Lüsong 呂宋 Mexico

Ma Zhanshan 馬占山 general in the Nationalist Army

Maak Ding 麥定 personal name

Maak Tou 麥圖 personal name

Maak Yuk Bing 麥沃炳 personal name

mahjong 麻雀牌 gambling game

mama 媽媽 mama

Mei Gwok 美國 United States of America

Mei Ho 美好 personal name

meiren 美人 beautiful woman

Min, King 愍王 ruler during the Jin dynasty

Min Ziqian 閔子騫 (Min Sun 閔損) one of Confucius's disciples

Mo Shee 毛氏 personal name

Mock Chung Nien (John Mock) 麥松年 personal name

Mock Ging Sing (William Mock) 麥景勝 personal name

Mock Mei Hon (Philip Fong) 麥美漢 personal name

Mock Yee Keung 麥億強 personal name

Mon Hing Bo 文興報 newspaper

Mount Tai 泰山 sacred Taoist mountain in Shandong

mu 畝 1.5 acres

mui jai 妹仔 slave girl

mui nui 妹女 slave girl

muk uk 木屋 wooden house

Mulan Ci 木蘭辭 "Poem of Mulan"

Nam How 南頭 town in Sunwui District

Nan Jiyun 南霽雲 defended Suiyang in An Lushan Rebellion

Nanhai (Namhoi) District 南海縣 in Guangdong

ng ga pei 五加皮 Chinese liquor

Ngim Ah Oy 嚴亞愛 personal name

ngow 牛 cow

Niulang Zhinü 牛郎織女 Cowherd and the Weaver Maiden

Nom Hong 南坑 village in Toishan District

Northern Zhou dynasty 北周朝

Ow Soak Yong 歐淑容 personal name

Oy Hoi 外海 village in Sunwui District

pai gow 牌九 Chinese dominoes

Pang Juan 龐涓 official in the state of Wei

peng 鵬 giant, mythical bird

Pong Tou 龐頭 village in present-day Chungshan District

Punti 本地 local people in Guangdong

Qi 齊 former state in present-day Shandong

Qianlong xia Jiangnan 乾隆下江南 *Emperor Qianlong Travels to the South* (novel)

Qin dynasty 秦朝

Qing dynasty 清朝

qingyi 青衣 blue clothing worn by lower social classes

Ruan Ji 阮籍 scholar who lived during the Three Kingdoms period

Sai Gai Yat Po 世界日報 newspaper

Sam Hop 三合 town in Toishan District

Sam Yup 三邑 three districts in Guangdong—Namhoi, Punyu, and Shuntak

sang gai jook 生雞粥 chicken congee

Sanshui District 三水縣 in Guangdong

seung ngon! 上岸! Landed!

Shaanxi 陝西 province in central China

Shandong 山東 province in China

Shang dynasty 商朝

Shanxi 山西 province in northern China

Shanyu 單于 title used by the Xiongnu

Shekki (Shiqi) 石岐 administrative center of Heungshan (Chungshan) District

Shi jing 詩經 Confucian classic of poetry

Shu jing 書經 Confucian classic of history

Shun Lee 信利 sewing factory in San Francisco Chinatown

sik fan la! 食飯喇! time to eat!

Sin Tung 仙洞 village in Sunwui District

Sing Chong 成昌 grocery store in San Francisco Chinatown

siu mai 燒賣 dumpling

siu ye 宵夜 midnight snack

Soon Din 順進 personal name

Soto Shee 司徒氏 personal name

Su Qin 蘇秦 scholar who lived during the Warring States period

Su Wu 蘇武 envoy to the Xiongnu during the Western Han dynasty

Suiyang 睢陽 ancient city in present-day Henan

Sun Bin 孫臏 official in the state of Qi

sun hei 呻氣 vent or moan in sorrow

Sun Hung Heung 新杏香 restaurant in San Francisco Chinatown

Sun Yat-sen 孫逸仙 (Sun Zhongshan 孫中山) first president of Republic of China

Sunning 新寧 former name of Toishan District

Sunwui District 新會縣 in Guangdong

sup ng wu 十五胡 gambling game

Sze Yup 四邑 four districts in Guangdong—Sunwui, Toishan, Hoiping, and Yanping

Tai Foo Lay 大夫里 village in Yanping District

Taigongwang 太公望 (Jiang Taigong 姜太公) Zhou dynasty minister and marquis

Tam Kai 潭溪 village in Hoiping District

Tang dynasty 唐朝

Tangong 檀弓 chapter in *Book of Rites*

Tangkou 塘口 village in Kaiping District

Taozhugong 陶朱公 (Fan Li 范蠡) wealthy merchant and minister in the state of Yue

Tian Heng 田橫 nobleman who failed to reestablish the state of Qi

tien gow 天九 Chinese dominoes

tien wong 天王 heavenly god

Toishan District 台山縣 in Guangdong

Toising 台城 city in Toishan District

Tom Fat Kwong 譚發光 personal name

Tom Yip Jing 譚業精 personal name

Tong Guan 潼關 strategic pass in Shaanxi

Tongmenghui 同盟會 Chinese United League, founded by Sun Yat-sen in 1905

Tsamgong 湛江 city in Guangdong

Tuck Chong Company 德祥號 dry goods store in San Francisco Chinatown

Tung Sen Tong 同善堂 benevolent association for Longdu people

Wang Can 王粲 official who lived during the Later Han dynasty

Wei 魏 former state in present-day Shanxi

Wei River 渭河 major river in Gansu and Shaanxi

Wen, Emperor 漢文帝 ruler during the Han dynasty

Wen, King 周文王 founded the state of Zhou

Western Han dynasty 西漢朝

Western Jin dynasty 西晉朝

Western Wei 西魏 state in ancient China

Wing Hung Chong 榮紅昌 Gold Mountain firm in Hong Kong

Wong Chung Hong 王仲康 personal name

Wong Gung Jue (Henry Wong) 黃拱照 personal name

Wong Leung Do 黃梁都 region in present-day Dowmoon District

Wong Poy Yen 黃培英 personal name

Wong See Chan 黃氏陳 personal name

Wong Shee 黃氏 personal name

Wong Ting Cheong 黃廷章 personal name

Wong Woo 橫湖 village in Toishan District

Wong Yen Yi (Henry Wong) 黃仁儀 personal name

Woo Tong 胡棠 personal name

Wu 吳 former state in present-day Jiangsu

Wu, Emperor 漢武帝 ruler during the Han dynasty

Wu, King 周武王 founded the Zhou dynasty

Wu Yun 伍員 (Wu Zixu 伍子胥) official in the state of Chu

Wuchang 武昌 uprising that ended the Qing dynasty

xi 西 west

Xiajia 下滘 village in Nanhai District

Xiang Yu 項羽 military leader and overlord in the late Qin dynasty

Xianggang 香港 Fragrant Harbor, Hong Kong

Xiangjiang 香江 Fragrant River, Hong Kong

Xiangshan District 香山縣 in Guangdong

Xiao Lüsong 小呂宋 Philippines

Xie Chuang (Xavier Dea) 謝創

xie-xie! 謝謝! thank you!

Xinhai Revolution 辛亥革命 1911 Revolution that toppled the Qing dynasty

Xinjiang 新疆 province in China

Xinning Zazhi 新寧雜誌 Taishan magazine

Xiongnu 匈奴 nomadic people who lived north of the Chinese empire

Xishi 西施 famous beauty in the state of Yue

Xiyou ji 西遊記 *Journey to the West* (novel)

Yan Gaoqing 顏杲卿 Tang dynasty official who was defeated in the An Lushan Rebellion

Yan Hui 顏回 poorest of Confucius's disciples

Yandi 炎帝 Emperor Yan, one of the legendary sovereigns of ancient China

Yangzi River 楊子江 longest river in China

Yanping District 恩平縣 in Guangdong

Ye Keliang 葉可梁 a consul general of China in San Francisco

Yee Tet Ming (Tet Yee) 余達明 personal name

yeung kam 揚琴 butterfly harp

Yi jing 易經 *Book of Changes*

yi wu 二胡 two-stringed fiddle

Yijing 以敬 village in Kaiping District

Yim Tai Muey 嚴大妹 personal name

Yingtai 瀛臺 Sea Terrace Island near the Forbidden City in
  Beijing where Emperor Guangxu was imprisoned
Yingyang District 榮陽 in Henan
Yoen Oi 潤愛 personal name
Yu Xin 庾信 Liang dynasty official
Yue 越 former state in present-day Zhejiang
Yuen Lan Heung (Helen Hong Wong) 院蘭香 personal name
Yung Dung 楊棟 personal name
Yung Hin Biew 楊庭標 personal name
Yung Hin Sen 楊庭順 personal name
Yung, Judy 譚碧芳 personal name
Yunnan 雲南 province in China

Zhejiang 浙江 province in China
Zhongnan Mountain 終南山 in Shaanxi
Zhongshan District 中山縣 in Guangdong
Zhou 周 state in ancient China
Zhou dynasty 周朝
Zhou, King 紂王 last king of the Shang dynasty
Zizhihui 自治會 Self-governing Association
Zu Ti 祖逖 general during the Western Jin dynasty

BIBLIOGRAPHY

PRINTED MATERIALS

A Ying 阿英編, ed. "Ailun qiaobao zhi gejie shu" 埃侖僑胞致各界書 (A message from the Chinese on Angel Island to all). *Chinese World* 世界日報, August 24, 1923.

———. *Fan mei huagong jinyue wenxueji* 反美華工禁約文學集 (Anthology of anti-Chinese labor laws). Shanghai: Zhonghua shuju, 1960.

———. "'Huaqiao xuelei,' you ming 'Guan boshi lizheng keli'" 「華僑血淚」，又名「關博士力爭苛例」 ("Blood and tears of Chinese Americans," also titled "Professor Guan vigorously contests harsh laws"). *Young China Morning Post* 少年中國晨報, February to April, 1911.

———. "Muwu juqiu chi jin ku" 木屋拘囚吃盡苦 (Suffering from imprisonment in the wooden building). In *Jinshan Geji* 金山歌集 (A collection of Gold Mountain songs), 13B–14A. San Francisco: Daguang shulin, 1911.

———. "Muwu juliu xu" 「木屋拘留序」 (Preface to Imprisonment in the wooden building). *Chinese World* 世界日報, March 16, 1910, 1.

———. "Tianshidao ke bei kun" 天使島客被困 (A visitor imprisoned on Angel Island); "Tianya jiongku zhong zhi aisi" 天涯窘苦中之哀思 (Sad thoughts in the midst of suffering); "Dui Mei xin yimin lü zhi beifen" 對美新移民律之悲憤 (Indignation at the new immigration laws). In *Yuequ Jinghua* 粵曲精華 (Essence of Cantonese arias), 1–7. San Francisco: Jinmen lequn she, 1925. Also in *Yuediao Gequ Jinghua* 粵調歌曲菁華 (Essence of Cantonese songs), 103–8. San Francisco: Xin dalu tushuguan, 1926.

———. "You Meizhou bei qiukun muwu shu" 遊美洲被囚困木屋疏 (Imprisoned in the wooden building while visiting the United States). In *Yuehai Chunqiu* 粵海春秋 (Spring and autumn annals of Guangdong), 23B–26A. Guangzhou: Dacheng shuju, 1923.

Angel Island Immigration Station Historical Advisory Committee. "Report and Recommendations on Angel Island Immigration Station." San Francisco, 1976.

Architectural Resources Group. "Angel Island Immigration Station Detention Barracks Historic Structure Report." Prepared for National Park Service, California State Parks, and Angel Island Immigration Station Foundation, San Francisco, 2002.

———. "Historic Structures Report: Hospital Building, Angel Island Immigration Station." Prepared for the National Park Service, California State Parks, and Angel Island Immigration Station Foundation, San Francisco, 2002.

Architectural Resources Group and Daniel Quan Design. "Final Interpretive Plan, Phase 1 Project Area, Angel Island Immigration Station." Commissioned by the California Department of Parks and Recreation, Sacramento, 2006.

———. "Poetry and Inscriptions: Translation and Analysis." Prepared by Charles Egan, Wan Liu, Newton Liu, and Xing Chu Wang for the California Department of Parks and Recreation and Angel Island Immigration Station Foundation, San Francisco, 2004.

Askin, Dorene. "Historical Report, Angel Island Immigration Station." California Department of Parks and Recreation, Interpretive Planning Unit, Sacramento, 1977.

Bamford, Mary. *Angel Island: The Ellis Island of the West.* Chicago:

Woman's American Baptist Home Mission Society, 1917.

Barde, Robert. *Immigration at the Golden Gate: Passenger Ships, Exclusion, and Angel Island.* Westport, CT: Praeger, 2008.

Barde, Robert, and Gustavo J. Bobonis. "Detention at Angel Island: First Empirical Evidence." *Social Science History* 30, no. 1 (Spring, 2006): 103–36.

Bolten, Joseph. "Cerebrospinal Meningitis at Angel Island Immigration Station, Calif." *Public Health Reports* 36, no. 12 (March 25, 1921): 593–602.

Brownstone, David, Irene Franck, and Douglass Brownstone. *Island of Hope, Island of Tears.* New York: Barnes and Noble, 2000.

California State Board of Control. *California and the Orient: Japanese, Chinese and Hindus.* Sacramento: California State Board of Control, 1922.

California State Senate. Special Committee on Chinese Immigration. *Chinese Immigration: Its Social, Moral, and Political Effect.* Sacramento, CA: State Office of Printing, 1878.

Camacho, Julia Maria Schiavone. *Chinese Mexicans: Transpacific Migration and the Search for a Homeland.* Chapel Hill: University of North Carolina Press, 2012.

Cannato, Vincent J. *American Passage: The History of Ellis Island.* New York: Harper, 2009.

"Carved on the Walls: Poetry by Early Chinese Immigrants." In *The Heath Anthology of American Literature*, edited by Paul Lauter. 2nd ed. Vol. 2. Lexington, MA: D.C. Heath, 1994, 1956–63.

Chan Juan 蟬娟. "Ailisidao shang aisi chang: Yi ge beicang lao yimin zhuiyi qiuju dao shang de qiku suiyue" 哀離思島上哀思長: 一個悲滄老移民追憶囚居島上的凄苦歲月 (Recollections of Ellis Island: An old immigrant remembers his plight in the island prison). *China Times* 中國時報, September 25, 1984.

Chan, Sucheng. *Asian Americans: An Interpretive History.* Woodbridge, CT: Twayne Publishers, 1991.

———, ed. *Chinese American Transnationalism: The Flow of People, Resources, and Ideas between China and America during the Exclusion Era.* Philadelphia: Temple University Press, 2006.

———, ed. *Entry Denied: Exclusion and the Chinese Community in America, 1882–1943.* Philadelphia: Temple University Press, 1991.

———. *This Bitter-Sweet Soil: The Chinese in California Agriculture, 1860–1910.* Berkeley: University of California Press, 1986.

Chang, Iris. *The Chinese in America: A Narrative History.* New York: Viking, 2003.

Chen Fengli 陳鳳麗. "Xiri huaren shangxin di rujin youke zhuisi chu: Tianshidao shang wu tianshi" 昔日華人傷心地如今遊客追思處: 天使島上無天使 (The former place of sorrow for the Chinese is now a place of reflection for tourists: No angels on Angel Island). *Huanqiu Shi Bao* 環球時報, November 10, 2000, 15.

Chen, Helen. "Chinese Immigration into the United States: An Analysis of Changes in Immigration Policies." Ph.D. diss., Brandeis University, 1980.

Chen, Wen-hsien. "Chinese Under Both Exclusion and Immigration Laws." Ph.D. diss., University of Chicago, 1940.

Chen, Yong. *Chinese San Francisco, 1850–1943: A Trans-Pacific Community.* Stanford, CA: Stanford University Press, 2000.

Cheng, Lucie, and Edna Bonacich, eds. *Labor Immigration Under Capitalism: Asian Workers in the United States before World War II.* Berkeley: University of California Press, 1984.

Chew, Ng Poon. *The Treatment of the Exempt Classes of Chinese in the United States: A Statement from the Chinese in America.* San Francisco: Chung Sai Yat Po, 1908.

Chi Chan 次塵. "Min shi fu Jia kunyu Yunbu yiminjian" 民十赴加因于雲埠移民監 (En route to Canada in 1921, imprisoned in the Vancouver immigration jail). *Taishan Huaqiao Gongzuo Baogao Zhoukan* 台山華僑工作報告周刊, no. 1, November 1929.

Chin, Tung Pok, and Winifred C. Chin. *Paper Son: One Man's Story.* Philadelphia: Temple University Press, 2000.

Chinn, Thomas W., H. Mark Lai, and Philip P. Choy. *A History of the Chinese in California: A Syllabus.* San Francisco: Chinese Historical Society of America, 1969.

Chiu, Ping. *Chinese Labor in California, 1850–1880: An Economic Study.* Madison: State Historical Society of Wisconsin, 1967.

Chow, Christopher, and Connie Young Yu. "Angel Island and Chinese Immigration." *San Francisco Journal*, June 30, July 21, August 4, 11, 18, 25, 1976; April 25, 1979.

Choy, Philip P., Lorraine Dong, and Marlon K. Hom. *The Coming Man: 19th Century Perceptions of the Chinese.* Hong Kong: Joint Publishing Company, 1994.

Coolidge, Mary Roberts. *Chinese Immigration.* New York: Henry Holt, 1909.

Daniels, Roger. *Asian America: Chinese and Japanese in the United States since 1850.* Seattle: University of Washington Press, 1988.

——. *Guarding the Golden Door: American Immigration Policy and Immigrants since 1882.* New York: Hill and Wang, 2004.

——. "No Lamps Were Lit for Them: Angel Island and the Historiography of Asian American Immigration." *Journal of American Ethnic History* 17, no. 1 (Fall 1997): 3–18.

Delgado, Grace Pena. *Making the Chinese Mexican: Global Migration, Localism, and Exclusion in the U.S.-Mexico Borderlands.* Stanford, CA: Stanford University Press, 2012.

D'Emilio, Frances. "The Secret Hell of Angel Island." *American West* 21 (May–June 1984): 44–51.

Deng Shusheng 鄧蜀生. "Tianshidao—sa xiang renjian dou shi yuan" 天使島—灑向人間都是怨 (Angel Island—a tale of woe). In *Shidai beihuan "Meiguo Meng": Meiguo yimin licheng ji zhongzu maodun* 世代悲歡 "美國夢": 美國移民歷程及種族矛盾 (Generations of the "American dream": The course of U.S. immigration and racial contradictions), 228–44. Beijing: Zhongguo shehui kexue chubanshe, 2001.

"Edith Eaton he Tianshidao shige" 伊迪絲·伊頓和天使島詩歌 (Edith Eaton and the Angel Island poems). In *Xinbian Meiguo wenxueshi* 新編美國文學史, 第 2 卷, 1860–1914 (History of American literature, vol. 2, 1860–1914), edited by Liu Haiping and Wang Shouren 劉海平, 王守仁編, 539–52. Shanghai: Waiyu jiaoyu chubanshe, 2002.

Egan, Charles. "Voices in the Wooden House: Angel Island Inscriptions, 1910–1945." Manuscript, 2008.

Fairchild, Amy L. *Science at the Borders: Immigrant Medical Inspection and the Shaping of the Modern Industrial Labor Force.* Baltimore, MD: Johns Hopkins University Press, 2003.

Fang Daming 方大明. "Mulou xiezhen" 木樓寫真 (A realistic description of the wooden building). *Chinese Pacific Weekly* 太平洋週報, August 24, 1978.

Fang Minxi 方民希. "Mulou ti bi shi zhushi" 木樓題壁詩注釋 (An annotated explanation of the wall poems in the wooden building). *Chinese Pacific Weekly* 太平洋週報, August 24, 1978, 11.

Fanning, Branwell, and William Wong. *Images of America: Angel Island.* Charleston, SC: Arcadia Publishing, 2006.

Fowler, Josephine. *Japanese and Chinese Immigrant Activists: Organizing in American and International Communist Movements, 1919–1933.* New Brunswick, NJ: Rutgers University Press, 2007.

Fu, Chi Hao. "My Reception in America." *Outlook*, August 10, 1907, 770.

Gai Jianping 蓋建平. "Ganxing yu shiqing: Zuowei huaren shengcun jingyan de muwu shi" 感性與詩情: 作為華人生存經驗的木屋詩 (Perception and poetic sentiment: "Wooden building poems" as life experiences of Chinese Americans). *Huawen Wenxue* 華文文學 2 (2009): 59–66.

——. "Muwu shi yanjiu: Zhongmei xueshujie de jiyou chengguo ji xiancun nanti" 木屋詩研究: 中美學術界的既有成果及現存難題 (Research on the "wooden building poems": Past achievements and current problems in Chinese and American academic circles). *Huawen Wenxue* 華文文學 6 (2008): 79–86.

——. "Zaoqi Meiguo huaren wenxue yanjiu: Lishi jingyan de chongkan yu dangdai yiyi de chengxian" 早期美國華人文學研究: 歷史經驗的重勘與當代意義的呈現 (Research on early Chinese American literature: Reexamination of its history and contemporary significance). Ph.D. diss., Fudan University, 2010.

Gee, Jennifer. "Housewives, Men's Villages, and Sexual Respectability: Gender and the Interrogation of Asian Women at the Angel Island Immigration Station." In *Asian/Pacific Islander American Women: A Historical Anthology*, edited by Shirley Hune and Gail M. Nomura, 90–105. New York: New York University Press, 2003.

———. "Sifting the Arrivals: Asian Immigrants and the Angel Island Immigration Station, San Francisco, 1910–1940." Ph.D. diss., Stanford University, 1999.

Gold, Martin B. *Forbidden Citizens: Chinese Exclusion and the U.S. Congress: A Legislative History*. Alexandria, VA: The Capitol Net, 2012.

Guan Lin 管林. "Fu Mei huaren de xuelei shishi—shi lun Tianshidao shige" 赴美華人的血淚史詩—試論天使島詩歌 (Epic poems of blood and tears by Chinese immigrants—a discussion of the Angel Island poems). *Jinan Xuebao (Zhexue shehui kexue ban)* 暨南學報 (哲學社會科學版) 2 (1992): 30–34.

Guan Minqian 關敏謙. "Tianshidao shang huagong lei" 天使島上華工淚 (Tears from Chinese laborers on Angel Island). In *Shewai suiyue huimou* 涉外歲月回眸 (A look back at my foreign sojourn), 388–91. Beijing: Zhongguo funü chubanshe, 2002.

Guo Kedi 郭克迪. "Tianshidao shang hua jinxi" 天使島上話今昔 (Angel Island: Past and present). *People's Daily* 人民日報, November 23, 2011.

Guo Zhengzhi 郭征之. "Yimin lei hua zuo cui xin shipian" 移民淚化作撼心詩篇 (Immigrant tears, heart-wrenching verses). *Huaqiao Ribao* 華僑日報, October 26, 1985.

Gyory, Andrew. *Closing the Gate: Race, Politics, and the Chinese Exclusion Act*. Chapel Hill: University of North Carolina Press, 1998.

Hannaford, Alex. "Scarred by an Angel." *South China Morning Post*, May 1, 2004, C5.

Healy, Patrick J., and Ng Poon Chew. *A Statement for Non-Exclusion*. San Francisco, 1905.

Helmich, Mary. "Angel Island Immigration Station, Interpretive Plan, Phase II." Interpretive Planning Section, Office of Interpretive Services, Sacramento, 1987.

Hing, Bill Ong. *Making and Remaking Asian America through Immigration Policy, 1850–1990*. Stanford, CA: Stanford University Press, 1994.

Hom, Marlon K. *Songs of Gold Mountain: Cantonese Rhymes from San Francisco Chinatown*. Berkeley: University of California Press, 1987.

Hsu, Madeline. *Dreaming of Gold, Dreaming of Home: Transnationalism and Migration between the United States and South China, 1882–1943*. Stanford, CA: Stanford University Press, 2000.

Huang, Yunte. "The Poetics of Error: Angel Island." In *Transpacific Imaginations: History, Literature, Counterpoetics*, 101–15. Cambridge, MA: Harvard University Press, 2008.

Huang Zhongji 黃仲楫. "Xiang lang ge" 想郎歌 (Songs about missing my husband). *Xinning Zazhi* 新寧雜誌 3 (2000): 38.

Huang Zunxian 黃遵憲. "Zhu ke pian" 逐客篇 (The unwelcome guests). In *Renjinglu shi cao jianzhu* 人境廬詩草箋註 (Renjinglu collection of poems), 126–30. Kowloon: Zhonghua shuju, 1963.

Jann Mon Fong 鄭文舫. "Jinshanke de zishu" 金山客的自述 (A Gold Mountain man's monologue). *Renjian Shi* 人間世, March 5, 1935, 15-16.

———. "Qiupeng ji: Ji ruozhe xinsheng juan" 秋蓬集: 集弱者心聲卷 (A collection of autumn grass: Voices from the hearts of the weak). Manuscript, 1932.

Jian Ni 堅妮. "Ailisidao juliu ying cesuo qiangbi shang faxian duo shou zaoqi huaren yimin shicao: Huabu lishi yanjiushe zheng xiezhu jianding kaoju gongzuo" 愛麗絲島拘留營所牆壁上發現多首早期華人移民詩抄: 華埠歷史研究社正協助鑒定考據工作 (The discovery of numerous poems left by early Chinese immigrants on the bathroom walls of the Ellis Island detention center: Chinatown History Project assisting appraisal and research). *Huaqiao Ribao* 華僑日報, July 24, 1985, 16.

———. "Ailisidao shang duanju canpian qizhong yi shou shu Zhongguo minyao: Lishi yanjiushe yi chengyuan you ci faxian" 愛麗絲島上斷句殘篇其中一首屬中國民謠: 歷史研究社一成員有此發現 (A Chinese folk song among the poetry fragments on Ellis Island: Discovery made by a member of the Chinatown History Project). *Huaqiao Ribao* 華僑日報, August 3, 1995.

———. "Ailisidao yimin shichao wangshi bu kan huishou: Sawu nian qian jingxiang lilizaimu lao huaqiao gankai tan xinsuan wangshi" 愛麗絲島移民詩抄往事不堪回首:卅五年前景象歷歷在目老華僑感慨談辛酸往事 (Unbearable memories in Ellis Island immigrant poems: An old Chinese American speaks of bitter experiences thirty-five years ago). *Huaqiao Ribao* 華僑日報, August 5, 1985.

———. "Yimin shichao yi zi yi lei Ailisidao ling ren duanhun" 移民詩抄一字一淚愛麗絲島令人斷魂 (Immigrant poetry: Heartbreaking verses from Ellis Island). *Huaqiao Ribao* 華僑日報, September 12, 1990.

Jing Nan 景南. "Lan yantong yu zongtong lun" 藍煙通與總統輪 (Blue chimneys and President liners). *Chinese Pacific Weekly* 太平洋週報, November 14, 1974.

———. "Tianshidao" 天使島 (Angel Island). *Chinese Pacific Weekly* 太平洋週報, November 21, 1974.

———. "Tianshidao de shenwen" 天使島的審問 (Interrogation on Angel Island). *Chinese Pacific Weekly* 太平洋週報, December 5, 1974.

———. "Tianshidao shang de dai xin ren" 天使島上的帶信人 (The mail carrier on Angel Island). *Chinese Pacific Weekly* 太平洋週報, November 28, 1974.

Jorae, Wendy Rouse. *The Children of Chinatown: Growing Up Chinese American in San Francisco, 1850–1920.* Chapel Hill: University of North Carolina Press, 2009.

Kvidera, Peter. "Resonant Presence: Legal Narratives and Literary Space in the Poetry of Early Chinese Immigrants." *American Literature* 77, no. 3 (2005): 511–39.

Kwong, Peter, and Dusanka Miscevic. *Chinese America: The Untold Story of America's Oldest New Community.* New York: The New Press, 2005.

Lai, David Chuenyan. "A 'Prison' for Chinese Immigrants." *Asianadian* 2, no. 4 (1979): 16–19.

Lai, David Chuenyan 黎全恩. "'Zhuzi wu' nei zhi kejia shan'ge" 「豬仔屋」內之客家山歌 (Hakka folk songs in the "Pigpen"). *Huabu Tongxin* 華埠通訊 10, no. 1 (April 2008): 18.

Lai, Him Mark. "Angel Island Immigration Station." *Bridge Magazine*, April 1977, 4–8.

———. *Chinese American Transnational Politics.* Urbana: University of Illinois Press, 2010.

———. "Chinese Detainees at NY's Ellis Island Also Wrote Poems on Barrack Walls." *East West*, November 6, 1985, 1.

———. "The Chinese Experience at Angel Island." *East West*, February 11, 1976, 1–2; February 18, 1976, 1, 4; February 25, 1976, 1–2.

———. *Him Mark Lai: Autobiography of a Chinese American Historian.* Los Angeles: UCLA Asian American Studies Center and Chinese Historical Society of America, 2011.

———. "Island of the Immortals: Angel Island Immigration Station and the Chinese Immigrants." *California History* 57, no. 1 (Spring 1978): 88–103.

———. "Potato King and Film Producer, Flower Growers, Professionals, and Activists: The Huangliang Du Community in Northern California." *Chinese America: History and Perspectives* (1998): 1–24.

Lai, Him Mark, Joe Huang, and Don Wong. *The Chinese of America, 1785–1980.* San Francisco: Chinese Culture Foundation, 1980.

Lau, Estelle. *Paper Families: Identity, Immigration Administration, and Chinese Exclusion.* Durham, NC: Duke University Press, 2007.

Lee, Erika. *At America's Gates: Chinese Immigration during the Exclusion Era, 1882–1943.* Chapel Hill: University of North Carolina Press, 2003.

———. "Exclusion Acts: Chinese Women during the Chinese Exclusion Era, 1882–1943." In *Asian/Pacific Islander American Women: A Historical Anthology*, edited by Shirley Hune and Gail M. Nomura, 77–89. New York: New York University Press, 2003.

Lee, Erika, and Judy Yung. *Angel Island: Immigrant Gateway to America.* New York: Oxford University Press, 2010.

Lee, Moonbeam Tong. *Growing Up in Chinatown: The Life and Work of Edwar Lee.* Berkeley: published by author, 1987.

Lee, Robert. *Orientals: Asian Americans in Popular Culture.* Philadelphia: Temple University Press, 1999.

Li Wenyun 李文雲. "Tianshidao shang huaren lei" 天使島上華人淚 (Tears of Chinese immigrants on Angel Island). *People's Daily* 人民日报, July 4, 2006, 16.

Liang Biying 梁碧瑩. "Tianshidao de xuelei pian" 天使島的血淚篇 (A tearful chapter from Angel Island). In *Jiannan de waijiao: Wan Qing Zhongguo zhu Mei gongshi yanjiu* 艱難的外交: 晚清中國駐美公使研究 (Difficult diplomacy: A study of late Qing Chinese envoys to the United States), 357–63. Tianjin: Tianjin guji chubanshe, 2004.

Lim, Genny, and Judy Yung. "Our Parents Never Told Us." *California Living, San Francisco Examiner and Chronicle*, January 23, 1977, 5–9.

Liu, Fu-ju. "A Comparative Demographic Study of Native-Born and Foreign-Born Chinese Populations in the

United States." Ph.D. diss., University of Michigan, 1953.

Liu Lingchen 劉凌塵. "Zhongguo yimin dao Meiguo zaoyu de yimu: Jiujinshan Tianshidao yiminju" 中國移民到美國遭遇的一幕: 舊金山天使島移民局 (A scene from the Chinese immigration experience: Angel Island Immigration Station in San Francisco). M.A. thesis, Tsinghua University, 2004.

Lo, Shaura. "Chinese Women Entering New England: Chinese Exclusion Act Case Files, Boston, 1911–1925." *New England Quarterly* 81, no. 3 (September 2008): 383–409.

Lu Ke 魯克. "Tangrenjie he Tianshidao" 唐人街和天使島 (Chinatown and Angel Island). *Qiaoyuan* 僑園 6 (2002): 17.

Ma, L. Eve Armentrout. *Revolutionaries, Monarchists, and Chinatowns: Chinese Politics in the Americas and the 1911 Revolution.* Honolulu: University of Hawai'i Press, 1990.

Mai Liqian (Him Mark Lai) 麥禮謙. *Cong huaqiao dao huaren: Ershi shiji Meiguo huaren shehui fazhan shi* 從華僑到華人: 二十世紀美國華人社會發展史 (From overseas Chinese to Chinese American: History of the development of Chinese American society in the twentieth century). Hong Kong: Joint Publishing Co., 1992.

———. "Tianshidao cangsang shi" 天使島滄桑史 (The history of Angel Island). *East West* 東西報, February 11, 1976, 15–16.

———. "Tianshidao juliusuo shenxun huaren xiangqing" 天使島拘留所審訊華人詳情 (Interrogation of Chinese immigrants at the Angel Island Immigration Station). *East West* 東西報, February 18, 1976, 15–16.

———. "Tianshidao zhong shici su jin yimin jianku" 天使島中詩詞訴盡移民艱苦 (Angel Island poems: A full account of the plight of immigrants). *East West* 東西報, February 25, 1976, 14–16.

Mark, Diane Mei Li, and Ginger Chih. *A Place Called Chinese America.* Dubuque, IA: Kendall/Hunt Publishing Company, 1982.

Markel, Howard, and Alexandra Minna Stern. "Which Face? Whose Nation? Immigration, Public Health, and the Construction of Disease at America's Ports and Borders, 1891–1928." *American Behavioral Scientist* 42, no. 9 (June–July 1999): 1314–31.

Marshall McDonald & Associates. "Report and Recommendations on Angel Island." Oakland, CA, 1966.

Martin, Mildred Crowl. *Chinatown's Angry Angel: The Story of Donaldina Cameron.* Palo Alto, CA: Pacific Books, 1977.

McClain, Charles J. *In Search of Equality: The Chinese Struggle against Discrimination in Nineteenth-Century America.* Berkeley: University of California Press, 1994.

McClellan, Robert. *The Heathen Chinee: A Study of American Attitudes toward China, 1890–1905.* Columbus: Ohio State University Press, 1971.

McCunn, Ruthanne Lum. *An Illustrated History of the Chinese in America.* San Francisco: Design Enterprises of San Francisco, 1979.

McKee, Delber L. *Chinese Exclusion versus the Open Door Policy, 1900–1906.* Detroit: Wayne State University Press, 1977.

McKeown, Adam. "Chinese Families and Chinese Exclusion, 1875–1943." *Journal of American Ethnic History* 18, no. 2 (Winter 1999): 73–110.

———. *Chinese Migrant Networks and Cultural Change: Peru, Chicago, Hawaii, 1900–1936.* Chicago: University of Chicago Press, 2001.

———. "Ritualization of Regulation: The Enforcement of Chinese Exclusion in the United States and China." *American Historical Review* 108, no. 2 (April 2003): 377–403.

Miller, Stuart Creighton. *The Unwelcome Immigrant: The American Image of the Chinese, 1785–1882.* Berkeley: University of California Press, 1969.

Moreno, Barry. *Encyclopedia of Ellis Island.* Westport, CT: Greenwood Press, 2004.

"Muwu shi pian" 木屋詩篇 (Poems from the wooden building). In *Zhongwai Shihua* 中外詩話 (Chinese poetry and works from other countries), edited by Yu Zhi 余之編, 58–59. Beijing: Zhishi chubanshe, 1983.

Natale, Valerie. "Angel Island: 'Guardian of the Western Gate.'" *Prologue: Quarterly of the National Archives and Records Administration* 30, no. 2 (Summer 1998): 125–35.

Ngai, Mae M. *Impossible Subjects: Illegal Aliens and the Making of Modern America.* Princeton, NJ: Princeton University Press, 2004.

———. "Legacies of Exclusion: Illegal Chinese Immigration

during the Cold War Years." *Journal of American Ethnic History* 18, no. 1 (1998): 3–35.

———. *The Lucky Ones: One Family and the Extraordinary Invention of Chinese America.* Boston: Houghton Mifflin Harcourt, 2010.

Nishi, Thomas. "Actions and Attitudes of the United States Public Health Service on Angel Island, San Francisco Bay, California, 1891–1920." M.A. thesis, University of Hawaii, Manoa, 1982.

Pangu huang 盤古皇. "Shi shi er shou" 詩十二首 (Twelve poems). *Tiansheng Zhoubao* 天聲週報, July 17, 1979.

Peffer, George Anthony. *If They Don't Bring Their Women Here: Chinese Female Immigration before Exclusion.* Urbana: University of Illinois Press, 1999.

Pegler-Gordon, Anna. *In Sight of America: Photography and the Development of U.S. Immigration Policy.* Berkeley: University of California Press, 2009.

Pfaelzer, Jean. *Driven Out: The Forgotten War against Chinese Americans.* Berkeley: University of California Press, 2008.

Pitkin, Thomas M. *Keepers of the Gate: A History of Ellis Island.* New York: New York University Press, 1975.

Polster, Karen L. "Imagined Communities: Nationalism and Ethnicity in Twentieth-Century American Immigration Literature." Ph.D. diss, University of California, Riverside, 2000.

Quan, Daniel. "Angel Island Immigration Station: Immigration History in the Middle of San Francisco Bay." *CRM*, no. 8 (1999): 16–19.

Reimers, David. *Still the Golden Door: The Third World Comes to America.* New York: Columbia University Press, 1992.

The Repeal and Its Legacy: Proceedings of the Conference on the 50th Anniversary of the Repeal of the Exclusion Acts. San Francisco: Chinese Historical Society of America and Asian American Studies, San Francisco State University, 1994.

Riggs, Fred. *Pressure on Congress: A Study of the Repeal of Chinese Exclusion.* New York: Columbia University Press, 1950.

Romero, Robert Chao. *The Chinese in Mexico, 1882–1940.* Tucson: University of Arizona Press, 2010.

Sakovitch, Maria. "Deaconess Katharine Maurer: 'A First-Class Favourite Anytime.'" *The Argonaut* 22, no. 1 (Spring 2011): 6–27.

Salyer, Lucy. *Laws Harsh as Tigers: Chinese Immigrants and the Shaping of Modern Immigration Law.* Chapel Hill: University of North Carolina Press, 1995.

Sandmeyer, Elmer Clarence. *The Anti-Chinese Movement in California.* Urbana: University of Illinois Press, 1973.

Saxton, Alexander. *The Indispensable Enemy: Labor and the Anti-Chinese Movement in California.* Berkeley: University of California Press, 1971.

Shah, Nayan. *Contagious Divides: Epidemics and Race in San Francisco Chinatown.* Berkeley: University of California Press, 2001.

Shan, Te-hsing 單德興. "Angel Island Poetry." In *The Multilingual Anthology of American Literature: A Reader of Original Texts with English Translations*, edited by Marc Shell and Werner Sollers, 577-81, 729-31. New York: New York University Press, 2000.

———. "Carved on the Walls: The Archaeology and Canonization of the Angel Island Chinese Poems." In *American Babel: Literatures of the United States from Abnaki to Zuni*, edited by Marc Shell, 369-85. Cambridge, MA: Harvard University Press, 2002.

———. "'Yi wo Ailun ru quanfu': Tianshidao beige de mingke yu zaixian" 憶我埃崙如螗伏: 天使島悲歌的銘刻與再現 ("I am ashamed to be curled up like a worm on Island": The inscription and representations of the Angel Island poems). In *Zaixian zhengzhi yu huayi Meiguo wenxue* 再現政治與華裔美國文學 (Politics of representation and Chinese American literature), edited by He Wenjing and Shan Dexing 何文敬與單德興主編, 1-56. Taipei: Zhongyang Yanjiuyuan Ou Mei Yanjiusuo, 1996.

Shen Lixin 沈立新. "Ailun shiji zhong suo shu lü Mei huaren kunan shi" 埃崙詩集中所述旅美華人苦難史 (The bitter story of Chinese sojourners in America as told in the Island poems). *Lishi Zhishi* 歷史知識 4 (1983).

Siu, Paul C. *The Chinese Laundryman: A Study in Social Isolation*, edited by John Kuo Wei Tchen. New York: New York University Press, 1987.

Soennichsen, John. *Miwoks to Missiles: A History of Angel Island.* Tiburon, CA: Angel Island Association, 2005.

Stolarik, M. Mark, ed. *Forgotten Doors: The Other Ports of Entry to the United States.* Philadelphia: Balch Institute Press, 1988.

Sun, Shirley. *Three Generations of Chinese—East and West.* Oakland, CA: Oakland Museum, 1973.

Takaki, Ronald. *Strangers from a Different Shore: A History of Asian Americans.* Boston: Little, Brown and Company, 1989.

"Tianshidao" 天使島 (Angel Island). In *Bai nian cangsang yimin Meiguo shi hua* 百年滄桑移民美國史話 (A hundred-year history of Chinese immigration to the United States), edited by Zhang Zherui Law Office 張哲瑞聯合律師事務所編著, 128–33. Beijing: Zhongyang bianyi chubanshe, 2004.

"Tianshidao shige: Beiyu he kangsu" 天使島詩歌: 悲郁和抗訴 (Angel Island poems: Dejection and denunciation). In *Shuangchong jingyan de kuayu shuxie: Ershi shiji Meihua wenxue shi lun* 雙重經驗的跨域書寫: 二十世紀美華文學史論 (Writing about the crossing of dual experiences: A historical perspective of twentieth-century Chinese American literature), edited by Liu Denghan 劉登翰主編, 30–39. Shanghai: Joint Publishing Co., 2007.

Toogood, Anna Coxe. "A Civil History of Golden Gate National Recreation Area and Point Reyes National Seashore, California." Historic Resource Study, U.S. National Park Service, 1980.

Tsai, Shih-shan Henry. *China and the Overseas Chinese in the United States, 1868–1911.* Fayetteville: University of Arkansas Press, 1983.

——. *The Chinese Experience in America.* Bloomington: Indiana University Press, 1986.

Twain, Mark. *Roughing It: The Works of Mark Twain.* Berkeley: University of California Press, 1972.

U.S. Department of Commerce and Labor. *Annual Report of the Commissioner-General of Immigration.* 1903–11. Washington, DC: Government Printing Office.

U.S. Department of Immigration and Naturalization Service. *Lists of Chinese Applying for Admission to the United States through the Port of San Francisco, California.* Microfilm Publication M1476, Record Group 85, National Archives, Washington, D.C.

U.S. Department of Labor. *Annual Report of the Commissioner-General of Immigration.* 1912–32. Washington, DC: Government Printing Office.

——. *Annual Report of the Secretary of Labor.* 1933–40. Washington, DC: Government Printing Office.

Wang De'en 王德恩. "Liu Mei yimin bei ju ji" 留美移民被拘記 (Chinese immigrants put in detention). *Huatian Sheng Dong San Sheng Liu Mei Xuesheng Nianbao* 華天省東三省留美學生年報, August 15, 1926.

Wang, Ling-chi. "The Yee Version of Poems from the Chinese Immigration Station." *Asian American Review* (1976): 117–26.

Wang Xiaoyun 王曉雲. "Meiguo huaren juliu suo jintou Zhongguo yimin lei" 美國華人拘留所浸透中國移民淚 (The detention center is soaked with the tears of Chinese immigrants to the United States). *Wenshi Yuekan* 文史月刊 11 (2010): 36–37.

Wang Xingchu 王性初. "Shi de linghun zai diyu zhong yongsheng: Meiguo Tianshidao huawen yi shi xin kao" 詩的靈魂在地獄中永生: 美國天使島華文遺詩新考 (The soul of poetry is alive and well in hell: A new look at the Chinese poems left on Angel Island). *Huawen Wenxue* 華文文學 1 (2005): 17–22.

Wei, William. *The Asian American Movement.* Philadelphia: Temple University Press, 1993.

Wei Yu 衛瑜. "Wo ju Mei qijian zui zhide jiyi de yijian shi" 我居美期間最值得記憶的一件事 (The most memorable event during my sojourn in the United States). *Chinese Pacific Weekly* 太平洋週報, April 29, 1955, 18–19.

Wen Juan 溫娟. "Zaoqi huayi Meiguo shige yanjiu: Ping *Jinshan geji* yu *Ailun shiji*" 早期華裔美國詩歌研究: 評<金山歌集> 與 <埃侖詩集> (A study of early Chinese American poetry: A critique of *Songs of Gold Mountain* and *Island*). M.A. thesis, Fujian Normal University, 2008.

Wickberg, Edgar, ed. *From China to Canada: A History of the Chinese Communities in Canada.* Toronto: McClelland and Stewart, 1982.

Wong, K. Scott, *Americans First: Chinese Americans and the Second World War.* Cambridge, MA: Harvard University Press, 2005.

Wong, K. Scott, and Sucheng Chan, eds. *Claiming America:*

Constructing Chinese American Identities during the Exclusion Era. Philadelphia: Temple University Press, 1998.

Wong, Li Keng. *Good Fortune: My Journey to Gold Mountain.* Atlanta, GA: Peachtree Publications, 2006.

Wong, Wayne Hung. *American Paper Son: A Chinese Immigrant in the Midwest.* Urbana: University of Illinois Press, 2006.

Wu Rijun 吳日君. "Tianshidao shou nan zhe: Mai Jingsheng le guan jin qu" 天使島受難者: 麥景勝樂觀進取 (Mai Jingsheng: An optimistic survivor of Angel Island). *World Journal* 世界日報, April 6, 2001.

Wu Ruiqing 吳瑞卿. *Meiyou tianshi de Tianshidao* 沒有天使的天使島 (No angels on Angel Island). Shijiazhuang: Hebei Jiaoyu chubanshe, 1995.

Wu Qixing 吳琦幸. "Tianshidao" 天使島 (Angel Island). In *Taojin lu shang* 淘金路上 (On the way to pan for gold), 46–62. Shanghai: Shanghai guji chubanshe, 2003.

"Xi wei qiujin suo, jin bian youlechang: Ailisi yimin bowuguan juanke lishi cangsang erhu luopan zhuliu Zhongguo yimin dangnian xinsuan" 昔為囚禁所, 今變遊樂場: 愛麗絲移民博物館鐫刻歷史滄桑二胡羅盤貯留中國移民當年辛酸 (Former detention center now a park: Ellis Island Immigration Museum historical engravings, *erhu*, and compass hold bitterness of former Chinese immigrants). *Huaqiao Ribao* 華僑日報, September 12, 1990.

Xie Chuang 謝創. *Chongyang nan zu baoguo xin* 重洋難阻報國心 (Seas and oceans cannot block an intention to serve the nation). Guangzhou: Hua'nan Shifan Daxue yinshuachang, 1993.

"Xie Chuang." *Guangzhou Local History.* http://www.gzsdfz.org.cn/dqzt/jcgcdy/201106/t20110626_3615.htm (accessed March 21, 2013).

Xing Zhi 醒之. "Huaqiao shou nüedai zhi yiban" 华侨受虐待之一斑 (The abusive treatment of overseas Chinese). *Chung Sai Yat Po* 中西日報, August 14, 1936, 1.

Xu Xiong 徐熊. "Xuelei yin'e Tianshidao" 血淚吟哦天使島 (Tearful murmurings from Angel Island). In *Hua shuo Meiguo* 話說美國 (Let's talk about America), 283–87. Beijing: Zhongguo guoji guangbo chubanshe, 2003.

Ya Cheng 亞程. "Jiliu Dingzhi Ailun you gan" 羈留丁治埃侖有感 (Thoughts on being detained on Angel Island).

Morning Sun 公論晨報, January 2, 1931.

Ya Zong 亞宗. "Huiyi wushi qi nian qian de yimin jingguo" 回憶五十七年前的移民經過 (Remembering my experiences as an immigrant fifty-seven years ago). *Suyuan Jikan* 溯源季刊 31 (August 31, 1994): 71–76.

Yans-McLaughlin, Virginia, and Marjorie Lightman, with The Statue of Liberty–Ellis Island Foundation. *Ellis Island and the Peopling of America: The Official Guide.* New York: The New Press, 1997.

Yao, Steven G. *Foreign Accents: Chinese American Verse from Exclusion to Postethnicity.* New York: Oxford University Press, 2010.

Yep, Laurence, and Kathleen S. Yep. *The Dragon's Child: A Story of Angel Island.* New York: HarperCollins, 2008.

Yi Shuqiong 易淑瓊. "Zhongguo wei du xia 'Tianshidao shige' shishi xing yu wenxue xing zai jiedu 中國維度下 "天使島詩歌" 史詩性與文學性再解讀 (A Chinese reinterpretation of the epic nature and literary quality of the Angel Island poems). *Jinan Xuebao (Zhexue shehui kexue ban)* 暨南學報 (哲學社會科學版) 10 (2012): 41–49.

Yin, Xiao-huang. *Chinese American Literature since the 1850s.* Urbana: University of Illinois Press, 2000.

Yu, Connie Young. "Rediscovered Voices: Chinese Immigrants and Angel Island." *Amerasia Journal* 4, no. 2 (1977): 123–39.

Yu Yaopei 余耀培. "Meiguo yiminju jujin rujing huaqiao canzhuang" 美國移民局拘禁入境華僑慘狀 (The pitiful condition of Chinese Americans taken into custody and denied entry by the U.S. Immigration Service). *Liu Mei Xuesheng Yuekan* 留美學生月刊 1, no. 5 (April 1936): 15–18.

Yuan Guoqiang 袁國強. "Niuyue Ailisi dao huaren yimin xuelei bainian yihen zai: Meng duan guguo shanhe, cancun tuya zuopin ling ren yi sa lei" 紐約愛麗絲島華人移民血淚百年遺恨在: 夢斷故國山河•殘存塗鴉作品令人一灑淚 (The sorrows of Chinese immigrants on Ellis Island linger for a hundred years: Hills and streams of the native land gone as in a dream, remnants of graffiti poems invoke tears). *Zhong Bao* 中報, August 30, 1985.

Yuan Liangjun 袁良駿. "Tangrenjie he Tianshidao: Kan bainian qian yiwei lao huagong de riji" 唐人街和天使島: 看

百年前一位老華工的日記 (Chinatown and Angel Island: A look at a hundred-year-old diary of a Chinese laborer). *People's Daily* 人民日報, August 1, 2001.

Yung, Judy. "'A Bowlful of Tears': Chinese Women Immigrants on Angel Island." *Frontiers* 2, no. 2 (1977): 52–55.

———. "'A Bowlful of Tears': Lee Puey You's Immigration Experience at Angel Island." In *Asian/Pacific Islander American Women: A Historical Anthology*, edited by Shirley Hune and Gail Nomura, 123–37. New York: New York University Press, 2003.

———. "'A Bowlful of Tears' Revisited: The Full Story of Lee Puey You's Immigration Experience at Angel Island." *Frontiers: A Journal of Women Studies* 25, no. 1 (2004): 1–22.

———. "Detainment at Angel Island: An Interview With Koon T. Lau." *Chinese America: History and Perspectives* (1991): 157–68.

———. *Unbound Feet: A Social History of Chinese Women in San Francisco.* Berkeley: University of California Press, 1995.

———. *Unbound Voices: A Documentary History of Chinese Women in San Francisco.* Berkeley: University of California Press, 1999.

———. "'We Were Real, So There Was No Need to Be Afraid': Lum Ngow's Long Detention on Angel Island." *Chinese America: History and Perspectives* (2012): 19–26.

Yung, Judy, Gordon H. Chang, and Him Mark Lai. *Chinese American Voices: From the Gold Rush to the Present.* Berkeley: University of California Press, 2006.

Zhang Zhengping 張正平. "Huaren yimin de xuelei shishi: Tianshidao zhi ge" 華人移民的血淚史詩: 天使島之歌 (The tearful epic poems of Chinese immigrants: Songs of Angel Island). *East West* 東西報, February 2, 9, 16, 23, 1977.

———. "Tianshidao de lao jian qiu" 天使島的老監囚 (An old prisoner from Angel Island). *East West* 東西報, February 15, 1976.

Zhang Ziqing 張子清. "Huayi Meiguo shige de xiansheng: Meiguo zuizao de huawen shige" 華裔美國詩歌的先聲: 美國最早的華文詩歌 (The precursor of Chinese American poetry: The first Chinese poems in the United States). *Dangdai waiguo wenxue* 當代外國文學 2 (2005): 153–58.

———. "Lishi yu shehui xianshi shenghuo de kua wenhua shenshi—huayi Meiguo shige de xiansheng: Zai Meiguo zuizao de huawen shige" 歷史與社會現實生活的跨文化審視—華裔美國詩歌的先聲: 在美國最早的華文詩歌 (A cross-cultural examination of history and real life experiences—the precursor of Chinese American poetry: The first Chinese poems in the United States). *Jianghan Daxue Xuebao (Renwen kexue ban)* 江漢大學學報 (人文科學版) 5 (2008): 18–23.

Zhao Yijuan 趙義娟. "Meiguo yimin shi shang nankan de yi ye" 美國移民史上難堪的一頁 (An embarrassing chapter from U.S. immigration history). M.A. thesis, Huazhong Normal University, 2012.

Zhong Wen 鐘文. "Tianshidao shang huaren xuelei" 天使島上華人血淚 (Blood and tears of the Chinese on Angel Island). *Qiaoyuan* 僑園 6 (2007): 36–37.

Zhu Bangxian 朱邦賢. "Tianshidao shang wu tianshi" 天使島上無天使 (No angels on Angel Island). *Lianhe Bao* 聯合報, May 21, 1994, 7.

Zhui Chen 追陳. "Ailun shixuan" 埃侖詩選 (Selected poems from Angel Island). *San Francisco Weekly* 舊金山週報, April 10, 1974.

———. "Tianshidao" 天使島 (Angel Island). *San Francisco Journal* 時代報, November 14, 1973.

MULTIMEDIA PRODUCTIONS

Chen, Amy. *The Chinatown Files.* Videorecording. New York: Filmmakers Library, 2001.

Chen Zhuoling 陳卓玲. "Huaren yimin shi, di san ji, meiyou tianshi de Tianshidao" 華人移民史, 第三集, "沒有天使的天使島" (Roots old and new: Stories of Chinese emigrants, North America, episode 3—No angels on Angel Island). Radio Television Hong Kong (RTHK) 香港電台, 2012.

"Huaren zuji: Ailun shiji" 華人足迹:埃侖詩集 (Footprints left by the Chinese: The poetry and history of Chinese immigrants on Angel Island). CCTV International 中國中央電視台國際頻道, 2012.

Lowe, Felicia. *Carved in Silence.* Videorecording. San Francisco: Felicia Lowe Productions, 1987.

Moyers, Bill. *Becoming American: The Chinese Experience.* Videorecording. Princeton, NJ: Films for the Humanities and Sciences, 2003.

Wong, Eddie. "Angel Island Profile: Robert Hong." Leapman Productions, 2009. http://www.youtube.com/watch?v=42kRfovnVeE.

——. "Angel Island Profile: Tyrus Wong." Leapman Productions, 2010. http://www.youtube.com/watch?v=5rz5whByOts.

——. "Discovering Angel Island: The Meaning Behind the Poems." KQED, 2004. http://www.kqed.org/w/pacificlink/history/angelisland/video/.

——. "Angel Island Immigration Station Tour—AIISF." J. J. Media Labs, 2011. http://www.youtube.com/watch?v=ZnpgiUY5ip4.

Yip, Garman. "Poetic Waves: Angel Island." 2006. http://www.poeticwaves.net.

ORAL HISTORY INTERVIEWS

Chan, Ted. Interview in Cantonese with Him Mark Lai and Judy Yung, April 17, 1977, San Francisco. Interview 23 (Mr. Chan), Angel Island Oral History Project, Ethnic Studies Library, University of California, Berkeley.

Ja Kew Yuen. Interview in Cantonese with Him Mark Lai and Judy Yung, March 24, 1976, San Francisco. Interview 43 (Mr. Dea), Angel Island Oral History Project, Ethnic Studies Library, University of California, Berkeley.

Jang, Ruth Chan. Phone interview with Judy Yung, July 8, 1984.

Jann, Smiley. Interview in Cantonese with Him Mark Lai and Judy Yung, January 4, 1976, San Francisco. Interview 32 (Mr. Ng), Angel Island Oral History Project, Ethnic Studies Library, University of California, Berkeley.

Lau, Koon T. Interview in Cantonese with Judy Yung, June 10, 1990, San Francisco. Interview 36, Angel Island Oral History Project, Ethnic Studies Library, University of California, Berkeley.

Law Shee Low. Interview in Cantonese with Sandra Lee, May 2, 1982, San Francisco.

——. Interview in Cantonese with Judy Yung, October 20, 1988, and October 30, 1989, San Francisco. Interview 5 (Law Shee Low), Angel Island Oral History Project, Ethnic Studies Library, University of California, Berkeley.

Lee, Edwar. Interview with Him Mark Lai, Genny Lim, Judy Yung, and Paul Chow, May 8, 1976, Oakland, CA; interview with Felicia Lowe, April 9, 1984, Oakland, CA. Interview 50 (Immigration Interpreters), Angel Island Oral History Project, Ethnic Studies Library, University of California, Berkeley.

Lee Puey You. Interview in Cantonese with Him Mark Lai and Judy Yung, December 14, 1975, San Francisco; interview in Cantonese with Felicia Lowe, April 11, 1984, San Francisco. Interview 11 (Mrs. Chan), Angel Island Oral History Project, Ethnic Studies Library, University of California, Berkeley.

Lee Show Nam. Interview in Cantonese with Judy Yung, Oakland, CA, December 3, 2010.

Lee Suk Wan. Interview in Cantonese with Judy Yung, Oakland, CA, September 3, 1992. Angel Island Oral History Project, Ethnic Studies Library, University of California, Berkeley.

Leung, Mr. Interview in Cantonese with Judy Yung and Him Mark Lai, San Francisco, December 28, 1975. Interview 40 (Mr. Leung), Angel Island Oral History Project, Ethnic Studies Library, University of California, Berkeley.

Lin Sun Lim. Interview in Cantonese with Him Mark Lai, Genny Lim, and Judy Yung, September 12, 1976, San Francisco. Interview 10 (Mrs. Lim), Angel Island Oral History Project, Ethnic Studies Library, University of California, Berkeley.

Mock Ging Sing. Interview in Cantonese with Felicia Lowe, April 9, 1984, San Francisco. Interview 41, Angel Island Oral History Project, Ethnic Studies Library, University of California, Berkeley.

——. Interview in Cantonese with Him Mark Lai, November 13, 1995, San Jose, CA. Him Mark Lai Collection, Ethnic Studies Library, University of California, Berkeley.

Mock, John. Interview in Cantonese with Him Mark Lai, May 3 and November 2, 1969; April 26 and May 17, 1970, San Jose, CA. Him Mark Lai Collection, Ethnic Studies Library, University of California, Berkeley.

——. Interview in Cantonese with Him Mark Lai and Judy

Yung, December 27, 1975, San Jose, CA. Interview 19 (Mr. Low), Angel Island Oral History Project, Ethnic Studies Library, University of California, Berkeley.

Sims, Emery. Interview with Genny Lim, Judy Yung, and Him Mark Lai, June 29, 1977, San Francisco. Interview 47 (Immigrant Inspector), Angel Island Oral History Project, Ethnic Studies Library, University of California, Berkeley.

Tom Yip Jing. Interview in Cantonese with Him Mark Lai and Judy Yung, April 17, 1977, San Francisco. Interview 23 (Mr. Tom), Angel Island Oral History Project, Ethnic Studies Library, University of California, Berkeley.

——. Interview in Cantonese with Judy Yung, November 20, 1986, San Francisco.

——. Last will and testament in Cantonese, November 16, 1987, San Francisco.

Wong, Helen Hong. Interview in Cantonese with Judy Yung, June 17, 1982, San Mateo, CA; interview in Cantonese with Nellie Leong, 1992–2001, Chicago.

Wong, Mr. Interview with Judy Yung, San Francisco. Interview 35 (Mr. Wong), Angel Island Oral History Project, Ethnic Studies Library, University of California, Berkeley.

Wong, Mrs. Interview in Cantonese with Genny Lim and Judy Yung, August 15, 1976, San Francisco. Interview 3 (Mrs. Wong), Angel Island Oral History Project, Ethnic Studies Library, University of California, Berkeley.

Yee, Tet. Interview in Cantonese with Him Mark Lai, Genny Lim, and Judy Yung, August 15, 1976, Oakland, CA; interview in Cantonese with Felicia Lowe, April 9, 1984, Oakland, CA. Interview 33 (Mr. Tong), Angel Island Oral History Project, Ethnic Studies Library, University of California, Berkeley.

HIM MARK LAI, a mechanical engineer by profession, devoted his life to researching and writing about Chinese America in English as well as in Chinese. He is the author of more than one hundred articles and ten books on the subject, including *The Chinese of America, 1785–1980*, *Cong Huaqiao dao Huaren* (From overseas Chinese to Chinese American), *Becoming Chinese American: A History of Communities and Institutions*, and *Chinese American Transnational Politics*.

GENNY LIM, a native San Franciscan, is a poet, playwright, performer, and educator. She is the author of three poetry collections, *Paper Gods and Rebels*, *Child of War*, and *Winter Place*, and the award-winning play *Paper Angels*, about Chinese immigrants detained on Angel Island. A noted jazz poet, Lim has performed at numerous jazz festivals throughout the United States and at World Poetry Festivals in Caracas, Venezuela, and Sarajevo, Bosnia-Herzegovina.

FIG. 3.56
Editors Judy Yung, Him Mark Lai, and Genny Lim at a book launch, 1983. Photo by Henrietta Lai.

JUDY YUNG is a native of San Francisco Chinatown and professor emerita of American studies at the University of California, Santa Cruz, where she taught courses in ethnic studies, Asian American studies, and oral history. Her publications include *Unbound Feet: A Social History of Chinese Women in San Francisco*, *Chinese American Voices: From the Gold Rush to the Present*, *The Adventures of Eddie Fung: Chinatown Kid, Texas Cowboy, Prisoner of War*, and *Angel Island: Immigrant Gateway to America*.

KATHY ANG is a third-generation Chinese American living in Northern California. Her interest in family history has led her to research the stories of members of her family and her husband's family who went through Angel Island. She is humbled by their struggles and inspired by their spirit.

DAVID CHUENYAN Lai, a native of Canton, is professor emeritus of geography at the University of Victoria, Canada, where he taught for thirty-five years. Upon retirement, he was appointed research affiliate at the Centre of Aging in Victoria. His publications include *Chinatowns: Towns within Cities in Canada, The Forbidden City within Victoria: Myth, Symbol and Streetscape of Canada's Earliest Chinatown*, and *Building and Rebuilding Harmony: The Gateway to Victoria's Chinatown*.

CHARLES EGAN is professor of foreign languages and literature at San Francisco State University and specializes in classical Chinese poetry. He was the lead scholar in the Angel Island comprehensive study "Poetry and Inscriptions." His book *Clouds Thick, Whereabouts Unknown: Poems by Zen Monks of China* won the 2011 Asian Translation award from the American Literary Translators Association.

MARLON K. HOM teaches Asian American studies at San Francisco State University. He is the author of *Songs of Gold Mountain: Cantonese Rhymes from San Francisco Chinatown* and the coeditor, with Philip P. Choy and Lorraine Dong, of *The Coming Man: 19th Century American Perceptions of the Chinese*.

PENELOPE WONG spent twenty-five years in advertising at Ogilvy & Mather, the Franklin Mint, Brann Worldwide, and Wong Wong Boyack. Game-changing clients included Nike, Cisco, Mattel, SINA.com, Pixar, Hewlett-Packard, the Walt Disney Company, American Express, and Intuit. An award-winning screenwriter for *The Shanghai Café*, she is now planning a documentary on her father's Angel Island experience as well as a narrative feature that connects Mainland Chinese and Chinese Americans.